The End of Agriculture in the American Portfolio

The End of Agriculture
in the
American Portfolio

Steven C. Blank

Q

QUORUM BOOKS
Westport, Connecticut • London

Library of Congress Cataloging-in-Publication Data

Blank, Steven C., 1951–
    The end of agriculture in the American portfolio / Steven C.
Blank.
      p.   cm.
    Includes bibliographical references and index.
    ISBN 1–56720–165–2 (alk. paper)
    1. Agriculture—United States—Finance. 2. Agriculture—Economic
aspects—United States. 3. Agricultural industries—United States.
4. Investments—United States. I. Title.
HD1761.B565 1998
338.1′3′0973—dc21   97–21995

British Library Cataloguing in Publication Data is available.

Library of Congress Catalog Card Number: 97–21995
ISBN: 1–56720–165–2

First published in 1998

Quorum Books, 88 Post Road West, Westport, CT 06881
An imprint of Greenwood Publishing Group, Inc.

Printed in the United States of America

The paper used in this book complies with the
Permanent Paper Standard issued by the National
Information Standards Organization (Z39.48–1984).

10 9 8 7 6 5 4

This book is dedicated to Glenn and George, my two grandfathers, who showed me the entire food chain and made me appreciate the hard work involved therein.

Contents

Acknowledgments

The work that led to this book was conducted over a period of years and benefited greatly from the inputs of many people. In particular, Brian Schmiesing and Dorothy Kaufman gave generously of their time and ideas as they reviewed early drafts of the manuscript.

Chapter 1

Not Made in America

America's unsurpassed ability to produce plentiful and inexpensive food is coming to an end. The signals are all there, the economic trends are in position to bring about this inevitable conclusion. America, "the world's breadbasket," is currently producing at its peak, but it is going out of the food business.

What could cause such a dramatic turn of events? No, Americans are not all going on a crash diet at the same time. No, we are not going to lose some war, real or economic. In fact, winning the Cold War is a small part of the push that will put an end to the world's most efficient agricultural industry. In the simplest terms, the production of food and other agricultural products will disappear from the United States because it will become unprofitable to tie up resources in farming and ranching. This means that we will voluntarily leave agriculture behind in favor of better opportunities—a process that has been going on since American history began. The completion of the process was not visible before. It is now.

Is this good or bad? Well, where you stand on an issue depends on where you sit. Therefore, all possible opinions will be expressed during the final stages of this national transformation because food affects every person in the country. This statement encapsulates two of the many obvious but necessary assumptions that must be made when discussing food in America: (1) Americans will continue to eat at least their share, and (2) everyone has an opinion about food and likes to express it often. Another assumption that can be made is that air, water (in some form), shelter (if you live in an unpleasant climate) and food (in some form) are the only true "necessities" in life. (This assumption is less obvious to new-car dealers, fashion designers, toiletry manufacturers and a few others in corporate America who think we can't live without their product.) Other assumptions will be noted as the story is laid out.

If you sit in a tractor seat there is a good chance that you will think that the end of raw food production is not a pleasant part of our future. American farmers and ranchers are in their occupations by choice. The news that your chosen profession is terminally ill is rarely welcome. Most current agricultural producers are descendants of agricultural families and probably wish to pass on the family business to future generations. Unlike other businesses, agriculture is often referred to as a "way of life." The unique aspects of agriculture, like the rural setting and the fact that no two operations are identical due to location and other factors, make the experience quite different than that of most other types of business. Thus, people in agriculture often resist leaving the industry more strongly than do operators of other types of firms.

If you sit behind a desk in a large agribusiness firm, such as a food processor, the end of American agricultural production creates modest challenges but does not seriously threaten your livelihood. Assumption number one is that *Americans will continue to eat*, thus demand for the output of American food processors and distributors will grow at least as fast as our population.

If your only direct contact with food comes when you sit down to eat, you might never notice the changes as they gradually occur. There will be no change in the quantity or quality of the products available. The only sure change is that the *range* of available products will continue to expand over time. As a nation of eager food consumers, the cost of food relative to other products in America will not noticeably change, but it could continue to decline.

For those people with a seat in Congress or some state legislature, the end of food production will generate hot air (depending on the tone of telephone calls received) but will ultimately come to be viewed as one less thing to argue about. All politics may be local, but food is global, and this fact will eventually be faced. The screaming and crying will be loud as each sacred cow is slaughtered, each hot potato is passed, and as the pork in each barrel is replaced by some nonagricultural topic, but the end result remains inevitable.

WHY NOW?

America is probably at its peak of agricultural production right now, with sales in 1996 of $200 billion and a record net income of about $50 billion. Is this a strange time to forecast the end of American agriculture? No more so than a dockside warning for the captain of the doomed ocean liner, *Titanic*, about the risks involved in his planned course would have been. Indeed, worrying about the timing of the message is missing the point. The message is the key. Even though American agriculture is "plowing ahead," any warning of obstacles ahead may facilitate adjustment. The *Titanic* was sailing along at a record pace and the passengers were enjoying the ride, yet had those passengers known the hazards of their course, they might have demanded changes.

Contrary to what many people in agriculture seem to think, The Future Is Not Obvious. The fact that Americans will continue to eat does not directly equate to job security for American agricultural producers. Nor should it. Many of those producers will, in a number of ways, be better off after they make the difficult decision to leave agriculture voluntarily. Many of them will not believe it at the time. Almost none of them will believe it now. Nevertheless, it is important to hear the news—whether it is judged to be good, bad or ugly—that the future can go either way; it can be filled with good prospects or bad, depending on how we react to the limited range of options available.

THE STORY

The story in this book is an attempt to bring to light the broad range of events and issues that make the end of American food production a coming reality. The story tries to explain what is happening and why. To a great extent people will judge the events described in this book to be good or bad based upon their individual perspectives. However, *understanding*, rather than judging, the background and logic of the personal, political and economic decisions involved is more important here. The story is fascinating in its global scope and is relevant to everyone because the simplicity of the economic logic can (and probably will) be repeated in the story of other industries.

The story begins with broad observations from history and the current status of agriculture around the world, then proposes how the decisions of individuals combine to make the end predictable and rational. The inevitable progress of international economic development is shown to be the sum of individual cases facing producers across America and around the world. Also, the individual trauma of making decisions regarding operating an agricultural business is described as being derived from many inter-related peculiarities of the industry, both in America and elsewhere.

The story is explained using the logic of an investor managing his or her portfolio. The logic is the same for individual businesses and national economies. America's portfolio of investments has included food production since the birth of the nation because it was a profitable use of resources. Over time, the American portfolio has expanded to include many new industries. In the eighteenth and nineteenth centuries, much of the new investment could be made using newly acquired resources, like new land as the country expanded westward and new people as the population grew rapidly. During the twentieth century, America has been able to keep investing in new and more profitable industries by using resources shifted from less profitable industries. One of the less profitable industries in recent decades was agriculture. The proportion of our population working directly in food production has decreased steadily down to its current level of about 1.3 percent. The reason for decreased labor needs in agriculture was the constant improvements made in the efficiency and productivity of agricultural resource use. It required fewer and fewer people to produce all the food we wanted plus surpluses for sale to other countries. In the twenty-first century, other industries will continue to draw our increasingly scarce resources away from agriculture as the nation adjusts its portfolio to maintain the best possible return on its investments. At some point, agriculture must be dropped entirely from the portfolio because it cannot compete with the profitability of newer industries.

That is the story, "in a nutshell." The "meat" of the story is in the details that follow. Its telling will include a constant stream of food- and agriculturally based sayings and clichés as an illustration of how important agriculture has been in our past. Agriculture was once the "main course" of American industry and still deserves our attention as we enter the final "weaning" process. It is in our language and in our hearts (through our stomachs).

At this point, some readers may be thinking that this story is too wild to be true and may be reluctant to read on. Can the world really change that much? Consider this: the author's maternal grandfather was born on a farm in Missouri within a month of the Wright brothers' first flight in a motor-powered airplane, and he lived to see live television coverage of men walking on the moon. America is a dynamic country; nothing stays the same for long. Some of us can remember a time before McDonalds hamburgers. Food and agriculture in America are changing along with everything else being pushed (or pulled) along by the tidal wave of economic development. Read on and see.

Chapter 2

Agriculture: First In, First Out

In the global scale of economic development, farming is an entry-level job. Also, providing raw food products for the population is the first job that must be done by any developing country. Yet, being the *first* job is different than being an *entry-level* job. Agriculture is both. An obvious point that explains why agriculture must be the first job in an economy is that *hungry people do not work very long*. This means that the job must be performed continuously by someone. Being an entry-level job implies that it is something that everyone has to go through, but it is not a highly desirable occupation and is one that, eventually, everyone wants to get out of as they move up. This is true for national economies as well as for individual people, although no national governments have realized it (or admitted it) yet.

The story is easier to understand if we begin with the case of individuals. We all know that many immigrants to America are first employed as farm laborers. That was true 200 years ago and remains true today. Agriculture is a vast industry, literally spreading out across the country. It exists in some form in every part of America, as well as in every country in the world. Thus, it is readily available to anyone looking for work. It remains a labor-intensive industry, meaning that it needs a lot of people at some point in the production and/or harvest process. Much of the labor needs continue to be for unskilled people willing to do physical work. Anyone who has done much farm or ranch labor can attest to its difficulty. Chopping weeds with a hoe, moving irrigation equipment, tending to ill livestock, mending fences, bending over or climbing a ladder to harvest crops, and any number of other jobs could be listed as examples of physically tough ways to try to earn a living. What may be worse, in America it is rare that one person doing any of these jobs can earn enough money to support a family. As a result, agriculture often becomes the *family's* occupation, with more than one member working to generate sufficient income to keep the group going. There are strong incentives for workers to learn skills that earn higher incomes outside of agriculture. Asking virtually any agricultural workers who do not own a farm or ranch whether they hope to stay in the industry until retirement produces a near unanimous chorus of #@&* NO! The reasons for workers' desire to get the heck out of the fields? the work is too physically demanding and the financial rewards are too small. These responses are rational and understandable. The reasons why farm and ranch owners would leave agriculture are also rational and understandable and are discussed in the next chapter.

The story is more complex when considering countries. Also, only a few highly developed countries are just now beginning to face the exit decision. It is easier to understand the story if the conclusion is presented first. So, if the conclusion for individuals is that people leave agriculture for better paying jobs as soon as possible, then the same conclusion can be rephrased for countries: national economies leave agriculture for more profitable industries as soon as possible. Whereas people leave agriculture by literally moving to another location, countries "leave" agriculture by shifting resources, like land and labor, into other uses. In America, land leaving agriculture often goes into residential or commercial use. Also, once land leaves agriculture for alternative uses, it virtually never comes back. Of course in the past, American farmers and ranchers did not worry much about land leaving agriculture in one location because there was always more somewhere else. Even today there is marginal land which could be (and is) brought into production if food prices get high enough to make it profitable. However, as improved methods of transportation for food products created a true world market, land taken out of production in wealthy, developed countries was increasingly replaced by land going into production in less developed countries.

EXITING THE ENTRY LEVEL

The exit from agriculture does not happen voluntarily at the national level. Most countries resist the necessity to leave agriculture. The most common excuses given for overstaying in agriculture are because governments wish "to avoid economic blackmail" by potential foreign suppliers of food and because agriculture is "vital for the national security." Japan is a good example of a country using the latter excuse. The Japanese government spent decades claiming that self-sufficiency in rice production was necessary to avoid the evils of shortages during some future war. This was a comical argument for a country that has not even had a real army since World War II. Whatever war they were supposedly anticipating would have been very short without the means to defend themselves. In the meantime, Japanese consumers paid up to eight times more for domestic rice than they could have paid for rice from California. Nevertheless, in the 1980s the rate of decline in the number of farms was twice as fast in Japan as in the United States. In recent years, the Japanese government began shifting from the ridiculous national security excuse to the economic blackmail excuse. As a result, there are still a significant number of people working in agriculture and small mom-and-pop food retailers in Japan. Today some California rice is entering the Japanese market, but an ancient, labor-intensive Japanese rice industry still exists because its government still enables it to get prices several times higher than those that foreign rice producers would charge. The current excuse? to preserve the country's "rural heritage."[1]

Small, rich European countries were the first to be forced to face the end of their agriculture. Switzerland, Belgium, and the Netherlands are examples of countries that have nearly abandoned agriculture. They had no choice. They did not have much land, so their populations' food demands had outgrown their ability to produce long ago. What little agriculture that remains in the two small, coastal countries (primarily intensive livestock operations such as dairies) represents a holding action before residential and recreational needs take over. The end of agriculture is being hastened by regulations imposed as a reaction to the public's recent awareness that hog manure is being hauled 40 miles through villages and towns to central processing plants.[2] In the Alps,

---

[1] Nevertheless, Japanese are eating more imported food. Their food imports in 1995 climbed 9.3 percent over 1994 to a record $41.8 billion, according to the Japan External Trade Organization. It was the fifth straight year of record highs. The reason for the increase is costs. For example, it costs 10 times more to produce beef in Japan than it does in Australia.

[2] The Netherlands' 14 million pigs have contributed to a huge manure mountain—close to 17 million tons in 1995—which some say threatens the country's environment and which has soured relations between farmers and the government. The Hague, pledging to cut the manure surplus, proposed an emergency package of measures including a 475 million guilder ($299 million) grant to farmers over the period 1995-2002. In other

the same holding action is occurring except that the weather limits residential potential and supports recreational potential. As the production of various food products was given up and reliance on imported products increased, the countries were able to pay for the imports with their incomes from the sale of other, more valuable products that were produced domestically. A lot of Swiss farmers found that making cuckoo clocks (and other manufactured goods) during the cold winters rewarded them with higher incomes and more comfortable lives than did tending to snow-bound livestock. It was not difficult to convince many of those farmers to make the switch. Other Swiss farmers may have decided that they liked the rural life, but they now support their farming addiction by running winter ski resorts or other tourist businesses.

A few large European countries are also well on their way toward the end of agriculture. In 1995, Germany's agriculture minister said that the government was planning to increase aid to rural Germany in order to develop commercial alternatives to the shrinking agriculture sector. Tourism and care for the elderly were alternatives to farming put forward by the ministry. It must have been a shock to many farmers to hear the *agriculture* ministry recommend tourism over farming, but the message could not have been clearer: get ready, the real world is coming.

In some European countries agriculture has been protected from the real world by government subsidies, but those barriers are finally coming down. For example, Austria's entry into the European Union sent Austrian producer milk prices into a tailspin, squeezing profit margins for the nation's 200,000 farmers and casting doubt on the survival of some smaller operations. "The problem must be tackled at once, otherwise it will be the death of our farm industry," one Austrian official said in 1995. Welcome to the real world. The only reason that so many Austrians were still in agriculture was the ridiculously high prices that their government allowed farmers to get; but when the country entered the Union and its farmers had to compete with lower-cost farming operations in other countries, the fate of those farmers was sealed.

Popular support for agriculture in Europe was dampened significantly in the aftermath of the floods of winter 1994-95. Experts reported that deforestation, ever-bigger farm fields, pesticides, efforts to

words, countries that used to pay Big Bucks to subsidize agriculture are now willing to pay Big Bucks to get rid of it.

contain rivers in straightjackets and more tarmac and concrete aggravated floods in northern Europe and may make such disasters more likely in the future. In the wake of these reports, European voters were much less excited about having to pay the artificially high prices necessary to keep farms next door. As a result, tighter constraints on production and more incentives for the importing of food are expected in wealthy European countries, which pushes the farming into less-well-off countries in eastern Europe. For example, strict limits on use of manure in farming could cost the tiny Dutch agricultural sector 24,000 jobs starting in the year 2000. The government wants farmers to use no more manure than what is strictly needed for crop growth in order to cut down the amount of phosphate and nitrogen being released into the environment.

The floods of 1994-95 were followed by the drought of 1995, triggering a debate that reveals the gap between European consumers and agricultural officials. At a meeting of European Union farm ministers, EU Farm Commissioner Fischler said that the Union could use spare funds to provide some $390 million in aid for farmers hit by drought. In response, consumer groups said that they wanted more radical change in the EU's Common Agricultural Policy (CAP)[3] because food was still too expensive. The European Commission's agricultural spokesperson said that consumers had benefited greatly from stable food supplies and that the CAP's cost was not outrageous. Finally, the director of the European Consumers' Organization urged the EU to end farm price supports.

The inability of agriculturalists to get the message from consumers (and taxpayers) is illustrated by the French bread market. Bread has occupied a central place in French life, but for many reasons, including cost, the French people have cut back drastically on bread consumption. What has been the industry's response? French flour millers launched a publicity campaign using the motto "If we don't eat bread, one day there won't be any left."

"It's a stupid system," the Swedish Agriculture Minister said, as she asked for prompt reform of the European Common Agricultural Policy. "The system has no future," the minister continued, calling it "much too costly," because most support goes to the wealthier farmers and high costs "weigh heavier on the poor." The Swedish minister described the European Union's production control mechanisms of

---

[3] The CAP is a joint policy created and followed by all EU member countries that, in effect, has led to subsidized agricultural production and relatively high food prices.

quotas and set-aside payments as "overt signs of economic mismanagement on a grand scale." The largest single item in the EU's estimated $116.8 billion budget for 1996 was the $55.2 billion for agriculture expenses (up 10.6 percent from 1995)—mainly compensation plans for farmers—and some believe further financing will have to be sought.

Europe's potential food suppliers are urging change. Australia's prime minister said changes to European agriculture could dislodge the role of the Common Agricultural Policy and open the door to food from Asia-Pacific Economic Cooperation countries. He said that trying to maintain protection "is going to get very nasty indeed for European budgets," and "that is where I think APEC can be just the ticket." But being dependent on others for food scares many people. As a result, countries around the globe have tried every trick imaginable to stay in agriculture. For example, Europe's policies have taken it from being a food importer to being an exporter in recent decades. Unfortunately, every market distortion dreamed up hurts someone and eventually that person's complaints will be heard. By definition, anything that helps food producers hurts their input suppliers or the consumers of their output, and vice versa. Thus, farmers' efforts to raise their profitability through improved prices or lower costs directly affect the economic wealth of someone else. Even legislative efforts to increase demand for agricultural products fail to make those products profitable in the changing world market. For example, a proposal to help American corn producers by requiring that ethanol (which is made from corn) be used by some percentage of American cars by the turn of the century would backfire if implemented. An economic analysis found that American corn would probably not be used in ethanol production because the European Common Market recently changed its policy regarding corn, lowering its cost to ethanol manufacturers and other potential users. Lower European corn prices lower the world price of corn and make American corn unprofitable to grow for such uses. The final outcome of the proposal would be that demand would not increase for American corn and Americans would be required to fuel their vehicles with ethanol made from foreign corn.

The bottom line is that as countries develop, their food production gets "farmed out" to poorer countries. Just like unskilled individuals, national economies start in agriculture but stay only until they acquire the skills needed to move into a more profitable industry. The process is described next.

THE ECONOMIC FOOD CHAIN

Countries move up the "food chain" as they develop. This means that countries go through a series of development stages, each with a different focus. Ultimately, nations withdraw their resources invested in lower stages as those resources are needed for new investment in higher stages. Stated more directly, economic development starts by focusing on *food*, then it focuses on freeing labor and other resources from agriculture for use in other, more profitable production as opportunities arise. Food is the entry level, the base industry.

In the beginning, humans spent all of their time trying to keep themselves fed. Hunting and gathering were often risky because people could not always count on finding something to eat. Farming and tending livestock reduced the risk somewhat because people did not have to guess where the food was going to be. People liked that idea. Also, as people became better agricultural producers, they were able to generate all the food they could eat in less time. Eventually, everyone did not have to spend every waking moment worrying about food. The concepts of leisure and recreational uses of time were big hits.

At the point where all of a country's population was not needed "in the field" of agriculture, the base stage of economic development was completed. From then on, a country could begin to devote resources to other industries and move up through four higher stages of economic development (see Exhibit 2.1). Each successive stage emphasizes different types of industries because each stage focuses on developing a different combination of the four types of resources: labor, land, capital and management.

The first stage of development beyond agriculture focuses on exploiting a country's natural or human resources. Industries such as mining and forestry are developed by using surplus unskilled labor from agriculture to "harvest" the natural wealth of the country. The primary resource type used during this development stage (in addition to labor) is land. Countries with more land, like Russia, Canada and the United States, are more likely to have a wealth of natural resources available for harvesting. Countries with ocean frontage also harvest the seas as part of this development stage. Heavily populated countries, like China and India, may focus on harvesting their large pools of unskilled labor. The American colonies all had beaches, so fishing immediately got us into this stage. Forestry and mining followed, with each triggering the settlement and development of various regions of the country. Mining of precious metals, in particular, gave quick boosts to the development of places like California (gold), South Dakota (gold), Arizona (silver and copper), Nevada (silver), Alaska (gold) and New Mexico (uranium). Other parts of America are still known for their mining roots, like West Virginia (coal), or their forests, like Oregon and Washington, but in every case these industries are dead or dying. In 1994, for example, a consortium of 10 sawmill owners in the American Northwest instituted a plan which called for $70 million to be invested over a few years to facilitate the importing of logs from Russia. The mills were trying to assure a steady supply of logs as American logging continued to decline. This was quite a reversal, considering that a decade earlier Americans had been complaining that American logs were being sent to Japanese sawmills.

Exhibit 2.1 The Economic Food Chain

Development Stage	Economic Activities	Resources Emphasized
4th	Information production	Capital and management
3rd	Hi-tech manufacturing	Land, capital and management
2nd	Base manufacturing	Land and capital
1st	Exploit natural or human resources	Land and labor
Base	Food production	Land and labor

Countries enter the second development stage when they begin to produce goods from natural resources. This means that base manufacturing is occurring. An example to illustrate the difference between stage 1 and stage 2 is provided by comparing mining and steel manufacturing. A country in stage 1 only mines the iron ore needed to make steel; a country in stage 2 makes the steel. Countries normally move into stage 2 by using the accumulated wealth, called *capital* or money, earned from stage 1 harvesting activities to invest in the necessary hardware of manufacturing. That means stage 2 focuses on two types of resources (beyond the necessary labor): land and capital. Lots of land is still needed because manufacturing is a "big" business: big factories, big warehouses, big equipment and big messes. Lots of capital is needed because all those big inputs have big price tags. It takes a big pile of money to establish base manufacturing industries. Luckily, things like factories have very long useful lives so their big set-up costs can be spread over long periods. To facilitate these types of long-term investments, a country must develop capital markets internally or be willing to let foreign capital influence domestic development. America followed Europe into stage 2 during the industrial revolution of the eighteenth and nineteenth centuries. Most of the debris from this stage is spread across the eastern half of America. For over a decade during the last half of the twentieth century, the region was referred to as the "Rust Belt" because most of the big factories were idled and quickly became big messes. Much of the region is now in economic recovery due to a shift into stage 3 industries.

Stage 3 is triggered by the development of a skilled labor force, enabling a country to go into hi-tech manufacturing. This stage focuses on combinations of land, capital and management resources. Manufacturing, even hi-tech, requires big facilities, so land is needed, although these businesses are much less land-intensive than base manufacturing. Capital is relatively more important in this stage than land. The cash needs of industries that apply sophisticated technology are high. As the saying goes, "a billion here, a billion there, and pretty soon you are talking about real money." Nevertheless, it is the application of a third type of resource, management, which enables stage 3 industries to develop. Hi-tech products are much more complicated than those of base manufacturing, and it takes much more skill to organize the business structures needed to support this type of manufacturing. In other words, more skilled people are needed, both in the factory and in the company office, than was the case in stage 2 base manufacturing firms. The automobile industry was an early example of this stage 3 type of manufacturing, while the computer industry is a more recent case. In fact, it could be argued that the auto industry was a stage 2 industry that transitioned into a stage 3 industry. Cars were originally very basic, by today's standards, and easy to understand, but the industry kept applying the latest technological advances thus enabling them to create a modern vehicle that few people now can repair themselves. Computers, on the other hand, started off as magic boxes beyond the technical knowledge of most people. Still, technological advances are coming so quickly now that computer "generations" are about as long as the lifespan of a housefly. America led Europe and Japan into stage 3 during the twentieth century. Our push began with industries making products like cars and assorted electrical gadgets. The emphasis was on consumer goods first because they had the biggest markets, but other products followed. After telephones and phonographs came products like medicines, rocket ships and nuclear power plants. The really big costs of these industries and the fickle nature of the markets for these products make stage 3 industries prone to boom and bust periods. Just ask a long-time IBM employee about the agony and the ecstasy of their last few decades. This type of risk makes stage 3 development sustainable only for wealthy nations.

The fourth, and final, stage of development requires a highly educated population because people get "paid for what they know, not what they do." In this stage, the focus is on knowledge and information production, not the production of physical products, although products are being developed or services are being provided using the new information. The key resources required are capital and management. Capital is needed to fund the research that generates the new knowledge and information and to create the businesses that make the new products based on the research. Management and problem-solving skills themselves will be valued and marketed between firms. Stage 4 industries include firms engaged in research and problem solving, but may have begun with specialists such as doctors and lawyers.[4] Scientific laboratories, public and private educational entities and management consulting firms are current examples. The direct output of

---

[4] An early example of this type of business is the electrician who, in response to a customer's complaint about the stiff fee charged for connecting two of many wires in an electrical panel through which thousands of volts flowed, replied "you pay me for what I know, not what I do—you can stick your hands into the panel if you would prefer to do it yourself."

these companies may be nothing more tangible than patents and reports, but these pieces of information are valuable inputs for stage 3 firms. America is leading the way in the creation of this stage of economic development. We are making it up as we go.

Countries move up through the Economic Food Chain by shifting resources from lower-stage industries to higher-stage activities. According to an economic concept called *comparative advantage*, countries drop lower-level industries as opportunities in higher-level sectors develop. Comparative advantage involves specializing by investing resources in industries that generate the best return, given alternative investments available. This means that given the choice of investing a skilled laborer in a low-level industry that requires mostly unskilled labor, like agriculture, or in a higher-level industry, like those in stage 3 or 4, the country is better off doing the latter; the country's gross national product is higher if the laborer produces a more valuable product. In this sense, agriculture serves as a temporary holding area for land and other resources until a higher-and-better-use is available.

A dramatic example of agriculture's role as a holding area for labor is provided by China. An unnamed Chinese farm official said that much of China's 450 million rural workers are redundant. He said only 200 million are actually needed for farming. Also, in 1997 the *China Daily* reported that the number of workers in China's agricultural sector will decrease by 2.6 percent each year over the next five years while the number in manufacturing and the service sector will rise. By the year 2000, employees in China's agricultural sector will account only for 43 percent of the total labor force, compared to 52.2 percent in 1990 and 68.7 percent in 1980.

In more-developed countries the figures are not as dramatic, but the story is the same. For example, French farmers comprise about 2 percent of the country's population and are declining in number by 4.2 percent per year. In the European Union, the number of people working on farms plummeted to 7.3 million in 1995 from 12.3 million in 1979.

GRADUATION DAY IS COMING

America is moving into stage 4 along with Japan and some European countries. Our increasingly wealthy and educated country now invests most of its resources in stage 3 industries and is poised to make significant strides into stage 4. To reach this point we have pulled all but 1.3 percent of our population out of farming and ranching for use elsewhere, and we import food.[5]   Our stage 1 and 2 industries are virtually gone as well, and with less pain than predicted. For example, the *New York Times* reported in 1994 that efforts to protect the spotted owl had not hurt Oregon, as the state had posted its lowest unemployment number in a generation.   High-technology jobs are replacing timber industry work.[6] This shows that there is no looking back now.   The cow is out of the barn.   We are following other participants in stage 4, like Switzerland, and enjoying the good life.   The Swiss found long ago that developing specialized expertise, like banking, would enable them to make the Big Bucks by working with their brains rather than their bodies.

America doing agriculture is like a Ph.D. doing child's work— we can do it, but it is a waste.   Much of our labor, capital and management resources that remain in agriculture are there by choice but could be better invested elsewhere.   Agriculture is still profitable in general; American farm income in 1996 was a record $50 billion. However, the fact that an enterprise is making *some* profit does not make it a good investment.

Ironically, it is America's energetic aversion to waste that is causing much of the resource waste in our agriculture. We are a people of action that view unused resources as being "wasted," so we look for some use for everything. In our case, we have lots of land that can grow crops, so we feel like it should be in crop production. In many cases this production mentality is self-destructive. For example, in California's San Joaquin Valley there is land that can grow cotton, so cotton is grown on it despite the fact that publicly subsidized water has to be brought into the region from hundreds of miles away and that cotton producers receive additional government subsidies in the form of price supports for a product that often is in surplus around the world and, thus, must be stored in subsidized warehouses. This is waste raised to an art form.

Other countries are benefiting from our exit from development stages 1 and 2 by replacing us in those industries and gaining a base for their own moves into stage 3. As America removes resources from

---

[5] America's shift to being a food importer has been aided by the trend of globalization in agribusiness. This phenomenon is discussed in later chapters.

[6] The timber jobs were being lost to economics, not owls. A lumber company executive said that U.S. lumber producers are fighting a losing battle against their Canadian counterparts. Canadian lumber is one-third cheaper, on average, and it is shutting U.S. mills out of longtime markets (*Journal of Commerce,* November 1995).

agriculture and stage 1 and 2 industries, the resulting gaps in world output are filled by less-developed countries moving up into those stages of their development. For example, mining activities are disappearing from America and other developed countries and relocating in Southern Hemisphere countries. The smokestack industries that left behind our Rust Belt are now thriving in eastern European countries needing to find employment for large numbers of workers.

America has helped some of the world's poorest countries develop their agriculture so that they can progress enough to become our customers. By helping these countries free up agricultural labor for investment in stage 1 and 2 industries, we help them earn enough wealth to begin buying the products of our stage 3 industries.[7] However, in creating customers for our higher-value industries, we have hastened our departure from agriculture by aiding in the development of competitors. The absolute cost advantage of poorer countries enables them to underprice our agricultural/food products—thus the world's consumers buy food products from other nations' producers rather than ours. Egypt, for example, has a huge pool of unskilled laborers who are willing to work in agriculture for as little as $1 per day. That makes Egyptian cotton cheaper to produce than ours. America is not alone in this Catch-22. Japan has also aided many Asian countries that are now producing food for sale to Japan and using the money earned to buy Japan's hi-tech goodies. Of course, Japan has so little land that it was inevitable that the country would find alternative sources for some agricultural products (despite the continuing resistance from some groups in Japan), but the scale of the displacement of their agricultural sector was far smaller than the displacement of American agriculture. We are facing Graduation Day. We are leaving agriculture, but many

---

[7] Asian economies will lead global growth in the next century, with those in East Asia continuing to fuel the rise, the World Bank's managing director said. "Asian economies will no longer be impacted by the world economy but will impact the global economy," he explained. He went on to say that they will contribute about 50 percent of the growth of global gross domestic product in the next century. The economies of the Asia-Pacific region expanded at an average rate of 7.7 percent in 1994, compared with the global average of 3 percent, according to the United Nation's economic commission for that region (Agence France-Presse). China had the fastest growing economy, with a growth rate of 11.8 percent, followed by Singapore and Vietnam, with 9.8 percent and 8.9 percent, respectively. In fact, Singapore became Southeast Asia's first "developed" economy on January 1, 1996 (Reuters, December 1995). Three decades of spectacular centrally planned growth transformed the tiny city-state from a small tropical port to the world's ninth richest country in per capita terms, with an average income of $22,300— ahead of Britain and New Zealand.

Americans do not want to go.

WHO'S IN CHARGE HERE?

Many Americans still earn their living by working in agriculture, but the number continues to decline. Most of these people are owners or managers of farms or ranches.[8] The non-owners working for wages in American agriculture are mostly immigrants from developing countries in Latin America or Asia. These people are serving an important role in our current food production process. It will not last. This is just a phase we are going through.

Transitional immigrant farm labor will keep American land in agriculture after the U.S. population has "left for the city," but the supply of labor will dry up as poorer countries develop better and/or local jobs for their labor force.[9] Immigrant farm labor is "transitional" in that it is helping us through the final phases of our exit from agriculture. Immigrants fill jobs that American workers are not willing to do for the wages that farmers can afford to pay. If enough immigrants cannot be found, the work does not get done. As a result, a thriving new business called farm labor contracting has become the most common way for farmers to find workers in many parts of California and the Southwest. Contractors find workers for farmers (for a fee). However, even contractors cannot always find enough workers. The reason is that, gradually, the low wages available in American agriculture look less attractive to people who would prefer not to endure the hardships necessary to earn this income. As alternative sources of income become available closer to the homes of immigrant workers, they will make the rational choice to stay near their families. When faced with the same choices that drove Americans out of agricultural work, immigrants will make the same decisions and work in other industries.

In most of the debates over immigration law and policy that have taken place over the last 30 years, it has been an odd fact that

---

[8] During the 1995-96 crop year the number of people working on U.S. farms and ranches ranged from 2.46 to 3.39 million (depending on the season), according to the USDA. Of the total, self-employed farm operators numbered 1.4 to 1.59 million, along with 348,000 to 541,000 unpaid workers (usually family members) and 713,000 to 957,000 workers hired by farm operators.

[9] Central and South America are the United States' primary source of labor at present. India, Pakistan and Asia may be future sources of labor (considering their population trends), but only when (or if) wages increase enough to cover workers' costs of transport. In other words, they will come only if it is profitable for them to do so.

American farmers have had to argue in favor of allowing immigrants, legal or otherwise, into the country for one reason: without those workers, America would be much closer to leaving agriculture than it is now.[10] Without immigrants working at minimum wages or less, many crops in America would not be produced or harvested. Why don't American farmers pay higher wages to attract more workers? It makes their costs too high to profitably compete in world markets. In other words, it is because people are working for low wages (in absolute terms) in the agricultural industries of less developed countries that American farmers cannot afford to pay enough to get the workers they need to stay in business.

Thus, America, the most efficient producer of food in the world today is going out of business because it cannot compete with the upstarts in the market, many of whom it helped get going. America has moved far enough up the Food Chain that now our agricultural industry is being "eaten up."

---

[10] For example, in 1995, an official with the American Farm Bureau Federation told the Senate Judiciary Committee that a reform proposal aimed at controlling illegal immigration would have a negative impact on agricultural labor and force farmers to seek alternative sources of farm help (*Delmarva Famer*). He said that the committee should "review the adequacy of programs intended to meet agriculture's need for alien workers" if domestic labor cannot fill in the gaps. His message: let us have cheap labor or we are out of business. How bad is the labor shortage? In 1997 the *New York Times* reported that three men pleaded guilty to enslaving migrant workers in South Carolina as part of a scheme in which workers were threatened with violence if they sought to escape.

Chapter 3

Any Portfolio in a Storm

Why would an individual farmer leave agriculture? We know they would not make this decision easily because people in agriculture are aware of the physical and financial difficulties they face and choose to remain anyway because they like the life. An obvious assumption is that *farmers and ranchers will stay in agriculture if it is at all feasible.* The answer is that individual farmers and ranchers are forced to leave agriculture by the harsh realities of personal finance.

An agricultural producer is a resource portfolio manager in an industry with a decreasing number of profitable investments (crop or livestock enterprises). As profitability falls, a farmer is eventually forced to protect his equity by getting out of the market. He does this by shifting resources out of agriculture and into something more profitable. One of the first resources to leave is usually the producer's spouse, who is sent to work "in town" to bring home some cash to feed the farming habit. A producer's equity is of vital importance because it is his or her primary source of retirement funds in most cases, adding even greater urgency to the need for profits from the agricultural business. Thus, being rational people, producers will protect their families' future by leaving agriculture, if necessary, before losing their assets. Sometimes individuals misjudge the gravity and/or the volatility of their situations and do lose everything. For example, the mid-1980s was a particularly bad period during which farm foreclosures were common. However, most exits from agriculture do not occur due to foreclosures, they happen when one person sells to another. The resources sold, including land and equipment, may or may not stay in agriculture after the sale.

During the 1980s, most of the farming resources that were sold at foreclosure sales in the Midwest were bought by the neighbors of the seller, so the resources stayed in production even though their ownership changed. In that hectic decade, about 20 percent of farms were sold, but total acreage in agricultural production did not decrease by nearly that amount.

Agriculture never was a pot of gold. Sure, the 1970s were pretty good, and 1914-16 was great, but generally profits in this competitive industry were nearly always small compared to most alternatives. The rate of return on farm assets in the United States has averaged about 4 percent for several decades, while the stock market has averaged returns of 13 percent during the same period. But one of the attractions for most people who stayed in agriculture was the stability of the profits from food. Some crops did experience wild price swings over time, yet farming was a modestly profitable business on average. That was the past. Recent history paints a different picture. By the mid-1980s, total profits of all agricultural firms in Arizona's were estimated to equal the amount of government payments received by producers in the state. In other words, without government help, agriculture was, on average, just a break-even proposition. The market was sending a message: Arizona's resources are not well suited to agriculture and, as a result, they cannot profitably compete in today's markets.[1]

Individual farmers react to lower profit margins in one crop or livestock enterprise by investing the land and other resources in another enterprise that appears to offer better profit potential. This strategy works as long as there are alternative crops. For most of American history there have been more-profitable alternatives. Unfortunately, for most producers the search for more profits led them away from crops with relatively stable markets, like grains, to crops with volatile markets and prices, such as fruits and vegetables. Many producers making the shift from one market to another experienced a rude awakening.

The Great Zucchini War of Pinal County is a typical example.

---

[1] But could this book be judged guilty of agricultural slander just by saying so? Legislation dubbed the "veggie hate crimes bill" was signed into Arizona law in 1995. The measure allows farmers and produce shippers to sue anyone who maliciously spreads false information about Arizona farm products. The bill was prompted by a scare several years earlier involving Alar, a chemical sprayed on apples to promote uniform ripening, that cost the apple industry $500 million. (Arizona is not the only state that doesn't like people picking on their veggies. By 1996, 12 states had passed laws that provide a legal cause of action against anyone who disparages a perishable food product.) Honest, Judge, it's not slander to tell the truth.

Pinal County is between Phoenix and Tucson, Arizona. During the mid-1980s, cotton growers in the area were looking for alternative crops. One farmer experimented with 10 acres of zucchini squash. He was able to sell his entire output at a good price to a buyer in the Phoenix market. But then he bragged to his neighbor about the big pile of profits he had made. Predictably, the neighbor also planted 10 acres of zucchini for the next season, expecting to make some easy money. Come harvest time, the two neighbors were furious with each other because they both had lost badly on their zucchini crops. When all the yelling and finger pointing died down, it was discovered that 20 acres of zucchini was more than all of Phoenix could eat during the short season, so the market price had collapsed. The war casualties included two farmers in debt, a couple of handfuls of laborers out of work, and thousands of slain squash. It was not a pretty sight.

WHERE HAS ALL THE MONEY GONE?

Why is agriculture becoming less profitable? Simply because the world keeps changing. Agriculture is becoming more expensive as America moves up the Economic Food Chain. It takes increasingly higher investments to remain competitive and the risks involved keep getting greater. The bottom line indicates that profits are being cut by shifts in both technology and risk; the two work to "pull-push" agriculture towards its fate. The story concerning "risk push" is in the next chapter, the story about "technological pulls" is below.

Technological advances first encourage, then force farmers to adopt ever more expensive production methods to compete. These "technological pulls" gradually force marginal land out of agriculture as rising production costs per acre cannot be supported by the land's ability to generate cash flow. Land that is good (meaning land that is capable of generating high yields of valuable crops) is priced ever higher because more farmers are willing buyers, thus bidding up prices for "good dirt." These higher land prices add to fixed costs and lower the return on assets for the owner/investor who purchases the land. Eventually the costs of producing on even the best farmland exceed the returns available from commodities.

The effects of technology can be seen as a progression. It is apparent when considering the case of almost any tree or vine crop producer. Grapes, for example, can be grown wild, with little help from people, in many cool, wet microclimates. Unfortunately, this approach has not been profitable since the ancient Greeks started getting colored feet from making wine. Some wise guy discovered that growing grapevines next to one another, in rows especially, reduced the amount of walking needed to gather the output, thus lowering costs and improving profits. Other innovations followed over the centuries, leading to the current situation in grape vineyards in which hi-tech trellises, irrigation systems, wind machines, et cetera, require an investment of over $10,000 per acre above the cost of the land itself. With this level of investment required to establish a modern vineyard, only people with access to lots of cash can get into the business. Also, with this level of overhead costs to recover, small dips in wine-grape market prices quickly translate into big losses. Even under normal circumstances the average payback period for tree and vine crops, like apples and grapes, is 15 years or more. Thus, agriculture of this sort is an expensive, risky investment that fewer Americans can afford to make.

Technology has kept American agriculture competitive in world markets by keeping prices of commodities falling in real terms. As shown in Table 3.1, the nominal prices (not adjusted for inflation) of many unregulated food commodities have not changed much in the past three decades. When inflation is accounted for, the real prices of these commodities have fallen dramatically. This has been possible because new innovations have increased productivity and reduced production costs per unit. Thus, American farmers and ranchers have been able to remain profitable despite the lower real prices they receive for their output because they have been able to produce each unit with relatively fewer inputs (in terms of dollars).

**Table 3.1 Sample U.S. Food Commodity Prices over Time
(farm level, not adjusted for inflation)**

	1962	1972	1982	1992
Corn ($/ton)	40.00	56.07	91.07	73.21
Wheat ($/ton)	68.00	58.67	115.00	108.00
Rice ($/hundredweight)	5.04	6.73	7.91	6.10
Oranges ($/box)	4.50	2.83	8.80	6.90
Tomatoes, processing ($/ton)	28.42	35.21	71.57	58.04

Source: *Agricultural Statistics, Annual Summary*, USDA; *California Fruit and Nut Statistics*, California Agricultural Statistics Service.

Unfortunately, continued technological improvements may not be enough to keep American products competitive with products from less-developed countries. The cost of inputs is increasing at a faster pace in America than in poorer countries. One of the most important input costs is wage rates. As America needs a higher percentage of its population working in stage 3 and 4 industries, hi-tech wages will go up to attract more workers and, in so doing, will gradually drag up agricultural wages. These higher wages will further reduce the profitability of food production because the price of food commodities is set by competition in world markets, and supplies from less-developed countries will keep those prices relatively low. Eventually, America will not be able to generate profits or wages to reward farmers sufficiently to match urban wages. Farm workers will be even harder to find and nearly impossible to keep, and the financial rewards will not be worth the trouble for owners/investors.

HOME ON THE RANGE

In the face of the mounting financial reasons for leaving agriculture, a couple million Americans remain. This raises the question of how much a farm lifestyle is worth. Or, put more bluntly, how much less income will farmers accept to be able to stay on the farm? It has long been known that farm incomes, on average, are lower than those in the agribusiness sector, and that average incomes in agriculture as a whole are lower than those "in town." For example, Table 3.2 shows the situation in the 1970s, which was a relatively profitable period for agriculture. Interpreting this information leads to the conclusion that either farmers and ranchers are crazy or they value their rural lifestyle in non-monetary ways and are willing to give up additional income that they might earn working in some other industry.

Surely there must be something to rural life because thousands of city folks are trying to recapture it by moving back to rural locations, especially in the western United States. It may not be measurable, but there is plenty of evidence that rural magic exists. In southern California, for example, there is a region east of Los Angeles that was once settled by dairy farmers. As the city expanded toward those farmers the value of their land grew rapidly, reportedly reaching prices as high as $1 million per acre. And yet, there is still a 20-square-mile dairy reserve that has been completely surrounded by urban development. Across the street from some of the dairy barns are housing tracts and shopping centers. Why do the dairies not sell out?

Some of them have, of course, but many of the people who sold used their huge financial gains to buy bigger dairies for themselves and/or their children in northern California or some other state. They obviously like the lifestyle. To some people this is land speculation; to many other people this is evidence of insanity.

Table 3.2 Agriculture's Share of U.S. National Income and Employment, 1970

	Employment (% of U.S. total)	National Income (% of U.S. total)
Farming	5.3	2.1
Agribusiness	23.5	17.6
Public service	0.3	0.5
Total agriculture	29.1	20.2

Source: *Agricultural Statistics and Statistical Abstract of the United States*, USDA.

In reality, farmers and ranchers are hardly ever crazy. Crazy people do not survive for long in such competitive markets. Agricultural producers do have some minimum income requirements and they do question the sustainability of their lifestyle if their income needs are not met.

Consider the case of a cattle rancher in northwestern California. He is 45 years old and single. His 80-year-old father is still active but has handed over the daily management of their 7,000 acre ranch to him. "Dad has put himself out to pasture." The father's only income is his savings from the time that he ran the ranch. The ranch has 6,000 acres of grazing land and 1,000 acres suitable for cropping. The feeder cattle herd usually runs about 300 head during low-price periods (which describes most of the last decade). The rancher runs the entire operation and does all the labor with the assistance of just one handyman. For all of this he pays himself $500 per month and his handyman $900 per month. $6,000 per year for managing a multi-million-dollar operation! Few managers outside of agriculture are willing to work for less than minimum wage. And few business managers pay their employees 80 percent more than they pay themselves. Is this rancher crazy? No, he has a financial plan. He pays himself only what he needs for basic living costs to reduce the cash drain on the ranch during unprofitable periods. When cattle markets are up, so are his wages. He pays his handyman the going rate for live-in help in his area of the state; he knows that if he does not, someone else will hire away the handyman. He limits his herd size to the number that can be carried profitably on his best grazing land; he knows that a larger herd would reduce profits, not increase them. When he can hedge or contract to guarantee a better price, he expands his herd accordingly. He leases out the cropping land to local farmers during periods when he cannot profitably use it for grazing. And, finally, he keeps track of the market value of his land to enable himself to include capital gains (and losses) in his calculation of total returns on his investment over the short and long term. He can tell you what that ROI is at any time (it has been as high as 20 percent and now bounces around between a 2 percent loss to a 3 percent profit). When questioned as to whether he thinks he could get a better return in some other business, he always says yes. When asked whether he is considering leaving agriculture, he always used to say no, but in recent years the answer has become maybe. The rate of growth on his land value always used to be enough to compensate him for the lost income in agriculture; now it is not. He wants to stay on the ranch, but he does not want to be forced to sell pieces of it to do so; he would prefer to sell it all and leave if the situation requires it. He is surprised, but he realizes that his family's long history in ranching may die with him.

Similar pressures face ranchers across the West. In Montana there are regions where trout are more valuable than cattle. Ranchers with property containing trout streams currently have three alternatives: (1) continue producing cattle, (2) offer fishing vacation packages to tourists, or (3) sell their land to developers who will build second homes for city folks. As a cattle operation, the land will support only two animal units (two cows with calves per acre), which means that the annual revenues are the proceeds from selling the two calves, or a couple hundred dollars per acre (depending on calf prices). The going rate paid by tourist fishermen is $1500 per week. Finally, people are paying $200,000 for 5-acre parcels along trout streams. It doesn't take long to calculate that cattle ranching is the least profitable and most risky choice of the three. So, sooner or later ranchers cannot resist the urge to make some money.

Agriculture is getting to be a very expensive habit for some people, and yet they are willing to work hard to keep it. The U.S. Department of Agriculture itself reports the strange truth. For example, "the average off-farm income of farm operator households in 1991 was $32,542, compared with $3,994 of net income from farming operations. Only about 18 percent of farm operator households received more income from the farm than off farm in 1991" (Gale and Harrington). This means that average family farmers have already shifted part of their portfolios out of agriculture. They had to; they needed the money. The realities of personal finance are sending country folks into town to find the cash to keep the homestead going. In the countryside the livin' may be easy, but the work doesn't pay. At some point, cash becomes a concern and getting it becomes a necessity. But income is not the only factor bringing about changes in agricultural households.

The risk environment triggers shifts in the agricultural portfolio. Even profitable agricultural producers may be forced out of production by changes in the risks they face. Individuals choose to produce the portfolio of crops and/or livestock enterprises that best suits their resources and attitudes regarding the trade-off between risk and return from that portfolio. When changes in the market or business environment occur, producers reassess the trade-offs from their enterprise portfolio versus alternative portfolios and choose accordingly. The result can be significant changes in the agricultural output of one or more producers. In fact, entire regions can go through significant changes over relatively short time periods. California is an example: in recent years lenders have reacted to banking regulations and other changes, farmers have reacted to lenders, the state's product portfolio has changed, and these changes are just the beginning of the end. The next few chapters tell the story of this "risk-push." It is a story in progress in parts of America, a story that has already been told in other areas of the country, and one that will be told eventually in all places where Americans currently produce food.

Chapter 4

Reading between the Curvy Lines

Agriculture exists only as long as both producers and lenders believe it is profitable. Producers have to be *willing* and *able* to get into farming or ranching. America has no shortage of people who are willing, but their ability to produce is often limited by their lenders' willingness to provide the necessary money. The long delay between the time that farmers must spend money to get the inputs needed to cultivate, harvest and sell crops and the time that they receive payment for those crops means that almost all farmers must borrow cash to stay in business. Being in debt makes farmers very responsive to the lenders who provide the cash. As a result, lenders today have a great deal of influence over what crops and livestock are produced, in what quantities, and in what locations. Lenders focus on the bottom line, thus profits dictate where the money flows.

Agriculture has virtually disappeared from northeastern United States due to low profits based on the inadequacy of the area's resources. The climate, terrain and soil of the region are not especially suited to farming many products using today's technology. A few potatoes, berries and dairies are about all that hang on. In America's youth, this region's agriculture supported the country. New Jersey was nicknamed the Garden State because of its plentiful agriculture. Quite a change. What little agriculture remains consists of small, intensive operations that can still generate enough profit to mollify investors. In Rhode Island, for example, there are only 700 agricultural operations left, averaging 90 acres each. These operations manage to hang on because in 1993 they generated an average of $641 net income per acre, the highest average income per acre of any state in America. Rhode Island's average net income per operation ranks as the third best in the country, following only Arizona and California. Yet, agricultural operations continue to leave the state as more profitable investments come along.

Other regions of the country are losing their agriculture as well. The Southwest has been a desert for a long time, not the kind of place suited for agriculture. Yet, before technology developed food storage and transportation methods to get food into the region from elsewhere, settlers in places like Arizona, New Mexico and west Texas had to "do it yourself or do without." The settlers obviously chose to eat, so they established agriculture locally. Now the livestock roaming New Mexico's barren hills are giving way to beef from cooler climates. The dry-land cotton farmers of West Texas are having a tougher time justifying operations that in some years have yields of zero cotton per acre. The huge irrigated farms of Arizona cannot afford to buy the water in the canals of the Central Arizona Project. Despite Arizona's number one ranking in average net income per operation ($80,729 in 1993), its average of $18 net income per acre does not leave much room for buying expensive water. People are not surprise that most of these regions have abandoned agriculture; looking at the resources in places like the Northeast and Southwest it is easy to see that agriculture is not the best way to utilize them.

Yet, California, the King of American Agriculture, is on the same path as other regions and is leaving agriculture. Lack of profitability is still the reason for the exodus, but the cause of these failing profits is not the unsuitability of the state's resources, but "risk push." Real and perceived changes in the risks involved in agriculture are pushing the industry into making alterations in its operations that will force it out of business eventually. As California goes, the rest of the country will follow.

This is a startling thought: California out of agriculture! The state currently produces about 250 commodities, leading the nation in the production of over 50 of these. It has been the nation's leading agricultural state for more than half a century, generating over $24.5 billion in agricultural sales during 1996. There are about 80,000 farms and ranches in the state, and agriculture as a whole employs about 9 percent of the its workforce.

In California, the "risk push" is coming from lenders, government, and agricultural producers' rational reactions to the changing business environment. In summary, California's agricultural producers are behaving as if there has been a recent increase in the risk levels they face. This is leading to significant changes in the industry. The story follows.

CALIFORNIA, HERE IT COMES

Economic and natural factors have both helped to create a new risk environment in which California's agricultural producers must operate. Producers believe that a credit crunch developed in agriculture in the early 1990s as that is when they began having more difficulty gaining access to the credit they need. As a result, significant changes in resource allocation are occurring in the state while the agricultural sector adjusts its approach to risk management. These adjustments have wide-ranging economic implications for California and the country.

California producers' concern for production risk has traditionally been relatively low, given a moderate climate, irrigation control of water, and broad options for diversification. But recent events are challenging those attitudes. For example, a major freeze, a six-year drought, a couple floods, and farm lenders' new attitudes toward risks have combined to make production risk exposure a renewed concern of agribusiness people in California. In December 1990, a record-breaking freeze significantly damaged a number of crops in many regions of the state. Also, for the first time in its history, the state's water project suspended all water deliveries to agriculture during 1992 and, on average, the federal Central Valley Project made just 25 percent of water deliveries to agriculture. It was the sixth year of a six-year drought and there was not enough water in the state's reservoirs to meet urban needs. Then, the drought was broken with two years of floods in a three-year period. Producers think these events have caused agricultural lenders to weigh production risk more heavily in their lending decisions. Many lenders are now including a water supply questionnaire in their loan application process, and producers who have been creditworthy in the past have been turned down because they do not have a secure water supply. During the height of the water hysteria in 1992, a researcher put the six-year drought into perspective by reporting that data from the rings of ancient trees in California show that over the past 500 years droughts lasting 10 years have been common. Since 1992, urban water needs have overshadowed those of farmers.

There have been real changes in attitudes and operating procedures concerning risk management and credit in California agriculture. The "risk push" story for California is typical of the story being told across America.

How Producers Choose Enterprises

A person deciding whether to produce agricultural commodities must first identify the opportunities available in their particular market. These opportunities can be evaluated using methods similar to those used by portfolio managers.

To begin, if no land is available for lease, for whatever reason, only landowners can produce crops. In this situation, each landowner would choose to produce the crop portfolio (i.e., combination of crops) which best suits his or her desired level of tradeoff between risk and returns. This leads to different portfolios being produced by people who have different profit expectations or attitudes about risk.

If leasing land is possible, the opportunities available to growers are altered. Leasing in land enables tenants to become producers. When cash leasing is possible, all of a region's landowners that have the same profit expectations will choose to produce the same list of enterprises, although the composition of their selected commodity portfolios will still vary because they will have different risk attitudes. The portfolio that each person selects depends on their personal risk preferences and consists partly of the enterprises in the " optimal" portfolio[1] and partly of the risk-free alternative (i.e., cash leasing a portion of land owned). Therefore, even though two growers in the same market may have the same opportunities and expectations, they will still choose different crop portfolios if they react differently to risk. The difference between the portfolios of these growers is in the percentage of land used in production versus the amount leased in or out.

Effects of Increased Risk on Producers' Enterprise Selection

An increase in production risk,[2] either real or perceived, changes the risk/return tradeoffs available to all producers, meaning that a higher level of risk must be accepted at each level of returns. This new set of economic opportunities triggers a three-stage reaction that could occur quickly or may take several years to complete. First, it creates new

---

[1] The " optimal" portfolio consists of those enterprises that, as a group, have the best tradeoff between return and risk, given current market prices and yields for all products. This combination of enterprises will change over time with market conditions.

[2] Production risk is one source of what finance specialists call business risk. Business risk and financial risk are the two components of a firm's total risk.

production opportunities that encourage landowners to lease out more land rather than producing on it themselves. Second, the lower profitability of these production opportunities is not high enough to attract tenants in sufficient numbers to enable owners to lease out all the land they wish, thus leasing rates fall until enough tenants can be found, which establishes a new set of production opportunities. Finally, the new production opportunities are more profitable, which may cause landowners to want to use more land themselves to produce a less risky portfolio of enterprises. (This entire process is explained in detail by Blank 1995.)

Direct Effects of an Increase in Perceived Risk. The first question to be addressed is, What direct effects do perceived increases in risk levels have on a farmer's production decisions? To begin, it is assumed that a producer is using all of his or her land for production.

If the perceived level of risk increases (i.e., farmers think the situation has become more risky), production decisions change significantly. A transition period, which could be brief or could last years, begins as a new set of production opportunities becomes relevant. A producer's profitability is lower in this period. During the transition farmers will select a new optimal portfolio and use a smaller portion of their land for production, leasing the remaining acreage out. The composition of the new optimal portfolio will be more risky than that of the original portfolio. Hence, growers respond to increases in risk by producing a *more risky* combination of crops, but they produce on fewer acres during the transition period so they can lower their total risk exposure.

In response to the reduced profitability offered by the new production opportunities, tenants' demand for land will decline over time, causing cash leasing rates to decline which, in turn, causes changes in production plans as the transition period ends in a new period of equilibrium. If leasing rates drop, production decisions will change again. A third set of production opportunities become relevant. A producer's profitability is decreased further in this new market. The new selected portfolio in this case requires that the farmer produce less risky crops on more of his or her land and, possibly, lease in additional land.

In summary, portfolio analysis leads to a number of explanations regarding producers' operating procedures and strategies. First, a transition period began in California with the perceived increase in risk caused by the drought, regulatory changes and other factors.

During what could be a multiyear period of transition, the following producer operating strategies are expected: (1) acreage of "risky" crops will increase; (2) more risky cropping patterns will lead to increased demand for risk management tools; (3) more acres will be fallowed and/or leased out by landowners; and (4) water and other inputs will be concentrated on fewer acres to raise the return per acre on the land in production.[3]

The transition period will lead to a new period of equilibrium as the following expected trends are observed: (1) cash leasing rates per acre will decline; (2) less land will be leased out (thus limiting entry into farming by tenants); (3) farmland values will decline; and (4) land will be forced out of agriculture and developed due to agricultural income shortfalls, unless farmland prices fall enough to make crops that are less profitable/risky viable again. Ultimately, farmers will generally be producing less risky combinations of crops, compared to the crops grown before the increase in risk, but these low-value crops may not provide sufficient income for individual landowners to justify staying in agriculture. Until these trends are observed, the transition continues, and producers will face numerous short-term constraints.

Credit Limit Effects. An increase in the perceived level of production risk leads directly to a reduction in the amount of financial risk (measured as debt levels) that a firm can take on without raising its total risk exposure. Therefore, higher production risk will either cause interest rates charged to the firm to rise or the amount of credit extended to the firm to decrease.[4]

Credit limits tightened by an increase in risk levels can have a significant effect on a farmer's portfolio choice and the risk efficiency (tradeoff) of that portfolio as an investment. This point can be illustrated using the cases of an owner and a tenant who each would

---

[3] This means that farms with water shortages, for example, are expected to use the full amount required for normal output per acre on fewer acres rather than putting less efficient amounts on all available acreage. Also, it is expected that growers will, to the extent possible given agronomic and management capabilities, shift out of water-intensive, low-value crops such as alfalfa, cotton and rice and into higher-value, less-water-intensive crops such as processing tomatoes. However, growers of perennial crops will face significantly more constraints on their ability to make adjustments to their production portfolio and, therefore, will be less able to adjust their risk exposure in the short term.

[4] This assumes that the increase in risk is detected by the lender. If the lender is unaware of an increase in the potential for default of which the borrower *is* aware, the producer might "plunge" by borrowing as much as possible, taking the big gamble seen as the only way to stave off impending failure of the firm.

choose the same portfolio if possible. If the owner needs to borrow additional funds to lease in land, expand production or invest in new crops or technology, he has the equity in his land to serve as collateral, giving him borrowing capacity. The tenant (or fully leveraged landowner), however, faces a much greater chance of being unable to borrow the full amount needed because he or she needs more funds (a tenant is leasing in *all* the land to be used in production, not just part of it like the owner) and has no equity in land to serve as collateral, hence, that person may represent a more risky loan to the lender. If the tenant cannot borrow all the funds needed to produce the desired portfolio, he or she will have to select a less costly (and less profitable) portfolio for which adequate credit is available. This means that for all producers, credit constraints will, at some point, cut off production opportunities. The lower the credit limits of tenants or landowners, the more likely that they will be forced to select a less efficient (less desirable) and less profitable portfolio. As the cliché says, "it takes money to make money."

Risk Attitudes

To identify changes in operating procedures and strategies of California producers caused by recent events, the following questions were included in a survey of farmers (Blank 1995): (1) Have you increased your total acreage of high-value produce during the past three years? (2) Do you believe that producing more-valuable crops requires more attention to risk management? (3) Have you fallowed and/or leased out more acreage over the last three years than you do normally? (4) When fallowing some land, do you use more water and other inputs on the land remaining in production? (5) Have cash leasing rates per acre declined over the past year or two? (6) Have you decreased the amount of land leased out over the past year or two? (7) Have farmland values declined in recent years? (8) Has farmland been developed into nonagricultural uses in your area recently?

In general, the results show producer behavior indicating a "transition period" has begun but shows no signs of ending in the near future. The level of positive responses to the first four questions reported in Table 4.1 indicates that producers are reacting to the new risk environment as predicted by the portfolio analysis. If the transition period were complete, responses to the last four questions in Table 4.1 would have been much more positive. This means that the four trends expected to signal the end of the transition period and the beginning of the new equilibrium are not evident yet, but are expected to develop in the future.

Table 4.1 California Producers' Operating Strategy Changes

	% Answering Yes	
Trends Beginning Transition Period	Owners	Tenants
(1) Increased total produce acreage in past three years?	21	27
(2) Crops require more risk management?	58	61
(3) Fallowed and/or leased out more acreage recently?	34	—
(4) Concentrating water and other inputs on fewer acres?	43	—
Trends Ending Transition		
(5) Cash leasing rates declined recently?	12	12
(6) Decreased the amount of land leased out recently?	7	—
(7) Land values declined recently?	28	—
(8) Farmland developed out of agriculture recently?	15	—

To cross-check the responses to the first question in Table 4.1, published acreage data from the entire state were evaluated for recent trends. As shown below for a sample of risky crops, acreage in production did increase during the early years of the new risk era. Growers are shifting more acreage into high-value produce as expected.

	Land in Production (thousands of acres)	
	1988	1991
Tomatoes (processed)	226.1	312.0
Tomatoes (fresh)	37.5	40.0
Carrots	51.1	56.0
Peaches	53.7	54.1
Strawberries	17.6	21.1
Almonds (shelled)	407.0	411.0

Risky Business

To identify changes in producer attitudes toward risk management methods in California, the following questions were asked: (1) Is risk included in management decisions? (2) Do risk variables enter into plans and decisions about enterprise selection and/or resource use and management? (3) Were you able to make contingency plans for the drought and/or freeze using existing risk management strategies? If not, what did you do? (4) Did the freeze and/or drought alter your attitudes toward or estimates of risk? (4a) If so, how will your risk management efforts be affected in the short run? In the long run? (5) Has the credit crunch reduced the amount of credit available to you? (6) Have you changed crops to reduce your credit needs? (7) Are you satisfied with the risk/return tradeoff available on the crops you produce currently? The results are summarized in Table 4.2.

Table 4.2 Producers' Attitudes toward Risk

	% Answering Yes	
	Owners	Tenants
(1) Risk used in decision-making?	40	45
(2) Risk used in enterprise selection?	31	36
(3) Risk contingency plans?	23	35
(4) Drought/freeze altered risk attitudes?	51	57
(4a) New risk plans developed?	25	25
(5) Credit crunch reduced credit limits?	29	35
(6) Changed crops to reduce credit needs?	18	37
(7) Satisfied with current crops' risk/return tradeoff?		
Risk averse growers	71	52
Less risk averse growers	83	78

As a whole, the results indicate that producers are now very aware of risk, yet over half were unprepared, to some degree, for the shocks of the drought, freeze, and credit crunch. Forty percent of land-owning respondents indicated that they are currently considering risk in their decision making. Yet, many producers are apparently uncertain as to *how* to incorporate risk into their management plans. For example, the most obvious time that risk should be considered is when selecting enterprises, yet only 31 percent of owners are doing so. Those respondents not considering it when selecting enterprises often explained that they produced perennial crops, so they were "not selecting enterprises each year." Exhibit 4.1 shows the varied ways in which producers are considering risk in their operations. Another indication of weak risk planning is the response to question 3 in which only 23 percent of landowners claimed to have active contingency plans for major risks such as the drought or freeze. Question 4 results show that 51 percent of owners now have a better appreciation for the need to consider risk in management planning than they did before the drought. Yet, only 25 percent have developed new risk plans since that time. Nearly one-third are feeling the effects of the new credit environment, according to question 5. The example cited most often is a shift in enterprises to reduce credit needs by considering the timing of cash flows from particular enterprises in their portfolio (question 6). The responses to question 7 indicate that producers are generally satisfied with their degree of risk exposure, however the confusion evident in responses to other questions raises the issue of whether growers truly understand the concept of risk and its management.

One question from the survey dealt with ranking various sources of risk as they affect profitability. The sources of risk itemized in the question encompass natural phenomenon such as weather and temperature variability, variability in market prices and competition, and government intervention and regulation. Producers were asked to rank the sources of risk according to the magnitude of their effects on profitability. The survey results are presented in Table 4.3. Percentages associated with each ranking are reported for every source of risk. In general, the sources of risk deemed most influential by producers of all types are, first, market (price) attributes and, next, adverse variabilities in nature.

However, it is interesting to note how agribusiness firms view risk compared to individual producers. During interviews, managers of 26 agricultural cooperatives were asked about the risks their organizations faced and how the cooperative managed these risks. Weather was the most commonly mentioned risk with 92 percent of the respondents listing it. Pests and disease were also mentioned by nearly two-thirds of co-ops, especially cooperatives dealing with fruits and nuts that must maintain quality standards.

Exhibit 4.1 Do Risk Variables Enter into Producers' Plans and Decisions about Enterprise Selection and/or Resource Use and Management?

Nature of Responses to Survey Question

Risks considered in everyday and long-range plans
Change management practices
Change cultural practices
Diversify operation
Change from high-profit to low-risk crop
Limit exposure to regulations and lawsuits
Change labor practices
Change marketing method
With tighter profit margins, can withstand fewer loss years

Sample Comments of Individuals

* Switched from grain corn to silage corn because of low grain prices. Gone to seed crops because of forward contract availability.
* Vegetable farmer said he modifies his planting because of susceptibility of different fields to flooding (doesn't plant by the river in the rainy season). Switched out of dry beans and sugar beets because of low prices.
* Planting locations determined by susceptibility to flooding. Tries to keep about the same acreage in each crop and yields high to minimize the effect of price risk.
* Would not plant almonds in his riverbottom land due to frost. Has moved out of peaches into almonds due to price fluctuations in peaches.
* Got into almonds because they are not perishable and they are easy to grow.
* Risk is why they are diversified even though it would be easier to specialize.
* Would like to diversify even more. Has drilled wells to reduce risk.
* Yields tend to be steady in lima beans. Forward contract in broccoli seed removes much risk.
* No longer grows rice because cost of production increased while price went down. With peaches, market has been good and contracts have been available.
* California must move into high-value and low-water use crops and away from alfalfa and row crops.
* Uses labor contractors when timeliness is a factor.
* Grows more and more permanent crops due to high land values but tries to find crops with low labor requirements.
* Prefers commodities that can be insured. Consider availability of long-term water supply.

(Continued on next page)

(Exhibit 4.1 continued)

* With permanent crops, enterprise selection is hard to change, so risk enters into cultural decisions like spraying.
* Chose early-season tomato varieties.
* Chose tomatoes because of contracts. Switches between wheat and safflower because of price. Chose rice because of the government program.
* Cotton has stable yields and the government program.
* Sugar beets show consistent returns. Planted popcorn and sunflower because they fit into the government program.
* Moved out of sugar beets because of disease. Stick with grain because of the equipment they own.

The second most commonly mentioned risk was government regulations, cited by 88.5 percent of the cooperatives interviewed. When respondents were asked to specify the two most important sources of risk, regulations were mentioned by half the cooperatives, whereas weather was noted by just over one-third. This is a significant difference between agricultural producers and agribusiness: firms consider government regulations to be a major source of risk, but individuals do not.

Table 4.3 Sources of Risk

Sources Of Risk	1st	2nd	3rd	Rank 4th	5th	6th	7th	8th
				(%)				
Disease	16.6	17.0	13.1	16.3	14.0	11.2	8.8	3.0
Drought	25.5	15.7	11.9	8.9	9.4	10.2	11.7	6.6
Floods	1.5	6.6	3.3	3.9	3.6	6.3	13.5	61.3
Freeze	19.9	16.8	8.9	7.6	7.8	11.2	14.8	13.0
Inp price	12.5	21.3	21.1	13.6	14.9	9.7	4.6	2.2
Labor	8.9	12.4	13.5	13.1	15.7	16.9	11.3	8.2
Otpt price	32.0	25.9	14.6	11.1	7.1	4.4	2.9	1.9
Pests	12.4	17.9	20.4	14.3	17.2	8.8	5.9	3.2
Other	35.6	15.6	13.3	17.8	6.7	2.2	2.2	6.7

Note: The table lists the percentage of respondents that ranked each source of risk as 1st most important, 2nd, etc. The percentages in each row are calculated on the total number of responses received for that item.

Regulations hit livestock cooperatives relatively harder than other commodities with all livestock cooperatives stating that regulations were one of the most important sources of risk to the cooperative. Regulations also seem to increase risk for smaller cooperatives relatively more than for larger ones. Of the smallest co-ops surveyed (those with less than 100 members), 75 percent mentioned government regulations as one of the two most important sources of risk. In contrast, about one-third of large cooperatives (those with over 1,000 members) listed regulations among the top two sources of risk.

A third group of risks that cooperatives face, that includes input and output price variability and labor costs, was mentioned by 54 percent to 62 percent of the respondents. As would be expected, supply cooperatives are more concerned with changes in input prices while cooperatives engaged in marketing care more about changes in output prices. Interestingly, labor costs are not ranked in the two most important sources of risk by any cooperative.

Producers' Views of Agricultural Credit

To assess how the credit environment is perceived by agribusiness (as represented by cooperatives) and by producers (as they have related their concerns to the cooperative managers), a series of questions was asked regarding requirements for borrowing. The survey results provide insight into a commonly held belief concerning credit. Producers think that lenders have tightened their requirements for getting credit. This is thought to be a direct result of the new risk environment in agriculture. It is also believed that producers have more difficulty getting credit than do agribusinesses.

The results concerning requirements for gaining credit indicate a large difference between the effects that recent changes have had on agribusiness firms and on individual producers. Over 70 percent of the co-ops surveyed felt that lender requirements were no more difficult to meet than in previous years, and 88 percent said that financing had not curtailed co-op activities. The other respondents tended to put a positive spin on their replies, stating that any restrictions on activity were due largely to internal discipline or that they helped to improve discipline. In contrast, over 95 percent of co-ops said that their members had complained of stricter lending requirements and over 46 percent said that activities of members had been curtailed due to a lack of financing or to timing problems in gaining credit. The results indicate that borrowing restrictions have shifted away from traditional measures of equity and toward sources of repayment.

Economic and Policy Implications

The results presented earlier, along with the responses to many open-ended questions on the survey, provide insight into how producers will react to perceived increases in risk and what the economic and policy implications of those risk factors might be. Some of the issues of concern in this new risk environment, and their economic and policy implications, are discussed below.

Credit Availability. The credit crunch, as a symptom of the new risk environment, is having a significant effect on many agricultural producers in California. Some people have not been able to borrow the amounts they had hoped to (question 5 in Table 4.2), and interest rates have gotten relatively higher for some borrowers in agriculture compared to urban borrowers due to the perceived risk differences between the sectors. It appears that many lenders have reassessed the risks involved in agriculture.

Effective Farm Size/Productivity. Effective farm sizes have decreased recently with water shortages. Producers facing shortages fallow marginal land because focusing inputs on fewer acres is usually more profitable than spreading those inputs too thinly across more acres. As shown in Table 4.1, 43 percent of owners used this strategy within the previous three years, therefore the effective sizes of the farms being operated by those growers have decreased. This also explains some of the incentive to lease out land in the short term. Yet, the lower productivity of marginal land would make it difficult to lease out. This trend in effective farm size is expected to reverse in the long term due to technological advances.

Land Prices. Land prices will follow crop income potential more closely as a result of the new focus in lending on an enterprise's expected cash flows. This could widen the range of prices for land. In general, prices will decline in the long term due to the lower profits that are generated when producers must operate under water limitations and with increased capital costs. Three-quarters of the growers that responded positively to question 7 in Table 4.1 cited lower production profitability as the primary reason for the recent decline in their land values. Lower land values lead to (1) lower property tax revenues to the state, and (2) lower borrowing capacity of producers. For producers with significant debt levels, the loss of equity for use as collateral needed to borrow capital could force reductions in production, at the least, and possibly liquidation of the business. The reduction in output would be due to reduced credit limits based on the lower equity level on a firm's balance sheet (Table 4.2, question 5). Liquidation might be caused if the lower level of credit will not support sufficient production to generate cash flows that meet expense levels. In other words, if using land for agricultural production will not pay the bills, the landowner has no choice but to find another use for the land that does a better job of providing cash flows and/or maintaining the market value of the asset. As a portfolio manager, farmers must eventually find a more profitable use for each land parcel and other resource.

More Firms at Risk. The lower level of income in the agricultural sector expected as a result of the perceived increase in risk means that there may be increased financial stress among producers. This may lead to increased demand for education and guidance on the part of those producers. Even firms able to absorb increased financial risk may experience difficult adjustments as they shift their enterprise portfolios (as evidenced by responses to question 6 in Table 4.2). Also, the entire agricultural sector may adjust its portfolio in the sense that enterprise acreages will be redistributed across the state and western region. All of these changes will add to the demand for credit. For example, to combat falling profitability, firms will need to invest in technology, thus raising the level of investment per acre that must be financed. This sounds a lot like Russian Roulette.

NEW RISKS, NEW RULES

The American farm financial crisis of the 1980s and the new risk environment of the 1990s illustrate that producers must take farming seriously or they will take it in the shorts. This is more true now than ever before. Producers need the support of lenders to stay in business, but lenders are changing the way they view agriculture. The lenders' story will be told over the next couple of chapters, yet what is already clear is that lenders have reassessed the risks involved in agricultural investments and have tightened their purse strings. Producers are now in a new ball game with new rules.

The effects of a perceived increase in the risk environment of agricultural production in California have significant economic implications not only for the leading agricultural state, but also for the entire country. From the results reported here for California it appears that agricultural producers are reacting in the rational manner expected. This has significant implications for the economic well-being of

California's agricultural sector: (1) producers will, on average, face lower incomes and/or higher levels of risk; (2) enterprise selections of individuals will be adjusted, leading to acreage redistributions across the state; (3) lower income levels may increase the degree of financial stress in the agricultural sector; (4) lower incomes may cause land values to decline, thus reducing equity needed as collateral for loans, adding to the credit crunch already evident; and (5) less land will be in agricultural production in the short term, leading to reductions in tax revenues to state and local governments and adding incentive to develop more land for nonagricultural uses.

It is unclear how long the final adjustments to the perceived risk increase will take because the degree of new business risk perceived to exist in the agricultural sector is not yet known; the transition period is still ongoing. Yet, it is clear that successive shocks such as the prolonged drought, severe freeze, and recent floods have altered attitudes about risk in California's agricultural sector and have caused risk management to become a more integral part of producers' decision making. This development, in turn, may lead to improved efficiency in resource use within the sector. Clearly, in the short run it is adding to shifts in production from less-credit-intensive to more-credit-intensive crops that are viewed as being more risky. And it is this "risk push" toward more costly enterprises that will eventually force producers to face the harsh reality that pouring more money into agriculture is a bad investment.

Chapter 5

Lenders Ride the Roller Coaster

Agriculture's history is full of thrills and spills. Profits and land values have ups and occasional downs. The ride is not for the squeamish. As traders on the futures exchange floors say, "What goes up comes down faster" when you are talking about agricultural products. Long ago, lenders were willing to take a chance on agriculture because it was the only game in town. Now that alternative investments are more plentiful, lenders are not so anxious to take the farming fun ride. This has immediate and long-term implications for agriculture because of the industry's strong dependence on credit. Without credit, agriculture cannot exist in the hi-tech form necessary for American producers to compete in global markets. This is true nationally, but it has become very evident in California during recent years.

The rapid expansion of the agriculture sector in the 1970s was financed largely by a dramatic increase in agricultural debt. In California, credit extended to agriculture increased from $4.1 billion to $15.7 billion, an increase of 285 percent over the decade, and continued to increase until 1984. This contributed to over-capitalization of the sector: too many dollars, too few investment opportunities. Land prices were driven up to levels that were not justifiable based on farm income. As prices for many commodities tumbled and agricultural real estate values crashed, the demand for credit fell. The strong reaction to the decline in real estate values by agricultural lenders and by Congress made the adjustment even sharper. The result was higher lending standards coupled with tighter regulation of all types of lenders. Consequently, there has been a perceived credit crunch in agriculture.

This crunch is a major threat to agriculture's survival.

In this chapter, on the current credit situation in agriculture, and the next chapter, looking at the prospects for the future, the California story is discussed because of its importance to the national farm picture. Key points in the story are that the lending game has changed due to the new emphasis on risk and that the changes are adding to the pressure on producers, which is pushing them closer to the exit sign.

THE PLAYERS

Credit for farmers is available from several sources, including commercial banks, the Farm Credit System, insurance companies, the Farmers' Home Administration (which has its name changed with each new government shuffle—it is now part of the Farm Service Agency), rural development corporations and agribusiness firms. In 1992, almost half (49 percent) of the market share for the $5.9 billion of non-real estate farm debt in California belonged to commercial banks. The other major non-real estate lenders in the state were the Farm Credit System (19 percent), individuals and others (19 percent), the Farmers' Home Administration (7 percent) and the Commodity Credit Corporation (7 percent).

The largest holder of the $7.6 billion in real estate debt in 1992 was the Farm Credit System (35 percent), followed by life insurance companies (30 percent), individuals and others (17 percent), commercial banks (15 percent) and the Farmers' Home Administration (3 percent). The distribution of market share has changed significantly over the past several decades. The Farm Credit System expanded its share of the market until 1985 and then gave up market share to government agencies (the Farmers' Home Administration and the Commodity Credit Corporation) and commercial banks.

Although the proportion of farm debt held by commercial banks increased, agriculture's share of bank loan portfolios has decreased steadily. For example, the country's three largest commercial lenders to agriculture are banks in California that each have less than 2 percent of their loan portfolio invested in agriculture. This means that banks have become more important to agriculture in recent decades, but agriculture has become less important to banks. This imbalance puts agriculture on shaky ground. Nevertheless, the volume of loans to agriculture has increased since 1987 in the United States and California. To understand these changes in market share and volume, it is important to look at the performance of the farm sector, the credit system and the general economy, and at government's response.

THE DUSTY TRAIL

Over the past three decades there have been boom, bust, and rebuilding periods for agricultural credit.

The 1970s Expansion: The Cliché Theory

Sadly, the story of agriculture is built, to a great extent, on The Cliché Theory of Inflation. The theory is:

Time is money. Money talks. Talk is cheap.

The translation is that over time money gets cheaper. What it has meant to farmers and ranchers is that they should borrow as much money as they can get now because by the time they have to pay off those loans, they will be using cheaper future dollars. "Borrow a real dollar now and pay it off later with a dollar that is worth only 75 cents." This reckless attitude reached its peak in the 1970s and early 1980s.

Several factors came together in the 1970s to create a strong farm economy and stimulate investment in agriculture. The dollar was taken off the gold standard and allowed to float, lowering its value abroad and making U.S. farm exports cheaper, stimulating export demand. Commodity prices were also pushed up by rapid inflation resulting, in part, from government expansion of the money supply to pay for the Great Society and the Vietnam War.

American agricultural debt from all sources nearly quadrupled between 1970 and 1984, from $49 billion to almost $194 billion (Klonsky *et al.*). In real terms, the credit expansion during this highly inflationary period was 60 percent and peaked in 1979. California farm debt also quadrupled from 1970 to 1984, increasing from $4 billion to $17 billion. This was an increase of 70 percent in real terms, peaking in 1983.

Lenders were facing strong demand from investors who had a great deal of equity and/or outside income. Large down payments made it possible to approve loans made on inflated land values. In other cases real estate appraisals were based on comparable sales and not income capacity, making loans to agriculture look attractive. In a highly competitive market, lenders were unwilling to turn away business that they knew their competitors would be happy to accept. And so the upward spiral existed both on the supply and demand side of the credit market.

Many growers saw land prices increasing and wanted to buy land before it became even less affordable. Expectations of continued inflation and low real interest rates encouraged investment. The investment activities of neighbors also fueled expansion. Farmer Smith wanted to keep up with Farmer Jones.

At the same time, groups from outside the sector invested in agriculture to take advantage of tax laws favoring agriculture. Capital gains laws encouraged speculation in agricultural land unrelated to productive capacity. Land was purchased and turned over for a short-term profit at relatively low tax rates. Limited partnerships allowed for tax write-offs of farming expenses while protecting nonfarm income.

Permanent plantings of trees and vines in California were particularly popular investments because of the ability to depreciate trees as a tax write-off. Other tax laws allowed for investment in citrus and almond orchards to be capitalized before the orchards came into bearing, providing an even more attractive tax write-off for high-income investors. As one expert put it, trees were planted "behind every rock" (Klonsky *et al.*).

Expansion in agriculture meant bringing poorly suited land into production simply because it was the most available. The results were higher operating costs per unit of output and an oversupply of commodities. These factors, coupled with the fact that land values had risen above their repayment capacity, made agriculture extremely vulnerable to market shocks affecting demand. Eventually reality had to set in.

The Downward Adjustment: Playing Chicken

In the early 1980s a worldwide recession cut back on demand for agricultural products, while a stronger dollar made American exports more expensive abroad. U.S. agriculture's increasing productivity resulted in excess capacity and huge, price-depressing stocks of commodities. The Green Revolution meant that many importing countries became net exporters of wheat and grain adding to world stocks. Lower-cost production areas farther down the Economic Food Chain began exporting to the United States, adding to already large supplies. Prices of all major commodities plunged.

At the same time, farmers' profits were squeezed as input prices were bid up by the inflationary boom and the Federal Reserve Board raised interest rates to control inflation, making interest the biggest cost increase for farmers. Many borrowers were unable to keep up payments on existing debt. Foreclosures forced about one in five out of business nationwide. The game was on. Farmers and lenders were "playing chicken," waiting to see who would blink first.

Real estate values dropped Big Time. Among California's diverse agricultural properties, certain sectors were hit harder than others. For example, in 1986 cropland, pasture and rangeland values were at their 1980 levels. Since then, the price of land in these sectors has risen slowly but steadily. In contrast, fruit and nut acreage values climbed more dramatically during the early 1980s, fell from 1984 through 1987 and leveled off at 1970s values.

As agricultural real estate values fell, the demand for credit declined. The capital gains on farm assets in California plummeted from a high of 17 percent in 1978, to a 13 percent loss in 1986. Bad loans were written off by lenders. By 1986, almost 8 percent of all loans to California agriculture had been dropped as being uncollectable (compared to only 4 percent on a national level).

There was an absolute decline in farm debt both in the United States and in California. American farm debt dropped from $188 billion in 1983 to $139 billion in 1991. In California, the absolute decline was from almost $17 billion in 1984 to just over $13 billion in 1991. On a national basis, farm debt fell from 5 percent of total U.S. debt in 1983 to less than 2 percent in 1991. Resources were shifting to other industries. Debt from businesses other than farming grew from $1.6 trillion in 1983 to $3.5 trillion in 1991. Trillion, with a T, is Big Money by anybody's standards.

Redesigning the System

There were strong reactions in the late 1980s on the parts of both lenders and Congress to the decline in real estate values that together may have caused an even faster decline in the supply of and demand for agricultural credit than would have occurred otherwise. Lenders were faced with deteriorating portfolios and Congress passed legislation that lengthened the process of cleaning up loan portfolios. Lenders found themselves in the costly situation of taking back agricultural properties and equipment in foreclosure (or in lieu of foreclosure) that they were not prepared to manage. Public auctions were held that were reminiscent of the Great Depression. Public relations for the lenders were damaged and real estate values further declined.

THE CURRENT SITUATION: FASTEN YOUR SEAT BELTS

The farm financial crisis of the 1980s was the last ride without seatbelts. The current agricultural credit situation involves a number of factors that are still changing, but virtually all recent changes have been making life more difficult for agricultural producers. Uncle Sam has gotten into the act as a result of the savings-and-loan mess. Also, the loan process has changed (tightened) in response to the shift from equity- to income-based lending. The story gets messy, but some of the main points follow.

Red Tape

The red tape is getting thicker. Depository institutions are regulated by a combination of the Federal Deposit Insurance Corporation, the Office of the Comptroller of the Currency, the Federal Reserve Board and state banking authorities. And this is *after* deregulation.

The deregulation of financial markets in the 1980s affected the structure and competitive relationships within these markets. In particular, legislation phased out interest rate ceilings on deposits, reduced reserve requirements and increased federal insurance coverage. The elimination of interest rate controls meant greater competition among banks, but at the same time meant greater risk taking. The riskier activities in the face of competition led to numerous bank failures and a general credit squeeze from 1988 to 1992.

In response to the taxpayer bailout of savings-and-loan institutions and poor liquidity within the banking sector, regulatory changes were instituted in an effort to stop bank failures and shore up the Bank Insurance Fund. An important provision of the new regulations was the introduction of risk-based premiums on January 1, 1994. Until then, the bank insurance rate had not been related to risk taking. The new system discourages risk taking and is intended to reduce the likelihood of bank failure as a result. Also, the Federal Reserve developed a system of weighting assets and liabilities based on risk.

Unfortunately, the new regulations require more reporting of information on bank loans to small businesses and farms. These increases in reporting, auditing and bank examinations increase the paperwork requirements of the loan process, make lenders more conservative and increase the cost of funds for banks. In effect, the regulations have already resulted in many farmers being cut off by lenders. For example, in a workshop organized in 1992 by the University of California, a farmer in the audience asked the local banker who was speaking why he had been denied credit that year after 20 years of being a steady customer and never missing a payment. The embarrassed banker acknowledged the farmer's good credit history but said that the bank had discontinued loans on the vegetable crop that the farmer produced. The product was now judged to be too risky for inclusion in the bank's portfolio of loans.

Lending Practices: Never Perfect

Lending standards changed across the industry as a result of the experiences of the early 1980s and in response to regulation. Few bankers or farmers are happy about it. While the general concepts of lending remain the same, the loan process has changed dramatically. Borrower repayment capacity has always been the basis of any loan. What has changed is (1) the analysis used to determine repayment capacity, and (2) the amount of information required to carry out that analysis. Consequently, the amount of paperwork has increased, making the loan process more arduous for both the lender and the borrower. Further exacerbating the problem is the fact that lenders can no longer fill out loan applications for their borrowers as a result of lawsuits that charged loan officers with being in partnership with borrowers and therefore responsible parties in bankruptcies. This is progress?

The current loan process is an expensive proposition. Real estate appraisals have become more sophisticated. Comparable sales is no longer a sufficient measure for a complete appraisal. The borrower's ability to generate income is now a key issue. However, estimating the income potential of dirt requires a knowledge of current agricultural production practices and market conditions, making appraisals much more complex than they were in the recent past.

A borrower is asked to provide financial records and a business plan projecting income and expenses. The most readily available records for farmers are income tax statements. However, virtually all farmers pay their income taxes on a cash basis. This allows for certain expenses to be prepaid and income to be delayed for tax management purposes. Unfortunately, this legal manipulation of cash flows disguises the true profitability of a farm. Therefore, current lending practices require that income and expense information now be provided on both an accrual basis and a cash basis.

Lenders get income from the interest collected on loans, loan application fees and origination fees. Many of the preparation costs (and the time involved in preparation) are the same regardless of the size of the loan, so banks prefer to make large, well-secured loans of at least $500,000. As a result, many lenders are not pursuing the business of small or new farmers.

Real Estate Values: It's Worth at Least Half of What It Costs

Investors in agriculture can be their own worst enemies. Some lenders fear that there may be a dangerous escalation in real estate prices. Despite the improved analysis of repayment capacity, improved appraisals and increased audits, real estate can still be leveraged beyond its productive level. For example, orchards in California's Sacramento Valley that cannot support more than $4,000 per acre of debt on an income basis are selling for $12,000 to $16,000 per acre. This means that two-thirds down is required for financing. It also means that land speculation is alive and well.

Recent prices for orchard crops have been high, spurring renewed investment in orchards. Yet few growers are willing to sell, which has led to the conversion of field-crop land into orchards. This land is often poorly suited for orchards. Too many dollars chasing too little land. The question becomes, "Is the land purchased for agricultural uses or for urban development after the city reaches the property?"

On the national level, one player to join the game recently is U.S. pension funds. These organizations have lots of money coming in, so they must invest it somewhere. In the booming markets of the early 1990s, the depressed prices of farmland looked good. Therefore, retirement money from the city flooded rural America. At the start of the decade, pension funds owned about $50 million worth of farmland. By the end of 1996, that amount had grown to about $1 billion. Too many dollars were looking for a home.

Availability of Funds

There is evidence that the improved loan analysis and the increase in regulatory efforts have been effective in some ways. Delinquencies on agricultural loans are now down, relative to other sectors of the economy, making these loans attractive to lenders once again. The situation in the general economy does not seem to have affected funds available to agriculture. It is generally agreed that agricultural lenders have plenty of money.

In summary, it is clear that what borrowers may consider to be a credit crunch in agriculture has been caused more by changes in both the loan process and loan analysis than by changes in the availability of funds. Also, these changes have been influenced by changes in the risk environment surrounding agricultural credit. That story follows.

Agricultural Loan Analysis: Number Crunching and Crystal Balls

The profitability and riskiness associated with each of the 250 commodities produced in California vary across markets, thus agricultural loan analysis can lead to differing results across products and locations. A look at current agricultural lending practices will illustrate how loan officers meet this challenge.

Lender Characteristics. The story reported here comes from the responses of 40 randomly selected lenders from across California who were interviewed during 1993. By lender category, the average loan sizes were: Farm Credit System, $327,000; large commercial banks, $1,095,000; small commercial banks, $371,000; life insurance companies, $1,100,000; Farmers Home Administration, $138,750; and agricultural processors, $387,500. By commodity, the largest loans were often made to dairies and vegetable farmers.

Table 5.1 provides a summary of basic information on the five types of lending institutions. The first two rows show the average high and low interest rates given by the institutions. Farm Credit System institutions tended to charge higher rates, while Farmers' Home Administration (FmHA) rates were lower. Not surprisingly, FmHA, the "lender of last resort," has the highest default and loss rates. Banks have drastically improved their default and loss rates since the 1980s.

Respondents were asked about their institution's portfolio, revealing important differences between lending types (see Table 5.1). Most lenders have diversified their portfolios across different crops, but several lend exclusively on one agricultural commodity, including one bank that specializes in dairy.

The Loan Process. Borrowers may compare getting a loan to "trying to squeeze blood from a turnip," but lenders view it as a necessary part of business. After the initial contact between lender and borrower, the next step is a completed application and package. A field visit is usually scheduled, often conducted by a specially trained field person or appraiser. The loan officer completes his or her analysis and, in most institutions, can grant the loan if it is within that officer's delegated authority.   Most institutions utilize a loan committee to evaluate the largest loans. Lenders reported that the average turnaround time for a short-term loan was 22 days after the borrower completes the package. For long-term loans, the average was 52 days because the appraisal could cause delays.

Table 5.1 Average Interest Rates, Losses and Portfolios of Lending Institutions in California

	FCS	Banks	Insurance	FmHA	Business
Interest rate (avg. high)	11.7	9.3	8.6	7.3	9.5
Interest rate (avg. low)	6.4	6.7	7.3	5.4	6.5
Default %	2.04	1.31	5.7	12.0	4.5
Loss %	0.54	0.19	0.7	4.0	2.5
Short term	35.5	74.6	0.0	65.0	100.0
Intermediate	7.1	5.7	0.0	12.5	0.0
Long term	57.4	19.7	100.0	22.5	0.0
Field crops	28.6	37.5	36.0	37.0	50.0
Grapes	15.1	15.4	21.0	2.0	4.0
Fruit	13.7	13.6	29.0	15.5	50.0
Nuts	12.0	18.9	22.5	19.5	5.0
Livestock	14.9	26.1	7.0	11.5	10.0
Vegetables	18.3	16.6	15.0	3.5	0.0
Other	1.8	0.2	1.0	1.0	25.0

Note: Concerning the portfolio composition across commodities, the values reported are the percentages of each institutions' borrowers that have loans for each commodity listed. The percentages do not total 100 due to multiple-commodity loans held by many borrowers.

The documents required from borrowers were largely consistent among lenders. Three years of tax returns, a current income statement, a market value balance sheet, and a cash flow budget were the standard. However, for real estate loans environmental questionnaires were required. In some areas, a water questionnaire, a water plan, or well tests were often required.

Half of the lenders interviewed said that the loan process has changed recently. Some of the changes they mentioned were a greater use of computers, stricter verification of information, separation of the appraisal and loan analysis functions, and increased requests by lenders for accrual financial statements from borrowers.

Lender's Reaction to Risk. Seventy-five percent of the lenders said yes when asked whether the riskiness of the commodities produced by the borrower alters the loan process. They reported that risk can make a difference in that underwriting standards may become stricter on risky commodities. Also, riskier loans will be priced at higher interest rates. The main change due to risk was a tightening of loan requirements, mentioned by almost 60 percent of the lenders. Several lenders noted that higher risks meant more work for the borrower to prove knowledge or profitability of a commodity. This implies that there are severe limitations on borrowers who lack a history of production in that commodity and could slow shifts from field crops to higher value fruit and vegetable production.

Commodity risk was evaluated through industry analysis by 42 percent of the lenders and by tracking price and production history by 35 percent of the respondents. Quantifiable means of assessing risk include historical measures such as 5-year yield averages or average profits. These were mentioned by 25 percent of the lenders surveyed. Industry trends, mentioned by 37.5 percent of respondents, are another quantifiable measure, but are less useful for assessing individual loans. Twenty-three percent of lenders mentioned borrower characteristics as another measure of risk. These characteristics are a combination of measurable factors (e.g., degree of crop diversification or percent of land owned) and more subjective factors (e.g., reputation and general knowledge). However, nearly half the respondents listed no fixed system of risk assessment. Many rely on personal experience or use committees of loan officers from the region or state to develop guidelines. Responses were consistent across lender types, though banks rely relatively more heavily on borrower characteristics. This is possibly a reflection of relationships that develop over time between producers and, in particular, small local banks. Evaluation of risk was done in different institutions by different personnel: loan officers, fieldpeople, or centralized staff economists. Several lenders pointed out that the riskiness of some commodities is not only comprised of price and production risk. Political, economic and environmental risk can play a big role in the variability of returns for some products. For example, the water situation in parts of California's Central Valley was often mentioned as a major source of risk to farmers (and to lenders).

Each lender was asked to rank the riskiness of the commodities produced by their borrowers. Vegetables, citrus, tomatoes, melons, strawberries and grapes were most frequently ranked as the first or second riskiest enterprises. Dairy, beef cattle, field and row crops, almonds and walnuts were ranked as the first or second least risky enterprises. However, the picture is unclear because several commodities, such as cotton, citrus and almonds, were ranked as most and least risky crops by different lenders. Several respondents noted that it is difficult to consider risk by commodity since, as lenders, they are more familiar with analyzing the riskiness of a borrower's total operation, which is often diversified.

Finally, lenders were asked whether they have perceived a shift in risk within agriculture in recent years. The majority of respondents (62.2 percent) said that their assessment of relative risks had changed, and this was consistent across lender types.

In summary, interviews with California agricultural lenders pointed out that differences in the degree of risk associated with the income from production of a commodity is a major factor influencing the loan analysis process. The perceived riskiness of a commodity can lead to stricter underwriting standards and to higher pricing on the loan. Also, loan evaluation standards did not differ significantly between types of lenders. This is somewhat surprising considering the differences in the average loan amounts between lender groups, such as large commercial banks and the Farmers' Home Administration. This indicates some degree of standardization in the loan analysis process. One form that standardization has taken is the use of financial ratios. Although there is still considerable variation in the range of standards used in interpreting tools such as financial ratios, it appears that agricultural loan analysis is becoming more sophisticated and focusing increasing attention on risk.

The story sounds like agriculture is in for an even bumpier ride. Lenders are making logical decisions in the face of the risky new business environment confronting them. Since lenders are finding agriculture less profitable, they are trying to discover ways to adjust their portfolios. As a result, agricultural borrowers are wondering if their lenders are going to get off the roller coaster and take the freeway back to the city.

Chapter 6

Will Agricultural Risks Chase Lenders Back to the City?

Risk has lenders running scared. The increase in risk associated with agricultural production and marketing that is believed to have occurred in recent years has forced many agricultural lenders to reassess their business strategies. This ongoing reassessment is important for all of agriculture. In particular, questions being raised include, "Is farming becoming too risky for continued inclusion in the portfolios of commercial banks that have urban alternatives?" and "Could risk be the 'poison pill' that scares off lenders, leaving only small, rural banks or the Farmers' Home Administration to serve farmers?" These questions are important because if funds are diverted away from agriculture, interest rates in that industry could go up, thus adding to the profit squeeze that reduces the international competitiveness of American farmers.

These issues were discussed during interviews with agricultural lenders. In general, the response of most lenders to the question "Will agricultural risks chase lenders back to the city?" was no, or not yet, depending on how the question and answer were interpreted. In fact, lenders said a lot of things, but what it all meant depended upon the time frame considered. No, lenders will not leave agriculture today, they probably will stick around for tomorrow, but the next day is no safe bet. The real answer appears to be, "Not as long as profitable lending is possible in agriculture."

Availability of funds is not the problem. We can always make more money. Start up the presses or loosen up the lending regulations. All the lenders interviewed said that they had plenty of money to lend.

The problem is that agricultural borrowers aren't as much fun as they used to be.

For example, farms have been toxic nightmares for some lenders. Farm chemicals are plentiful and are not always handled well by some individuals, causing toxic spills requiring Big Money to clean up. There have been some lawsuits in which lenders were stuck with the entire, huge cost of the toxic cleanup because they had loaned money to a previous owner who could not afford the cleanup. In one case, a new owner of a farm was shocked by what he found at the bottom of an open well. Apparently, the previous owner had a habit of dumping the near-empty containers of pesticides into the well everytime he sprayed for bugs. He figured, rather than waste the chemicals remaining in the containers, by dumping the cans into the well and turning on the irrigation system, he could set it up so that the water pumped out of the well would have the chemicals in it, therefore, would get applied to his fields during irrigations. Unfortunately, the new owner and all the neighbors found that the pesticides in the well had gotten into the groundwater and had contaminated a huge area. The bank paid. This "toxic liability" is just one type of new risk that makes agriculture look much less attractive to lenders than it did in the past. This does not mean that agriculture is considered to be the riskiest of all industries, but it has moved up on the list recently.

The relative risk-return tradeoff is a concern of lenders. As financial portfolio managers, lenders must monitor the prospects for each of their holdings. Just like other portfolio managers, lenders must constantly shift their holdings as prospects change. When new investment opportunities come along, or when the tradeoff available on existing investments changes, financial managers must react. Over time, agriculture has become a small and relatively risky part of lenders' portfolios, compared to other industries. As a result, agriculture will eventually be replaced by industries that do not have toxic liabilities, droughts, floods, pests, wild price swings and a seemingly endless list of other risks.[1] As America moves up the Economic Food Chain, new investment opportunities will continue to appear and compete for

---

[1] One problem with agriculture is that when it has problems, they are Big Problems covering Big Areas. For example, the House Banking Committee held hearings in July 1996 in Elk City, Oklahoma, to gather information on the most recent drought's effect on rural banks. There was a 40 percent increase in farm bankruptcies in western Oklahoma that year, 44 percent of producers with federal Farm Service Agency (Farmers' Home Administration) loans were delinquent, and 10 percent of Oklahoma farmers were expected to quit or go bankrupt because of the drought.

available loans. This chapter tries to explain lenders' current willingness to provide credit to agriculture in the face of risk and to look at future prospects for this partnership.

A SIMPLE STORY OF LENDING

The argument that a perceived increase in risk will chase lenders away from agricultural borrowers assumes that bankers have unlimited urban lending alternatives. But if that is not the case, as bankers claimed in interviews (Blank), a very different story arises.

Individual lenders try to maximize their profits while operating in a highly competitive world with two sectors: urban and agricultural. (This is how many farmers view the world, but it is just a simplification here—it makes the story easier to follow.) Nearly all lenders face similar demands from the urban sector. This leads to urban interest rates being "sticky" around their current level. For each bank, the quantity of loan funds demanded by their urban customers is determined by those borrowers' investment opportunities. World and national interest rate markets set current prices for money lent, while national and local markets determine prices for money borrowed from depositors. Both of these interest rates are effectively set by outside forces and must be accepted by individual banks. This means that a lender using both of the market rates will usually find that the quantity of funds available to lend out will exceed the quantity that urban borrowers want. This presents the bank with a choice of offering its depositors an interest rate lower than the going rate to reduce the funds supplied or raising the total amount of funds lent by making agricultural loans.

The second choice indicates that banks will lend their extra funds to agriculture despite that sector's higher risk. Agriculture's demand also leads to sticky interest rates, but at a higher level than the urban rate if bankers view the relative risks in the two markets as being different. The net effect is that the total amount of funds lent is increased by combining urban and agricultural loan demand.

The situation faced by an individual bank can be described as attempting to maximize profits from lending to both sectors by allocating each dollar supplied by depositors to whichever of the two sectors offers the highest risk-adjusted return. In reality, banks try to set each loan price within the narrow range available so as to raise loan profitability and reduce risk. A risk premium is charged to agricultural borrowers.[2] However, for a specific bank, the exact cost of risk is not known in the short run. It includes all actual costs for market insurance against losses from known risks, plus any income lost from maintaining a cash reserve for paying any self-insurance claims. (These measures were identified by lenders as being those most likely to be taken in the face of new lending liabilities.) Increases in risk will increase self-insurance activities, but will not necessarily increase self-protection activities.[3] Therefore, after all urban demands have been met, the bank faces a dilemma of deciding how much, if any, remaining funds should be allocated to the agricultural sector, given the uncertainty about risk costs.

Banks will sometimes take on new customers at interest rates that initially generate expected losses because, as banks get to know long-time customers (firms), they will be able to make profits from them. This explains banks' current willingness to take on new agricultural loans: as a bank becomes more familiar with a firm, the chance of losses from risks is more clearly known, which reduces the cost of the self-insurance steps the bank will take, thus raising the profitability of the loan over time. Also, a bank will hesitate to take self-protection steps (such as rejecting a borrower) to reduce the chance of incurring a loss as long as potential customers represent a chance to make a profit in the long run.

But if a current or new borrower's prospects for profitability turn gloomy, lenders could "drop them like a hot potato." This was illustrated in mid-1995 when statistics confirmed that credit conditions were worsening for farm loans in the U.S. heartland. The Kansas City Federal Reserve Bank, reporting these results, said that commercial banks were increasingly turning aside requests for new farm loans, and "expect some erosion in the quality of their loan portfolios" for 1995. The figures had gotten worse nearly across the board, validating fears that commercial banks see rising signs of financial stress, especially with respect to loans related to beef herds. In other words, farm and ranch profits were down and the prospects were not good, so bankers were backing off. One Reserve Bank officer advised agricultural

---

[2] A risk premium is an additional amount charged to customers who are considered to be riskier than the average. This premium is supposed to compensate the lender for accepting the additional risk, thus making the risk-return tradeoff for the investment in this customer equal to that for average-risk customers. The additional revenues are also used to cover losses on bad loans.

[3] Self-insurance includes activities that prepare one to pay liabilities, if incurred. Self-protection involves taking steps to avoid the possibility of incurring a liability.

borrowers that price protection could be used more, noting that it is a risk management tool that would protect producers and might help them get new loans and stay in business.

THE STORY'S MESSAGE

The lending story implies either that banks have few investment choices (they must lend money to agriculture in the short run despite the sector's higher risk, lower profits) or that they do not view the new risk assessments to be significant enough to drop agriculture from their loan portfolios. These two explanations for bankers' continued participation in agriculture despite a perceived increase in risk are based on interview responses from bankers. Each explanation, however, is based on a different view of agriculture.

The first possible explanation is based on responses from bankers that say that agriculture is viewed as a strategic reserve for holding surplus funds until they can be used in the primary market of concern: the urban sector. In this view, a bank does not want to chase potential depositors away to competitors, fearing that they will be lost forever, so whenever surplus funds are available, long-run profits are maximized by accepting all deposits and "storing" them in agriculture until they can be shifted into the urban sector.

The second explanation is based on the view that agriculture is just another investment alternative. Banks with this view will continue to operate in agriculture as long as risk-adjusted profits are being earned from agricultural lending. These banks are likely to be relatively confident of their ability to identify the real cost of bearing risks associated with agricultural production and marketing. As a result, this group of banks would be more willing to make long-run commitments to agricultural borrowers.

Each of these two perspectives of agriculture indicates that banks are willing to accept the risks in agriculture, at least for the short run. However, lenders are likely to set interest rates at high-risk levels for all agricultural borrowers to improve the chances that the risk premium collected covers their cost of bearing risk.

In general, accepting increased risks puts banks more at risk, making more bank failures possible, especially in rural areas, so banks with strong urban alternatives are more likely to be the major (surviving) agricultural lenders in the future. In turn, this dependence by agriculture on banks with strong urban portfolios for sources of capital puts the agricultural sector at risk of credit crunches anytime either urban alternatives improve or sources of capital decline. This has been true for some time—rural people have long viewed their deposits as being drained to fund the "city."

Three questions are key in evaluating the future of agricultural credit: (1) Will any of the current suppliers of credit leave agriculture? (2) Which lenders will serve agriculture's various sectors in the future? and (3) What additional sources of credit will agriculture draw upon in the future?

WHO WILL BAIL OUT?

Who will leave agriculture first? The answer appears to be clear: lenders with the best least-risk alternatives available to them. If lenders can invest all available money in safer industries, why should they take a chance on agriculture?

This trend is already evident as insurance companies come and go and large commercial banks focus on the top-end, Big Borrowers. Insurance companies have made real estate loans to agriculture off and on for decades. Their history is full of brief exits and new entrances. The reason is simple: they have a limited amount of money available for loans and often they are able to lend it all to urban borrowers. This is the most profitable strategy for them. When insurance companies do have money available for agriculture, they look for the most profitable loans first—Big Money real estate deals. Real estate markets are understood by insurance companies, agricultural production is not, so only land deals need apply. Also, land deals usually involve large amounts per loan application, so they are more profitable for the lender than small production loans.

"Brother, can you spare a dime?" "No, but how about a million bucks?" This has become a common refrain for all types of lenders. Lenders with the most money look for the biggest loans they can find. It is easier to loan billions when you hand it out in pieces of more than a million each. It is more cost-efficient to complete and monitor fewer loan applications than to deal with piles of paper. As a result, insurance companies and large commercial banks often have minimum loan sizes that keep small borrowers outside looking in. Those on the outside include many urban borrowers and a high percentage of agricultural borrowers in some regions. In California, for example, the average agricultural loan size for both large commercial banks and insurance companies is over $1.1 million.

Table 6.1 Lenders Likely to Leave Agriculture

Type of Lender Mentioned	% of sample
Large commercial banks, in general	20
Small commercial banks, in general	15
Specific large banks	20
Insurance companies	5
Production Credit Associations	3
None will leave	30
Uncertain	18

Note: The percentages do not total 100 due to multiple answers given by some respondents.

Lenders admit it. They are honest about the "economic pulls" that drag them out of agriculture. When asked about lenders heading back to the city, only 30 percent of those interviewed felt certain that no lenders would bail out of agriculture during the next decade.

The interview results in Table 6.1 indicate that one in five lenders in California expect that all large commercial banks in the state will quit lending to agriculture within the next 10 years. That is bad news for producers. What may be nearly as bad is that 15 percent of lenders expect that all small banks will give up on agriculture within a decade. Large banks are the biggest lenders at present and small banks often fill geographic holes in credit availability. Thus, if both groups do bail out, there could be a whole lot of shakin' goin' on! Without credit, agricultural production would virtually come to a halt. Even if only specific large banks leave, as expected by 20 percent of lenders, there will be big gaps in credit availability for many borrowers.

WHO WILL ANSWER "THE CALL OF THE WILD"?

With lenders admitting that they expect some bailouts from agriculture in the relatively near future, there are questions about the long-term structure of the lending industry. Who will provide the cash necessary for our farming habit? Lenders were asked to consider the situation that they expect to see in 10 years and predict which lenders will serve agriculture's various sectors at that time. There was no consistency in the responses to this question. Although virtually all lenders expected their institutions to remain in agriculture and to play a significant role, there were conflicting opinions about what competitors might do. "Yeah, we're staying, but I'm not so sure about those other guys."

One conclusion that can be drawn from lenders' comments is that there are identifiable segments in the agricultural credit market. There is no agreement on which type(s) of lender(s) will serve those segments, let alone which firms will be participants. Therefore, it is reasonable to conclude that the variety of lender types and the number of lending firms serving individual geographic markets and producers of specific commodities will continue to be uneven. This means that the supply of credit will vary for specific market segments. Lenders will make funds available based on each agricultural segment's profitability relative to that of alternative investments.

Two groups of lenders that are expected to stay in agriculture to the bitter end are the Farmers Home Administration and the Farm Credit System (FCS). They must stay, they have no alternatives. Some FCS lenders may have wanted to bail out during the system's recent financial crisis, but they are stuck.

Lenders in the Farm Credit System will to stay in agriculture because their charter does not allow them to leave. They have tried to change the charter, but failed. Therefore, it is agriculture or nothing for them, so they choose agriculture. But it is scary being limited to a market that is relatively risky and having to compete with big banks that are diversified globally. In recent decades, the FCS tried to compete head-on with the Big Boys by offering similar interest rates. Unfortunately, that strategy almost killed them during the 1980s, when the risks of agriculture ganged up on them causing Big Losses. To survive, the FCS learned that they must price loans higher to reflect risk. This strategy may kill them as well because charging for risks gives the FCS a less attractive product for borrowers. Also, with only agricultural loans in its portfolio, the FCS is more at risk of failure than are its competitors. This is a vicious cycle for the FCS. It must charge somewhat higher rates than commercial banks to protect its own survival, but in doing so it adds to its borrowers' cost squeeze and *shoves* agriculture closer to the end by reducing relative profitability. This, in turn, brings the end of the FCS ever closer.

The Farmers' Home Administration is viewed as a permanent fixture now, but it does not have a chance of surviving in the long run. It is a subsidy to agriculture that is not needed by viable producers. It is the "lender of last resort" in that a borrower must first be turned down by other lenders before the FmHA will even accept his or her loan application. This means that only hard-luck cases need apply. Marginal producers or people with marginal resources wind up at the FmHA. In the past, the existence of this subsidy was judged to be worthwhile because it supported the sacred institution of "the family farm." It still is viewed as being part of God's Gift to Agriculture, along with the many other government subsidies. With the high default rates on FmHA loans, it is hard to describe them as "loans." They are more like grants paid just for trying to farm. And they total Big Money. General Accounting Office (GAO) officials told Congress that lax rules and poor enforcement in the FmHA's direct loan program led to $12.5 billion in delinquencies and defaults over the five years between 1989 and 1994. A 1996 GAO report said FmHA wrote off $3 billion in bad loans over the three previous years and another $7 billion could be at risk. Many of the write-offs were on loans of over $1 million. Also, the report said that borrowers who defaulted on FmHA loans were allowed to borrow again from the agency. It said that FmHA employees had few incentives to settle delinquent loans but were urged instead to get them off the books. As a result, the current drive for change will not be enough to save the FmHA. As taxpayers tire of paying for these special gifts to bad farming operations, the plug will be pulled.

FUTURE CASH COWS

The third question concerning the future of agricultural credit is whether there are other potential sources of funds. During interviews, 95 percent of the lenders said that they expected some new sources of credit to become more significant in the future. These are listed in Table 6.2.

The funding sources listed can be categorized as being one of two types: internal (from within agriculture) or external. Obviously, most lenders expect internal sources to be the likeliest area of expansion for agricultural credit. Both product handlers, such as processors, and input suppliers have a strong interest in supporting agricultural production so as to maintain their own businesses. Thus, it is reasonable to expect these sources to expand to some extent. However, product handlers and input suppliers have historically offered a narrow range of financial services and there is no reason to expect them to diversify their credit services further. This means that internal sources of credit cannot be expected to become more numerous, only more readily available whenever product handlers and input suppliers perceive that credit to producers is needed in order to maintain their own businesses.

External sources of funds are not expected to expand widely, with the possible exception of "Farmer Mac." As shown in Table 6.2, over half of the lenders interviewed expect that the Federal Agricultural Mortgage Corporation will succeed in becoming a significant source of funds for agriculture. By selling securities to fund loans on agricultural land and residential property, Farmer Mac enables anyone to invest in agriculture. Unfortunately, Farmer Mac does not provide funds directly for agricultural production, although it may indirectly enable lenders to expand their production loan portfolios. Several lenders are actively involved with Farmer Mac because, in the case of some small commercial banks, it has enabled them to expand the size of their total loan portfolios and to serve a market segment (agricultural real estate) that they were not able to serve before. However, the legal limit on loan size reduces the potential use of this tool by large lenders. The flawed design of Farmer Mac is destined for revision.

Table 6.2 Future Sources of Additional Credit for Agriculture

Type of Source Mentioned	% of sample
Processor credit	68
Farmer Mac	55
Trade (supplier) credit	53
Hard money, private lenders	10
Leasing	8
Brokers	3
Doane Western	3
A consortium creating a pool of funds	3

Note: The percentages do not total 100 due to multiple answers given by some respondents.

In general, no knight in shining armor is expected to rescue agriculture from its credit squeeze. Individual agribusiness firms will help themselves by helping their suppliers or customers, but no replacement for the disappearing banks is apparent. Even Big Brother cannot find a way to get involved. Wisconsin's Agriculture Director Gordon Guyer said that changes in the way the federal government provides financial support for crops mean that private banks have to do more to help farmers survive. Wisconsin officials said that small farmers that used to get direct loans from the federal government are being shut out by a new system that channels federal loans through banks. The banks are less willing to take risks, they said. Guyer and other officials who testified at a Michigan Agriculture Commission meeting in 1995 agreed that something should be done to boost bank loans, but they had not determined what the state government should do.

THE CRYSTAL BALL, IN SUMMARY

The near-future supply of agricultural credit looks very similar to the present supply, based on the results of interviews with lenders. To begin, lenders generally believe that a few institutions will leave agriculture in the next decade. The doubts about the commitment to agriculture of certain commercial banks appear to be explained by the unanimous opinion that lending is a cyclical industry, indicating that individual lenders may come and go as profitability changes across investment alternatives.

Next, there are mixed views regarding which lenders will serve agriculture's various sectors in the future. All survey respondents said that competition between lenders has changed in recent years, but they disagreed on the nature of the change, some saying that the industry has become less competitive while others think that direct competition has increased. Again, the cyclical nature of the industry may be part of the explanation for this difference in opinions. It may be that the consolidation that occurred in the lending industry in the early 1990s is still in progress, thus making the final outcome difficult to anticipate.[4] What is clear is that virtually all lenders interviewed believed that their institution had no plans to leave agriculture yet. Also, it is clear that

---

[4] Certainly, bank consolidation is making many farmers nervous. For example, in 1996 a farm advocacy group in Wisconsin said that a Mount Horeb (Wisconsin) bank holding company should not be allowed to buy a Belleville (Wisconsin) bank because the Mount Horeb bank had deliberately cut back on its lending to farmers.

agriculture's various market segments will continue to attract and lose lenders based upon the profitability of each segment relative to alternative investments both in and outside of agriculture.

Finally, few additional sources of credit are expected to become available to agriculture in the future. Lenders believe that some existing internal sources will expand, but they will not necessarily diversify to serve new market segments. Farmer Mac is the only outside source of funds for agriculture that is expected to grow significantly. It offers another source of funds for borrowers seeking relatively small real estate loans, but its size limitations reduce its potential contribution.

In summary, with most current lenders expected to remain in the game, only occasional change in the current lending industry structure, and no real new sources of funds becoming available to agriculture, the near future looks very much like the present. Is this good or bad? In terms of the total supply of credit available to agriculture, it is good because lenders currently have more money available to them than they can profitably lend. For agricultural borrowers, this is good also. As agricultural borrowers become accustomed to the new loan process that is evolving in the new risk environment, the conditions that caused the credit crunch for some borrowers will gradually disappear. Part of the lending industry's shift in focus, emphasizing the reassessment of risks in agriculture, involves requiring borrowers to provide different information than they did in the past and, thus, a period of transition is to be expected before all borrowers have adjusted to the new record-keeping requirements. As borrowers "learn the new game" they will have less difficulty obtaining credit and, therefore, the credit crunch will no longer exist. On the other hand, the story is completely different for the long run, as alternative investments become more available to lenders. At some point, all lenders could get out of agriculture, just like insurance companies have done a couple of times. Eventually it is going to stick. The story of that end game is in the next chapter.

Chapter 7

Dueling Portfolios

Producers and lenders are dizzy from a circular problem. Over the last decade, lenders have been required to pay more attention to risk because of the savings-and-loan crisis, natural disasters and other factors that triggered banking regulators to start barking new orders. Lenders reacted by reassessing the degree of risk present in agricultural markets. This caused them to tighten lending requirements to rebalance the risk-return levels in their loan portfolios. Agricultural producers were somewhat surprised to hear that they were in such a risky business. Their reaction to this perceived increase in risks was to fight it with even more-risky crops (in the short run). Adjusting their crop portfolios to balance the new levels of risk and return, producers found themselves needing to grow crops that generate more cash flow, and potential profits, per acre. Unfortunately, these high-value crops have Big Time variation in their cash flows from year to year. This shift in crop portfolios to more-risky products has caused lenders to view individual borrowers as being riskier still. In reaction to growers' increased risk exposure due to cropping shifts, lenders may restrict those borrowers' credit even more, often to the point of dropping them as customers entirely despite long histories of good credit. This new uncertainty about credit sources often pushes borrowers to accept less favorable loan terms, which can lower their profit levels and increase their financial risk. Obviously, lower profits or higher levels of any type of risk make a producer less attractive to a potential lender, so it becomes increasingly difficult to get the cash needed to stay in business. The circle keeps turning and turning.

The story is confusing. Many things are going on at the same time, so it is impossible to establish who started the problem or how much blame belongs to whom. Blame is unimportant at this point. What is important is to see where the trends are leading. Clearly, in the short run the change in cropping patterns described in earlier chapters is adding to shifts in production from less credit-intensive to more credit-intensive crops which are viewed as being more risky. This shift, in turn, may increase the total demand for credit during a period in which borrowers believe that access to credit is being tightened. Ultimately, this will reduce the profitability of agriculture relative to other potential uses of land and cause individual producers to shift their resource portfolios into more profitable investments; they will leave agriculture.

Low-value products, like annual field crops, require relatively little cash investment in land preparation, labor or harvesting costs. Mechanized methods are the norm for field preparation prior to planting and for harvesting. These methods use relatively little human labor per unit because machinery is substituted. The machinery may be very expensive, such as combines for harvesting grain, but when the cost is considered on a per unit of output basis, it is not much. Also, firms such as custom harvesters are available for hire, so farmers do not have to own the equipment, which means that they do not have to come up with the big down payments to acquire it. The total cash outflows for these crops are smaller than for others and are covered more quickly by the inflows, which means that growers must borrow relatively small amounts and for relatively short periods of time.

High-value crops, on the other hand, require large cash outlays before, during and after the production process. Also, many types of high-value crops, such as tree and vine products, require cash investments years in advance of when the first crop revenues are received. In Oregon, for example, apple growers often have more than $10,000 per acre invested five years before the first Red Delicious is picked. After the trellises are set up and the new trees are planted, much costly hand labor is required to trim the trees into their most profitable form. Labor is required all through the productive years of a tree's life to keep it at peak yield. And, of course, labor is needed to harvest the fruit so as not to damage it and reduce its value. The total amounts per acre to be borrowed by growers of these crops, compared to field crops, are much higher and the loans must be carried much longer, usually for several years. The higher amounts involved and longer investment horizon gives these crops more potential for Big Losses, so they are considered to be more risky.

Using this perspective, agricultural products can be organized into a hierarchy. There is a "pecking order" of food products that is created by the economic push on individual growers and, collectively, on geographic regions, as described next.

THE FARMING FOOD CHAIN

Individual parcels of land move up the Farming Food Chain as the geographic area around them develops, land prices rise and the economic pressure on landowners increases. The productive capabilities of a parcel may restrict how far up the pecking order that parcel can climb, but the last step is always the same: out of agriculture. The farther up the Farming Food Chain that a parcel of land can be developed, the longer it will remain in agriculture; but eventually the profits will run out and that parcel will have to leave. And land development up the Food Chain toward urbanization is a one-way trip— land does not come back once it leaves agriculture.

Exhibit 7.1 illustrates the Farming Food Chain and the relationship between crop types, investment amounts and the flexibility of production assets. At the bottom of the chain are low-value annual crops, like grains, which require relatively low investments per acre and which involve assets that can be shifted into the production of another crop very easily. The second stage of land development involves low-value perennial crops, like alfalfa and other forages. These crops have a normal economic life of more than one year and require somewhat higher investments per acre, but they involve fairly flexible assets. The third stage requires relatively high investments in inflexible assets to produce high-value annual crops like lettuce and fresh tomatoes. Finally, high-value perennial crops such as tree and vine products lock growers into the highest and least flexible investments. In general, the risks and potential returns involved increase with each step up the chain.

Individual growers are willing to invest in more-risky crops if they expect to earn a higher average return on their investment. Yet, there are at least two reasons why a grower with land capable of producing a range of crops would prefer to invest in low-value annual crops: (1) the total cost per acre is lower, and (2) the risk of suffering a loss is lower. These are both attractive features to young, entry-level farmers who do not have much cash. Also, older farmers facing retirement may prefer to reduce their risk of loss by growing relatively low-risk crops. Ultimately, most individuals prefer a safe, sure thing, but are willing to accept some higher level of risk if they feel it is a good investment or if they think they must.

Exhibit 7.1 The Farming Food Chain

Development Stage	Crop Type	Investment, Asset Fixity
4th	High-value perennial	Very high, highly fixed
3rd	High-value annual	High, inflexible
2nd	Low-value perennial	Moderate, flexible
1st	Low-value annual	Low, very flexible

Unfortunately, two types of economic pressures move growers into higher stages of the Farming Food Chain where the risks are higher. First, as the land around a parcel is developed into higher stages, the value of all similar land in the area rises with the profitability of the new crops, thus offering an incentive for landowners to capture the higher value by either following their neighbors into the production of the new crops or by selling the land. Most farmers want to be farmers so they choose to keep the land and shift (although gradually) into the new crop portfolio.[1] This type of economic pressure comes from external sources

---

[1] Eventually, farmers get tired of "working for peanuts." In fact, that is exactly what's happening in Oklahoma. For the first time since 1939, Oklahoma farmers' peanut acreage is approaching the low levels of their Depression-era counterparts. Some 15,000 acres previously devoted to peanuts were planted to other crops or idled in 1996. An industry official said that the reason was farmers' perception of the relatively low profitability of peanuts (*Daily Oklahoman*).

and can be viewed as "opportunity pulling" the grower up the chain. The second type of pressure on growers comes from internal sources and can be called risk push. Growers are pushed up the chain by the need to increase their cash flows to maintain profitability at or above some minimum desired level given their risk exposure. The response of producers to lenders' reassessment of risk, described earlier, is an example of this type of pressure.

Land moving up the Farming Food Chain can leave agriculture from any stage. All roads lead out of agriculture. Although a landowner may shift pieces of parcels into a lower development stage (or fallow it) temporarily, once some portion of a grower's land is in a higher stage it stays there because the economic pressures never ease. Crops are often rotated through specific fields to condition the soil, so low-value crops may temporarily be grown where a higher-value crop was, but this just means that the higher-value crop has been moved to another field, not that it has been discontinued. In total, a grower's land moves up the Food Chain. At any stage, land may be taken out of agriculture whenever the "opportunity pull" becomes too great to resist or the land cannot keep up with the risk push. Even land in the first development stage may be sold if the owner chooses not to shift crops in response to the higher land values. Land in any of the first three stages that is incapable of profitably producing crops in higher stages ultimately faces the exit sign. And, obviously, land that reaches the fourth development stage has nowhere else to go but out of agriculture. When either the opportunity pull or the risk push causes a landowner to look for agricultural alternatives that generate more cash flow (and, hopefully, profits) than the high-value perennials in the fourth stage, he or she will find none. At that point, the choice facing the owner is to leave agriculture or to knowingly accept lower returns on his or her investment. Some owners do hang on for a while, but eventually they must face economic reality.

A classic example of how land moves up and out of the Farming Food Chain is provided by the experience of Stanislaus County in California. Located in the middle of the state's fertile Central Valley, Stanislaus is now one of the nation's most productive agricultural counties. At the beginning of the century the county was covered by dry-land wheat farms. During the Depression of the 1930s, public works projects helped develop irrigation systems that made producing other crops possible in the desertlike climate. Higher-value crops expanded along with the area's population. Wheat was replaced by products from the Farming Food Chain's second and third stages. Irrigated pasture made livestock grazing, especially dairy cattle, a more profitable alternative. High-value annual crops, such as tomatoes, began appearing soon thereafter. By the 1950s, the explosive population growth of the county helped push increasing amounts of land into tree and vine crops (fourth-stage products). Walnuts, almonds, peaches, apricots, grapes, and various other products were planted in the fertile soil around the county's many little farm towns. As a result, many of the new houses built at a frantic pace during the 1950s and 1960s had fruit or nut trees on the property; the residential subdivisions were carved out of orchards that had been producing just a few months earlier. The ironic story continues today. The county's largest town, Modesto, became a central processing area for much of the region's high-value agricultural products. For example, two local boys, Ernest and Julio Gallo, ran a family winery in town. As their winery grew to become one of the world's biggest (and most famous), Ernest and Julio saw their town grow. And that population growth caused prime agricultural land to be transferred out of agriculture forever. Forty years ago Modesto had a population of about 30,000; its current population is around 200,000. You can still see the new houses being built next to orchards. A few miles outside of town the orchards give way to irrigated crops and dairies. But everyone knows what's coming. The dairies will give up and trees will be planted in neat rows.[2] After trees have occupied the land for some span of years, the Farming Food Chain will have been exhausted and the land will leave agriculture for other, more profitable uses: shopping malls and tract houses.

THE GRASS IS ALWAYS GREENER . . .

The grass is always greener on the other side of the fence, in the next crop year, or with the next investment. Virtually all agricultural producers and many of their lenders are eternal optimists. They like to complain, but they don't really want to give up the game. Nevertheless, the rational response to the situation described in the last three chapters is for farmers (as resource portfolio managers) and lenders (as financial

2 There is a strong movement among California farmers to put their land in permanent tree crops, according to Bank of America. San Joaquin Valley almond plantings are fueling the trend, but growers in the south end of the valley are putting in more navel and Valencia oranges, too. The nine tree crops analyzed accounted for 1.22 million acres of California farmland in 1996, much of it valley land. That's a 22 percent jump from 1990 (*Modesto Bee*).

portfolio managers) to both gradually shift assets into more profitable investments (with better risk-return tradeoffs) out of agriculture.

Given the chance, farmers would plant fencerow to fencerow, like they were told to do during the 1950s and 1960s. For example, according to an October 1994 survey by the Soil and Water Conservation Society, farmers nationwide planned to return 63 percent of the acreage in the Conservation Reserve Program at that time to crop production—this was up from 53 percent from the group's 1990 survey. Farmers also planned to keep 23 percent in grass for hay or grazing, 4 percent in trees for wood products, 3 percent in grass and trees for wildlife, and planned to sell 3 percent. What this indicates is that farmers want to shift their resource portfolios so as to generate more cash flows. The economic pressures were stronger in 1994 than in 1990 and are going to continue increasing. The limitation faced is profitability.

As producers face the pressures and make their way up the Farming Food Chain, the future becomes clearer. The message is

Money doesn't grow on trees.

Farmers must be convinced, lenders can see it coming. Farmers currently making Big Money per acre find it especially hard to believe. Lettuce growers, for example, like making a couple thousand dollars net profit on each acre harvested. But ask their lenders how much fun it is in the years for which prices don't cover costs. The *Los Angeles Times* reported that lettuce growers in the Salinas Valley of California spent the summer of 1994 grappling with overproduction that caused losses of up to $1,500 an acre in a region that plants some 72,000 acres of iceberg each year. Growing lettuce is a gamble that most farmers in the area had been losing for at least 13 months. Lettuce growers along Arizona's side of the Colorado River make money, on average, in only two years out of five. The three Bad Years out of each five are no fun. Farmers may have the nerve to keep going after those years, but do they have the cash?

Although no lenders have withdrawn completely from the rural sector, large commercial lenders have tightened loan requirements, causing some borrowers to be dropped as customers. In particular, some lenders have raised the minimum size of loans, in one case to $750,000. This means that small-scale agricultural producers (which large lenders consider to be risky) will have to look elsewhere for operating capital.

Their best prospects will be small, rural lenders. This situation creates the danger that over time rural lenders may accumulate much riskier loan portfolios than large lenders, making the rural banks more likely to fail. To avoid such a situation, rural lenders may have to turn people away, leaving some agricultural producers without sufficient capital to operate effectively.

In summary, the problems exist at the farm and ranch level, not at the national level. In fact, some national observers give agriculture credit for solving most of the world's problems. For example, an editorial in the October 1994 issue of *Today's Farmer* quoted the Hudson Institute's director of global food issues outlining the benefits of the American agricultural system. He said that U.S. high-yield agriculture saves 10 million square miles of wildlife habitat from being plowed under and that soil erosion in America is nothing compared with that in other places. He claims that pesticides prevent cancer by making vegetables and fruit plentiful and that we must continue to increase yields so that we triple food output in the next 40 years. In the face of such praise, what self-respecting farmers can turn their backs on agriculture? The answer is, Anyone faced with declining prospects and a net worth that is shrinking each year. Thus, despite the value of agriculture to the country, exits from agriculture must be individual choices.

Chapter 8

Live Poor, Die Rich

Being a farmer or rancher means never having to say you are sorry for being a little short of cash. In fact, being a farmer or rancher is one of the surest ways to avoid having any money for most of your life. But if a farmer can get through life without losing the farm, he or she is in the chips. In much of agriculture people live poor, die rich.

A life in agriculture comes with many inherent problems, but the most irritating to many people is the poverty. Although many farmers are not poor by most measures, ask any farmer or rancher and they will tell you that they are cash poor. The irritation probably is created by the backwards timing of cash flows: when farmers are alive, they never have two dimes to rub together, but as soon as they die they are rich. So, when they need cash they do not have it, but as soon as they no longer need it, they have so much money that they get tax bills that sometimes run millions of dollars. For the entire United States, "wealth of farmers (over $300,000 per household) averages several times that of consumers (less than $100,000 per household) and taxpayers (some $150,000 per household). Net worth of commercial farms, defined as those with annual sales of over $100,000, averages nearly $1 million per farm" (Tweeten, p. 4). Cash poverty in the face of paper wealth is a virtually unavoidable problem in rural America.

THE AGRICULTURAL CASH CYCLE

The cash problem in agriculture varies during different stages of a producer's life. The problem never goes away, it just changes. From the first moment a person takes over a farm or ranch until the last moment of that person's life, the cash problem is an important factor influencing business and personal decisions. This problem must be understood in order to grasp why producers leave agriculture, often against their wishes, and why those producers still in agriculture so often need help from lenders, the government and other sources to keep going.

To begin, it takes a lot of money to set up even a modest family farming or ranching business. To be capable of supporting a family, a farm must have hundreds (if not thousands) of acres in its control and big pieces of expensive equipment around to help do the work. All of this requires Big Money. In California, for example, a survey of producers found that, on average, agricultural operations had about 1,300 acres of land and $2.5 million in assets. If the average debt of $756,000 is subtracted from the assets, the net result shows that California farmers are millionaires, on average. They are rich!?

How does a young person start a farm? He or she has to inherit it because there is very little chance of being able to borrow enough money to buy a farm. After taking over a farm, a young producer is immediately faced with restrictive credit limits.[1] Until enough years of successful management have gone by to convince a lender to provide all the cash necessary, a young farmer must either scale back the operation or produce less-cash-intensive crops than he or she might prefer to grow. Why are credit limits immediately a problem? First, the new person is an unknown to the lender, but more importantly, there is the built-in cash flow problem.

Once a farming or ranching business is set up, it requires cash outlays for inputs many months before an output can be sent to market, and the cash inflows from the sale of outputs often do not arrive for several months after the sale is made. Therefore, it is not uncommon for the cash flow cycle of some producers to be 18 to 24 months long. This means that the first cash payments can be made as much as two years before the final check is received. Few businesses outside of agriculture have a cash flow problem this severe.

The cash flow problems become more complicated when a young farmer becomes a mature farmer wanting to retire and pass the family business on to his or her children. Many agricultural businesses

---

[1] A 1995 article in *Top Producer* outlines the problems a young farm family has obtaining a promised Farmers' Home Administration loan. Two problems they face are the dramatic drop in the number of loans available and the length of time the loan process takes—up to two years, in some cases.

cannot provide retirement income without being sold—thus the next generation cannot stay on their parents' land unless the parents have enough land and profits to support additional people. Eventually, the pieces of the parents' (or grandparents') farm get split too small to be viable as separate farms.

Agriculture is usually a *negative* cash flow business. First cash must be borrowed to produce a crop. After the harvest, most of the profits need to be invested in long-term capital improvements (and technology) and expansion in order for the operation to remain competitive in the face of the technological pulls discussed in earlier chapters. Profits become "capitalized" into land values in that the more money invested into improvements to land, the more valuable that land becomes and, consequently, the higher the land's price becomes. This trend of investment in land means that more cash is needed for each expansion due to ever-higher land prices. Thus, land absorbs cash. Farmers live poor because they are forced to pour all available cash into their land.

As a result, at retirement (near the end of the life cycle), a farmer's only significant asset is land, so it must somehow provide a *positive* cash flow for a change. The only way it can do that is by being leased out—which never provides as much income as would alternative uses of the money invested in that land—or by being sold so that alternative uses can be made of the money. Both of these approaches may interfere with the farmer's plan to turn the business over to the kids. Thus, cash flow problems put the next generation at risk of not getting their inheritance and, as a result, not being agricultural producers.

How many future American generations will continue to till the land is uncertain—especially with the federal government reporting that, nationally, the number of farms run by families has been declining, and these farms are breaking into smaller pieces. Over the past 40 years, family farms have been decreasing in size as larger operations have become more prominent. According to government statistics, small farms have been consolidated into larger, more efficient spreads, with the average farm totaling 491 acres in 1992, up 39 percent since 1964 (USDA). Competition has forced many family operations to fold, while others have scaled back or diversified their products to remain competitive for as long as possible.

COMBINING RETIREMENT AND ESTATE PLANNING

In agriculture there is a strong need to incorporate retirement planning into the estate planning process because most agricultural producers have few other sources of "pension" income. Their land has been their life, and it becomes their wealth. Estate transfer decisions affect retirement and vice versa.

When considering retirement, if expected income sources (including social security and any other nonfarm pensions) are not enough to meet all expected expenses, additional retirement and estate planning are required. In such cases, it may be necessary to shift the composition of a planned estate, for example, by selling some assets during retirement, thus reducing the value of the estate to be left to heirs. (Sadly, for many producers, "hitting pay dirt" means selling land to developers.) Unfortunately, many economic problems can be created when dividing up a farm or ranch as part of an estate settlement. Two of the most common problems involve (1) scale economies in production, and (2) the unique nature of agricultural assets.

The first problem arises because very often the pieces of a farm or ranch left to heirs may not be large enough to support a family. There are definite economic advantages that make larger agricultural operations more profitable per unit than smaller operations. Also, the productive capacity of land and other resources is limited, meaning that some minimum quantity of resources is needed to produce a particular income amount. If physical expansion is not possible (i.e., no additional land is for sale locally), heirs left with these small, inefficient parcels may be forced to sell them in the long run. This would defeat many agricultural producers' estate planning objective of maintaining continuity of the family business.

The second problem is faced because the pieces of an agricultural operation are not identical and rarely are perfectly divisible. Two pieces of real estate can never be perfectly identical (because of location), raising the possibility of disputes between heirs over the more productive resources. Also, trying to divide physical resources between heirs is another source of potential dispute. For example, many assets (such as houses and other buildings) and improvements to land (such as roads, fences and wells) cannot be divided because they cannot be moved. Sadly, many brothers and sisters have ended up fighting in court because they want particular pieces of a property that their parents intended for them to share.

The distribution problems noted above give agricultural estate holders a much higher probability, compared to urban estate holders, of facing difficulties in finding an equitable distribution of assets.

Equitable treatment of heirs does not necessarily mean *equal* treatment. The financial needs of the surviving spouse should be given priority, but an heir who has contributed time and money to build up the family farm or ranch may also deserve a larger proportion of the estate than other family members. Two especially difficult cases often faced in agricultural estate planning are the problem of having more heirs wanting to stay in the family business than the resources will support and the opposite situation in which no children want to stay in agriculture and the surviving parent cannot manage the operation without their help. Both situations lead to potential trouble because the estate holder has to prioritize in order to decide who gets what and when they get it. Somebody is always mad in these situations. To avoid hurting feelings, parents may go ahead and split a farm or ranch, hoping that the kids can somehow make it go. Unfortunately, two halves of a profitable operation are rarely profitable on their own.

Agricultural parents must often forego the full retirement they earned if they want their children to "keep the farm running." Smaller pieces of a farm are less able to support families, so retiring parents do not want to ask for the full rent on land, often because the financial burden of higher rents may cause their children to fail in farming. Also, parents do not want to sell part of their land to raise retirement cash because that strategy leaves smaller farms for their children as well. Therefore, many parents have to choose between their goals of a comfortable retirement and of being able to see their children and grandchildren running the family business.

For many in agriculture, retirement is simply impossible due to the problems described above. Across America the average age of farmers and ranchers is rising steadily, with many people working well beyond 70 years of age. Whether this is due to personal choice or economic necessity, it is a discouraging prospect when viewed by younger people. A young person considering a career in agriculture would like to think that the financial rewards that wait at the end of a rural life are the same as those available to urban retirees (no matter how dismal). The reality is that the odds are not good for cashing in on the farm.

But what about those families that score big and are able to build a very large-scale farm or ranch? Uncle Sam gets them. Dying rich is a very costly exit. As soon as you are gone, your estate feels the Big Bite. Estate taxes have to be paid before your heirs get anything. And the bite gets bigger as estate sizes increase. At present, estate tax rates start at 0 percent of the total estate (for small estates) but the tax rate goes up quickly to 55 percent. Thus, even the hard-working producer who has been able to build up some cushion over a lifetime cannot guarantee that his or her children will start with a comfortable operation.

In effect, Uncle Sam is helping to make some farms too small to survive—people get pushed off farms and into cities due to estate taxes.[2] The taxes are the same for rural and urban Americans, but they more often have lifestyle-changing effects on farmers and ranchers. The trouble is that darned cash problem described earlier. Agricultural producers have poured nearly all of their cash into their land over their lifetimes, so they do not have enough pocket money for retirement first, then Uncle Sam's Big Bite. The result is that some amount of land must be sold to pay for these two parts of the life cycle.[3] With Uncle Sam getting as much as 55 percent, the leftovers leave heirs either deep in debt (because they borrowed to cover the taxes) or nearly starting over. With these prospects, it is easy to understand why many people give up on agriculture and head to town with what is left of their inheritance. It is also easy to see that this added financial burden puts many of the remaining farms and ranches at risk of failure. The economics of agriculture in America do not make farming or ranching look like very attractive investments to many individuals, even those raised in a rural lifestyle.

This life of cash poverty makes agricultural producers very susceptible to financial disasters, which, they argue, gives them the need for a "safety net." They look to Uncle Sam for such protection. Apparently, they think that since Uncle Sam taketh away, he should also giveth. The story is in the following chapter.

---

[2] Many states are also taking a Big Bite out of agriculture. For example, Oklahoma agricultural leaders said in 1996 that elimination of the state's estate inheritance tax was deemed crucial for ensuring the survival of family farms.

[3] Two strategies used to avoid selling land to cover estate taxes are (1) using life insurance, and (2) incorporating the business, but each has drawbacks. The premiums on life insurance are a cash drain which may add to the burdens threatening the firm's survival. Incorporating can keep the farm's or ranch's assets intact, but heirs still may need to sell some of their inherited stock in the corporation to cover estate taxes on the value of their inheritance.

Chapter 9

Working without a Net

Agriculture's perpetual cash shortage has made producers come to expect subsidies, disaster programs, and bailouts, but they need to accept reality like businesses in other sectors do and face their risks. Farmers and ranchers are hard-working folks—just ask them, they'll tell you. They work year 'round, they are stable, most are owners of their businesses, they hardly ever break any big laws, and they are generous with friends and neighbors. But they are addicted to their safety net. They believe they deserve it. It has never been clearly explained, but something about "working the land" apparently makes people think that taxpayers owe them a good living.

Life on the farm does not offer a personal safety net for self-employed producers, so they look to Uncle Sam to provide one. The cash crunch, estate tax bite, and the dismal economics facing farmers and ranchers certainly put them in tight situations on a fairly regular basis, yet this should come as no surprise to anyone in agriculture. It always has been the case and should be expected. The tricky part is trying to understand why farmers and ranchers believe that they deserve help that is not available to other types of business owners, such as gas station jockeys, grocers, jewelers, bakers, tailors, car dealers, butchers, truckers, restaurateurs, clothiers, and about everyone else. Only the Big Guys like Chrysler and others who are Too Big To Fail get the access to taxpayer dollars that agricultural producers enjoy. The rest of the business world has to manage their risks on their own and suffer the consequences of their failure to do so.

Farmers and ranchers have gone Big Business one better. Big

Business gets subsidies and bailouts, but agriculture gets those two freebies and disaster programs too. And agriculture's safety net is up at all times, every year, not just in the bad times like it is for Big Business. Agriculture gets taxpayer dollars in good years too. For example, a Reuters article in October 1994 outlined the potential for a $2 billion increase in farm program payments because of dropping prices resulting from a record-breaking harvest. The article noted that even the increase to $12 billion in payments for the year was a far cry from the $26 billion paid out for commodity programs in 1986. However, $12 billion is still a lot of money when you consider that the 1990s were record-breaking years for profits in agriculture as a whole. So, farmers get taxpayer dollars when they produce too much as well as when they produce too little.

Also, farmers often get too many taxpayer dollars. By October 1995 Reuters reported that the crop price situation had reversed itself such that American farmers faced paying back almost $2 billion to the government because of bigger-than-necessary payments received earlier in the year. While it is not unusual for farmers to have to refund some payments to the government because of surprise price surges, the paybacks of 1996 were some of the largest on record and impacted many more producers than normal. Corn farmers were the hardest hit, having to return almost $1 billion in fall 1996 for overpayments received during spring 1995. At the time that the paybacks were announced, an official with the National Corn Growers' Association said, "the good news is that farmers don't have to pay it back for a year, because they wouldn't have enough income to pay it back from this year's short crop." That's right, farmers got to keep the overpayments for more than a year. In the meantime, taxpayers are required to *prepay* their income tax through the withholding system. Is this fair?

And the money goes to rich farmers as well as to poor ones. In fact, some of the richest farmers have been found to get disproportionately bigger slices of the tax money pie.[1] Sometimes it is

---

[1] This problem will probably exist for some time. Big farms will continue to get large government subsidies while payments for smaller farms will dwindle under the 1995 farm legislation, according to a rural advocacy group. "Once again, the rich and powerful are exempted from the rigors of deficit reduction, leaving farm families of modest means to shoulder the burden," said an analyst with the Center for Rural Affairs in Walthill, Nebraska. The center, a research group that focuses on problems of farm communities and advocates support for family farms, released their study in October 1995 with the pro-environment Campaign for Sustainable Agriculture, based in Washington, D.C.

legal. For example, one of the world's largest cotton producers was featured on a segment of the television show *60 Minutes* in the late 1980s in which it was shown that the farmer (a multimillion-dollar corporation) received subsidized irrigation water to grow subsidized cotton that was in such surplus at the time that it went into subsidized storage facilities. Other wealthy farmers featured during that broadcast admitted to receiving millions of dollars from government programs. When questioned as to why they take tax dollars they do not need, the farmers responded that they "deserved" the money for producing food for the starving masses. When it was pointed out that cotton in storage feeds no one, the response was that it was legal. The show went on to describe some of the not-so-legal ways that farmers have "milked" taxpayers. One of the best-known methods was to change the documentation of the property title to make it appear that a single, large farm was several small farms. This enabled the owners to take advantage of a government program that paid a maximum of $50,000 to the owner of each farm participating; large farms claimed to be several separate farms and collected $50,000 for each one.

Stories like these make agriculture a target during budget battles. For example, during the build-up to the 1995 Farm Bill, a coalition of environmental and taxpayer groups was lobbying to cut $33 billion from federal programs that it claimed wasted money, including irrigation subsidies used to grow surplus crops.[2] In another example, U.S. Department of Agriculture officials said that they were not consulted on a White House budget memo that listed about $16 billion in farm program cuts for the next five years. The memo, which was from the White House Budget Director, and was characterized by the White House as merely a "list of options," outlined several ways that farm program savings could be made. In response, one USDA official said the department had no current plans to seek additional farm program spending cuts as part of its recommendations for the 1995 Farm Bill. This indicated both that the USDA was a target and that it was not

---

[2] The General Accounting Office said that federal subsidies and various loopholes have allowed western farmers to pay only a fraction of their allocated share of the cost of irrigation projects that they use (*Modesto Bee*). The irrigators' share of costs for 133 water projects in 17 western states was $7.1 billion. As of September 1994, they had paid less than $1 billion, although they generally had kept up with their obligations and paid what they were billed. The difference has been made up with federal subsidies, fees transferred to other sources, such as power companies, and legislation specifically relieving irrigators of their obligations, according to the GAO (*Washington Times* November 22, 1994).

"in the loop" within the administration. Another USDA official said at the time that the department would focus on reshaping existing farm programs and "once we have the framework developed," the USDA may have to consider how to incorporate new spending cuts, but that issue is in the background for now. In other words, the USDA likes its big budget, is not anxious to reduce it, is not forward-looking in their programming, and has come to be seen within government as an advocate for agriculture rather than as an objective overseer. Only the Defense Department (because its budget is bigger) is considered to be more biased in favor of the industry it is supposed to monitor.

"Feeding at the government trough" has become a way of life in many rural areas. The *Omaha World Herald* reported in 1994 that cuts in federal entitlements would hit rural areas in Nebraska harder than urban areas because rural areas have a high percentage of elderly people and farm residents who are dependent on government payments. In the state's smallest counties, more than 23 percent of total income is in the form of government aid such as Social Security, Medicare and farm subsidies. According to an agricultural economist who was quoted in the article, rural economies are going to have to figure out, fairly quickly, ways to diversify their economies to cope with this loss of income. The Golden Era of Handouts is over. But that is considered to be a good thing by some people in agriculture. One executive, addressing a national conference of the Grain and Feed Association in Des Moines in December 1994, lay some of the blame for the slow decay of rural communities across the central United States on crop subsidies (*Washington Times* March 29, 1995). "Let's face it: the subsidy system we have developed in agriculture to save the Midwest farm has failed. We have tended to look to Washington in times of need. We're our own worst enemy."

WHO'S GOING TO PAY FOR THIS MESS?

Disasters happen too often in agriculture. A flood here, a drought there; it's always something. As shown in Table 9.1, the government passed out cash to agriculture in big wads during the 1980s, but as the annual deficit and total national debt grew to astonishing levels, something had to give. In the 1990s, the government has tired of paying for the endless stream of agricultural disasters, even though their cost is relatively low compared to that of many urban disasters, such as the Savings and Loan mess. The handouts to farmers set a bad example for other industries. Everyone is looking around and wondering why some industries get special treatment.

Table 9.1 Federal Outlays for Agricultural Disaster Assistance, 1980-93

Year	Disaster payments	Crop insurance	Emergency loans	Total
		(millions of dollars)		
1980	303	38	2,500	2,841
1981	1,422	0	4,900	6,322
1982	337	218	2,000	2,555
1983	128	330	566	1,024
1984	27	576	1,000	1,603
1985	18	506	500	1,024
1986	17	516	210	743
1987	668	454	103	1,225
1988	114	411	29	554
1989	4,017	1,103	80	5,200
1990	1,661	979	60	2,700
1991	141	770	53	964
1992	1,150	954	14	2,118
1993	1,319	867	38	2,224
Total	11,322	7,270	12,053	31,095

Source: H. Lee, J. Harwood, and A. Somwaru.

Within agriculture, some commodities and geographic regions have been treated to much more disaster cash than others. Feed-grain producers have been the biggest winners in the Disaster Lottery. Corn growers are usually the biggest recipients of disaster payments, with wheat and cotton growers next on the Hit Parade.[3] Also, Hoffman,

---

[3] Cotton's supporters in Congress are so determined to keep the money flowing that in 1995 they ignored 1994's legislation and tried to get $41 million in special disaster

Campbell and Cook showed that the top 10 congressional districts for disaster assistance received about one-third of the total disaster assistance from 1985 to 1993, and that over 60 percent of total disaster aid for that period went to the top 10 states: Texas, North Dakota, Minnesota, Kansas, Iowa, Illinois, Wisconsin, South Dakota, Michigan and Georgia.   They found that over 107,000 participants in the government disaster payment program received assistance four or more years out of the seven-year period from 1987 to 1993. Those producers received a total of $2.55 billion in payments. The authors concluded that too few people get too much of the benefits from this program and that agricultural production is being encouraged in risky geographic areas that would probably not be farmed without the program. In other words, the programs are failures by design unless their real purpose is simply to get a lot of money to the constituents of a few powerful congressional representatives from rural districts.

Agriculture as a whole has been treated differently throughout America's history, but conditions have changed. The midwestern floods of 1994 were the last straw. The government wants to shift away from the constant stream of disaster payments toward reliance on crop insurance and farmer-pays programs. In other words, farmers are going to be required to face the risks involved in their business just like everyone else must. No more free rides. If a farmer wants protection against the risk of bad weather reducing outputs and revenues, he or she must buy insurance. This is no different than a manufacturer buying fire insurance. All businesses face some types of risks and must take the responsibility of managing them or live with the consequences.

The economic effects of the movement toward holding everyone responsible for their own business risks include added momentum to America's exit from agriculture. Agriculture is not the only industry affected, but it has less control over how it can deal with the problem. The banking industry, for example, was hit with new regulations requiring more self-insurance measures in the wake of the savings and loan debacle. However, banks could simply pass along the resulting higher costs of doing business to their customers. Farmers cannot pass along any cost increases, they are price takers, not price setters. Thus, the need to pay for their own insurance, instead of getting it free in the

---

payments to cotton growers. The Senate denied the aid after opponents argued that payments would undermine a year-old reform of federal crop disaster aid. Senator Kerrey reminded Congress that just the previous year they had voted to reform disaster aid, making mandatory crop insurance the only way for producers to get payments.

form of disaster aid and other programs, makes agriculture more expensive and less profitable than it was before the change. Any decrease in profitability scares off more investors and producers.

It may have been accidental, but the changed perspective in agricultural policy will probably hasten the demise of farm programs. With the federal crop insurance reforms of 1994, the government signaled its goal of finding an insurance-based solution to the yield risks faced by farmers. However, federal crop insurance programs suffer from the same ills plaguing other government-designed risk management tools: they don't fit most people's needs. For example, 10 percent of citrus growers in California use federal frost insurance coverage, 90 percent use private frost insurance. In a nutshell, the reasons are the value and simplicity of private policies relative to federal policies. As shown in Table 9.2, private insurance policies offer a much lower deductible, higher coverage level and a quicker, easier application process than federal policies for just a slightly higher price. Anytime farmers are willing to pay more for something, it is sure sign that the cheaper product is a bad deal. Government programs have a bad reputation due to their complexity and, in places outside the Midwestern home of federal insurance, to their frequent unsuitability to the needs of growers. Their standardized design ignores the variability of different crops. In the case of California citrus farmers, yields rarely drop more than the 25 percent minimum deductible that is standard on federal crop insurance policies. This means that money spent on federal insurance by these growers usually generates no financial return: it is virtually wasted. Private policies, on the other hand, offer deductibles that are related to the level of need of local growers and often generate a cash inflow, as well as create some peace of mind. The one-size-fits-all approach of the Federal Crop Insurance Corporation and other federal agencies does not fit all too often.

The new, complicated federal crop insurance program may be the death knell for government farm programs. It is so confusing that it will turn off growers rather than encourage them to participate. In response to a survey about their risk management strategies, farmers and ranchers complained that few federal risk management tools fit their needs. Unfortunately, many of the standardized tools offered by private business, such as futures and options contracts for use in managing price risk, also were not able to completely fill producers' needs. Rather than use risk tools such as insurance or futures contracts, many producers rely on risk strategies that give them more control. For example, large-scale growers diversify geographically to reduce yield risk instead of insuring. Without widespread participation by producers, most federal programs will fail. Crop insurance, for example, needs a big pool of "good" farmers (those who do not have big yield swings over time) to buy policies so that the insurers can use those funds to help cover the losses paid out to "bad" farmers (those who have big yield losses). With the flaws in the standard design of federal crop insurance programs, good farmers do not view the program to be worthwhile and do not participate nearly often enough to cover the losses of the hordes of bad farmers that are attracted to the program by its subsidized insurance premium rates. So, the deck is stacked against federal insurance, like other poorly designed national "cookie cutter" programs. Local designs by private firms are likely to continue to be the risk programs of preference, leaving the pooling of risks from local programs as the only justification for the existence of federal programs.[4] Local tools still need national pools.

Table 9.2 Federal Crop Insurance Corporation vs. Private Citrus Frost Insurance in California

	Private	FCIC
Average Premium Rate	5.0 %	4.5 %
Deductible (% of liability)	10 % -15 %	25 %
Coverage Limit	$2,000	Yield x FCIC price (less than $2,000)
Advance Sign-up	21 days	12 months
Paperwork	Simple	Complex

Source: Insurance representatives who issue private and FCIC policies were interviewed.

---

[4] National insurance programs are probably the only way to manage the risks, and costs, of extraordinary disasters, like earthquakes. Even California could not create a large enough pool of local, private insurers to make earthquake insurance affordable to most homeowners.

On the whole, Uncle Sam would like to say good riddance to a bad investment. Of course it is not yet the majority view that agriculture is a bad investment. Certainly the U.S. Department of Agriculture is full of people who want the dollars to keep flowing into agriculture. But as the years go by and the budget battles get more intense, increased scrutiny will uncover the fact that, though agriculture has not been a bad investment in the past, other industries now offer a much better return on the invested tax dollars.

NO MORE FREE LUNCH

Agriculture is no longer made up of the group of helpless, little farmers that it was 150 years ago; it could take care of itself. But it does not want to because it thinks it can't after being so dependent on government intervention for so long. Unfortunately, the budget blues are going to cause increasing numbers of farmers and ranchers to be "weaned" from government dollars whether they like it or not. Uncle Sam has no choice.

Government support for tobacco, dairy, and other products and storage subsidies on subsidized crops such as cotton will be phased out due to concerns expressed by the urban public.[5] The bill is too big and the benefits to voting consumers are small or negative. In fact, as voters learn more about where the tax dollars are going, they could begin to view dairy, grain, and tobacco programs, respectively, as The Good, The Bad, and The Ugly. Millions of dollars go into dairy programs in the form of artificially high price supports that stimulate excess milk production. The extra milk goes into processed dairy products like butter and cheese. The good news is that at least most of the dairy output is consumed by Americans. The bad news is that huge quantities of grain produced in response to artificially high prices are exported. In this case, American taxpayers are subsidizing farmers and foreign consumers.[6] The news about tobacco gets ugly when the cost of

---

[5] It may take a while, however, because some products have regional support. For example, a *Journal of Commerce* columnist said that the 1995 congressional vote on the Farm Bill to cut $13.4 billion in crop subsidies while dishing out an incentive to cotton interests to increase production showed that cotton has clout. He noted that tobacco and sugar also were left alone in the Farm Bill, another victory for Southerners. He said cotton's hold on Congress could be a net loss to the South because the region's poultry industry is now likely to have to buy their feed from Midwestern producers, as Southern soybean production dips in favor of cotton, and that will raise costs to poultry producers.

[6] U.S. wheat production and exports would drop substantially from current projections if government subsidies were eliminated, according to a study done in 1995 for the

subsidies to farmers and cigarette companies is added to the healthcare costs of consumers and second hand sufferers. Taxpayers will not continue to pay farmers millions of dollars each year to grow a crop that is consumed by a minority of the population and that harms everyone with whom it comes in contact. Even ignoring the health issues, there is no reason to subsidize the production of tobacco because the cigarette companies are certainly capable of paying the full cost of their inputs; their annual profit reports show that very clearly.

Paying producers to do things that are not needed seems to be a common theme in farm programs. For example, the *Des Moines Register* (November 24, 1994) reported that the government loaned about $1 billion to corn farmers during fall 1994 to help them put 448 million bushels of corn into a low-interest loan program so that they could hold their grain until prices rose. The loan program, in effect, helps farmers speculate in times of low prices. Why should this be subsidized? If farmers want to speculate on corn prices, they can do it on the corn futures markets like the rest of us. What is worse, the loan program also has the effect of muting the market's signal that too many people are growing too much corn. Tax dollars are paying people to stay in corn farming even though other products may be needed much more.

And what boggles the mind even more are the many cases in which farmers are paid to do nothing. For example, in 1996 the Associated Press reported that 53 Colorado farmers who were leasing state-owned land were being paid $520,000 a year through the Conservation Reserve Program not to grow anything on the acreage. The article said the Colorado Land Board allowed the farmers to sign the "no-grow" leases because the state still reaps some financial benefit.

When confronted with details such as these, farm program advocates often respond in a manner that can be paraphrased as "Don't confuse me with facts." Well, the debate goes on anyway. Facts fly from one side of the argument to the other. Several newspapers have taken the position that everyone who eats is paying for Depression-era farm payments that just keep going. Farmers say they must be supported because they produce necessities and because commodity prices fall when farmers and Mother Nature do a good job of bringing in

---

House and Senate farm committees by the Food and Agriculture Policy Research Institute (*Washington Times* March 29, 1995). The point is, if America would still be exporting wheat without any subsidies, then there is no reason for taxpayers to continue paying for food eaten by foreign consumers.

a bountiful harvest. Consumers complain that farm price supports artificially raise food prices. Other types of businesses complain that they cannot get the level of protection and support that agriculture receives. Taxpayers complain that everything wastes money. One thing that has been proven in this debate is that confusion is contagious.

Independent academic researchers have tried to sort out fact from fiction in the arguments. The general result is typified by that of Bullock, who concluded that research and development subsidies and income transfers to agriculture grow politically incorrect as agribusiness firms receive a higher share of the benefits that are "deadweight losses" to the U.S. economy. In the good ol' days, taxpayers were willing to give farmers a little extra cash to assure a steady supply of food. Nowadays, people recognize that subsidies to tobacco farmers, for example, just make cigarette companies that much more profitable. This is a deadweight loss to the economy because the tax dollars spent on tobacco do not generate any output that would not have been produced without the subsidy: the tobacco still would have been grown because the cigarette companies would have paid for it. Those tobacco program dollars could have been invested somewhere else in the economy to generate additional output and jobs.

Even the USDA produces information that indicates that government farm programs keep a few small, inefficient operations in business unnecessarily. For example, a 1994 USDA report showed that 65 percent of U.S. crop subsidies go to just 17 percent of American farmers (*Washington Times* November 22, 1994). Only one-third of all farmers get subsidies, but the payments are a sizable part of small-farm income. The USDA economists said that the loss of government payments from budget cuts may affect small farms more than large ones. In other words, without the Big Handouts, a lot of uncompetitive farms would fail, but those operations can continue to waste their time and resources as long as tax dollars flow to them.

Proposed cuts in crop subsidies are numerous. For example, the World Resources Institute released a report in 1995 which said that cutting crop subsidies by 50 percent would save taxpayers $5 billion annually and improve the environment, with only a minimum loss of farm income (*Washington Post* April 29, 1995). Changes proposed in the report include making up to half of all cropland ineligible for subsidies and giving transition payments to farmers to encourage them to adopt environmentally friendly tillage practices and to take wetlands and ecologically fragile land out of production. With less land eligible for subsidies, farmers would pay more attention to finding profitable crop rotations and would put marginal land to other uses such as pastures, the report said.

Environmental issues are raising the pressure on subsidies. A *Washington Times* columnist said that farm subsidies trickle down into the environment through runoff of pesticides and fertilizer. He said a study by the Competitive Enterprise Institute indicates that elimination of farm subsidies could reduce farm chemical use by 35 percent, and he claimed that other studies back up such findings. The CEI study's author said that government behavior is bizarre, with the Environmental Protection Agency doing all it can to reduce pesticide use and the USDA spending taxpayer money to put more pesticides in use.

Unfortunately, it is not easy to cut through all the misinformation and cut farm subsidies. This was illustrated in May 1995 when the House of Representatives cut $17 billion from farm subsidies but did not touch the sugar support system—probably because of the myth that the $1.5 billion program doesn't cost a penny. The Government Accounting Office estimates that the sugar program has actually cost consumers more than $10 billion in the last decade by artificially inflating the price of sugar. Taxpayers also pay more indirectly when the government buys sugar at the inflated price for use in the federally subsidized school lunch program. The war of words set off by that vote was not "sugar coated".

The Candy Politics raged into fall 1995. One of the first blasts came in a *Washington Post* editorial which described the trade-off shaping up in the House of Representatives that would protect sugar and peanut programs from anything more than incremental change. It concluded with the question: "Who, except perhaps consumers of sugar and peanuts, will be losers from that?" The point of the editorial was that all Americans and their collective sweet tooth would lose. A vice president with the U.S. Sugar Corporation jumped in, saying that in truly free markets a sugar program wouldn't be needed or wanted, but, he claimed, the sugar market is rigged with dumped surplus, subsidized sugar (*Washington Times* September 30, 1995). He said that American consumers already pay less than most of the world's people for sugar and claimed that prices would rise if the United States relied on the world market for supplies. The United States, he warned, would lose much of its sweetener industry, and its 420,000 jobs, if the sugar program were eliminated. Things got sticky when U.S. sugar cane and sugar beet growers said that sugar users were motivated by "corporate

greed" in their efforts to have the sugar program dismantled.   In
advertisements in major daily newspapers, the American Sugar Farmers
group said that Hershey Foods Corporation was among a handful of
"corporate food titans bankrolling efforts to undo U.S. sugar policy"
(*Philadelphia Inquirer*). The group called on the states of California and
Michigan to sell their holdings in Hershey. In response, the Coalition to
End Welfare for Big Sugar said that the sugar growers were hypocritical
in their attack on Hershey Foods and criticized them for "hiding behind
mythical small farmers" in efforts to protect their benefits, pointing out
that most sugar program benefits go to a small number of farms
(*Washington Times* September 30, 1995).   A coalition official said
reforms being discussed in Congress did not go nearly far enough,
adding that the coalition would focus on repealing the sugar program
during the farm-bill debate. But Big Business As Usual won when the
leadership of the House of Representatives (headed by a Congressman
from Georgia) became "sugar daddies" by killing Congress' plans to
lower supports for sugar and peanuts. Ironically, at the same time the
International Sugar Organization was warning sugar-producing countries
about the consequences of oversupply.   An ISO official said that a
number of countries' plans for expanding sugar production worried him
because import markets are not expanding at the same rate as
production. In other words, the world has too much sugar, so there is no
reason for America to be subsidizing its production. If we needed more
sugar, we could call Australia, the world's largest raw sugar exporter; its
big and efficient sugar mills can satisfy the explosive growth of sugar
consumption in Asia, and they could take care of us as well.

What about peanuts? A *Washington Post* article examined
people who hold peanut quotas but rent them out to others who actually
are peanut farmers. A peanut quota is, effectively, a license to produce
some quantity of peanuts; without a license (quota), a farmer can't grow
peanuts.   Critics say that quotas divert as much as $200 per ton of
peanuts to an elite and unnecessary group.   The peanut quota lords
dispute the idea that they are unnecessary. Several points in the debate
are certain. First, the peanut quota program is opposed by peanut-using
industries. Second, a Government Accounting Office report says that
the quotas add up to $500 million a year to the cost of peanuts. Finally,
some of the peanut quota lords are large corporations with different
addresses than the farms that they run and some are the offspring of
peanut farmers who moved to town.   This is not unusual; by one
estimate, 37 percent of all U.S. farm program payments go to nonfarm

landlords. This does not jive with most programs' original intents, but it is a fact today.

Other subsidies have a proven record of paying big returns to America. A big piece of the subsidies to agriculture over the decades has gone to research and development of new and improved products. The inability of small, individual farmers to invest in research was a major argument for the creation of the USDA and, during the Civil War, the Land-Grant university system. In recent years the government research subsidy continues to "bear fruit." For example, over the past 30 years USDA scientists have tinkered with domestically grown produce, developing new varieties that resist disease and pests and have more nutrients. More than 730 varieties of vegetables, fruits and grains have been re-engineered since the 1980s. Examples of innovations include carrots with twice the vitamin A of their predecessors, and spider-proof berries. Developments of a more traditional nature include the recent success of a USDA scientist in breeding short rice plants that can be submerged in water for up to two weeks while yielding 20-40 percent more rice than tall varieties. In 1995, U.S. Agriculture Secretary Glickman said that agricultural research is a good investment, noting that every dollar invested in the American agricultural system has returned at least $1.35 (Heuer).

The questions now are who should, who can, and who will pay for this subsidy mess? The answer to the first is that only those people who receive benefits from the investment in agricultural research should be expected to pay for it. Most consumers fall into this category, hence the idea that federal programs are the easiest way to collect and distribute the money. But an increasing number of private agribusiness firms are benefiting from publicly supported research and, as Bullock found, taxpayers don't like it. As a result, the federal approach is fading away. This brings up the second question: Who *can* pay? Farmers can't unless they are very big. Big agribusiness firms are already paying for private research, so they could chip in for the public projects. However, they don't like to do that unless they can direct the research in some way and have control over the results—to make profits from the information generated. So, the third question arises: Who *will* pay for agricultural research in the future? The most likely candidates fall into two categories: (1) private companies will invest in relatively small projects aimed at making specific developments, and (2) the governments of the foreign countries in which future food production will take place will fund large projects and basic research.[7] Thus, as the role of producing food moves away from America and other countries high on the Economic Food Chain to less-developed countries, so too will the responsibility for investing in agricultural research. It will pay those countries to make investments in agriculture because they will receive the benefits of the results.[8]

For America, Japan, and Western Europe, the situation is reversed. Scientists from those countries will be paid (by foreign sources) to do the research and teach others how to do it, but the rewards for continued investments in agricultural research by those nations will continue to shrink with the volume of their agricultural output. The level of public research investment in those highly developed countries will not shrink as fast as the rewards, but it will eventually disappear with agricultural production. The safety net that seems to be such a fixture in current American agriculture will disappear in pieces, and the last piece to go will probably be subsidies for research and development.

WITH FRIENDS LIKE THESE . . .

In this day and age there is near universal agreement that the Three Greatest Lies are (1) "the check is in the mail," (2) "my wife doesn't understand me," and (3) "I'm from the government and I'm here to help you." The stories behind the first two lies may be more interesting, but it is the third lie that is most relevant to agriculture. It sums up the attitude of many producers toward Uncle Sam.

Agricultural policy and government programs have come to be viewed by those in the industry more as a source of risk than as a solution to the risks faced by agriculture, thus indicating the conflict between the perspectives of agriculture and the general public. Surveys

---

[7] Private businesses are funding a growing majority of agricultural research at U.S. public institutions, and that won't change anytime soon, according to the USDA. By 1997 private sources were funding 60 percent of the nation's agricultural research, the federal government 25 percent and states were contributing 15 percent (*Des Moines Register* January 23, 1997).

[8] An example of the research partnerships expected in the future is occurring in Brazil. To learn more about, watch over and protect the 2 million square miles of wild Amazon frontier, Brazilian authorities and the U.S. firm Raytheon Company planned in 1995 to launch a $1.4 billion project that would put the region under high-tech electronic surveillance. Pending final approval by the Brazilian Senate of the foreign financing, planners predict that it will be up and running by the turn of the century, helping to track problems such as deforestation, erosion, pollution, poverty and crime (*Los Angeles Times* October 19, 1995).

of producers in California showed that many people in agriculture rate government programs as one of the most important sources of risk that they face (see Table 9.3). This is true in both the farm and agribusiness sectors of the industry. This result is somewhat surprising, considering the close relationship that the USDA has with agriculture, but actually it is usually some other government agency, either federal or state, that is mentioned most often by complaining farmers. Environmental regulations, in particular, are becoming a common complaint with farmers and ranchers. The mood of the general public seems to favor policies that agriculture considers to be constraining and threatening to future profitability. For example, water is becoming less accessible and more expensive to farmers in many parts of the country, and ranchers are faced with higher costs for using public lands for grazing. On the whole, policy changes of the past decade have tended to make investment in agriculture relatively less attractive than some alternatives and, thus, have added incentive for farmers and ranchers to bail out.

Table 9.3 Sources of Risk to California Agribusiness

Source of Risk	Respondents Labeling it a Source of Risk (%)	Respondents Ranking it as One of Two Main Sources of Risk (%)
Government regulations	88	46
Weather	92	38
Pests	73	8
Disease	69	0
Input price variability	54	8
Output price variability	62	27
Labor cost changes	62	0

Even programs that are supposed to help agriculture are not popular with producers. For example, a University of Illinois survey found that only 37 percent of 9,754 farmers in 15 states want to keep the federal crop price-support system. This means that about two-thirds of farmers do not like the government's attempt to guarantee them at least a minimum price for their output. It does not mean that farmers want to depend entirely on the market for their prices, although many of them have said as much. All too often farmers' frustration with government cause them to say things that they would regret if anyone were listening. When farmers say that government programs do not work (the way that farmers want them to), and that they wish that Uncle Sam would get out of agriculture, they should remember the old saying, "Be careful what you wish for, it might come true."

Uncle Sam is now on the lookout for volunteers to leave the government charity list. If a few farmers speak up loudly enough, often enough, the end will be nearer than anyone realizes. In late 1994, the debate about the 1995 Farm Bill began with suggestions by key senators that farm subsidies could be dropped entirely. Farmers immediately said whoa, but the idea was already planted.[9] Agriculture had drawn too much attention and people were beginning to question seriously the need for future handouts to the industry. The announced consolidation or closure of 1,274 USDA field offices across the country over three years was the beginning. This action was designed to save $3.6 billion over five years while cutting 11,000 USDA jobs. As the Farm Bill debate went on, the tug-of-war over resources led environmental groups to point out agriculture's coziness with key members of Congress. For example, the Environmental Working Group said that direct subsidies to farmers, including commodity, disaster, emergency and conservation payments in the 19 states represented by members of the 1995 Senate Agriculture Committee had amounted to $52.4 billion in the previous 10 years, an amount equal to 26 percent of the estimated farmland value in those states (*Washington Times* October 12, 1995).   Such cozy connections may help agriculture fight off the budget cutters for a while, but it is a losing battle.

So, agriculture's uneasy alliance with, and dependence on, government is heading for the "last roundup." Although farmers often complained about the holes in their government safety net, they rarely refused to use it. It was the only net around. Without a private safety

---

9 A survey in 1995 by the American Farmland Trust showed that 10 percent of farmers felt that ending farm subsidies would force them off the land, but nearly 40 percent said that it would have little impact on their business. Clearly, marginal producers favor subsidies, but economically viable producers would be glad to see subsidies and those marginal competitors gone.

net, most farmers and ranchers realized that they had to depend on Uncle Sam. The trouble began when a few dissenters made enough noise to be heard during a bad budget period. Now the subsidies will be government inspected and eventually butchered. It is not a pretty thought. Farmers and ranchers will be left to face the real-world risks on their own. Although producers of some crops are used to working without a net, it will be a new experience for a lot of people who are unprepared for it. The casualties will mount and eventually the war will be lost, despite victories in a few battles. America is moving on to better investments.

Chapter 10

Why Not Switch
Rather than Fight?

Fighting the risks that are chasing off producers and lenders is more difficult for farmers than for agribusinesses. As a result, farming and agribusiness will go in different directions. Farming will fade away and agribusiness will continue to flourish. Farming won't go without a fight, but it is a battle that farming must eventually lose because the economic deck is stacked against it. On the other hand, agribusiness will not have to fight, only adapt. And as some farmers fight the inevitable, others will gradually see the light and embrace it. No, this story is not about a near-death experience (at least not in the normal sense), it is another case of natural economic evolution and the hard choices that confront people in the pursuit of happiness. It could also be called "making a silk purse out of a sow's ear."

"RAISE LESS CORN AND MORE HELL"

It has long been a source of irritation to farmers that the economics of agriculture are dismal. Farmers raise a big crop and they are punished by seeing prices fall; nature gives farmers a bad harvest and they have salt rubbed into the wound by seeing prices soar while they have nothing to sell. It is enough to drive a person crazy. And to make matters worse, the risks faced in agriculture are numerous and largely uncontrollable.

The reaction of agriculture has been to periodically take the advice of Mary E. Lease, a nineteenth century populist leader, to "raise less corn and more Hell" in times of strife. Thus, in the face of agriculture's demise in America, farmers should be expected to put up quite a struggle. Some will go out kicking and screaming. But, oddly enough, most farmers are not doing everything they can to manage the risks they face. Risk management tools are used less often by producers than by agribusiness firms. This makes one wonder, Why are farmers complaining about their predicament? It's their own fault for not doing all they can to protect themselves. Or is it?

Agriculture is a unique industry in many ways. The most obvious feature that makes it different from any other type of business is that agricultural production occurs outdoors over long periods of time, creating many opportunities for adverse results. Another characteristic that impacts producers' incomes is the economics of commodity markets and prices. Add in the highly perishable nature of many food commodities and you have a real manager's nightmare: very little truly is *manageable* at the farm level.

Tools do exist for managing risks of various sorts. Yet, farmers and ranchers across the country have not made much use of many of these. This seems odd considering the effects that risks have on producers' choice of crops and the income derived from those enterprises. As discussed in earlier chapters, risk is pushing agricultural producers down a path that leads to more-risky crops as they try to avoid the exit sign. This implies that risk tools should be showing increasing rates of usage over time, but they are not. For example, the USDA surveyed wheat growers in the mid-1970s concerning their use of futures hedging to manage price risk (Blank, Carter and Schmiesing). The results showed that only about 7 percent of growers who could hedge were hedging at that time. Similar surveys conducted during the 1980s and early 1990s found that only about 10 percent of potential hedgers were using the risk tool. Clearly, futures hedging is underutilized by agricultural producers. Producers also ignore other risk tools.

To determine why risk management tools have been underutilized, a survey was conducted in California in 1993. All types of farmers and ranchers were asked about their risk attitudes and strategies. The answers to three questions proved to be useful: (1) What risk management tools do California producers use? (2) Which of these tools are preferred? and (3) How do producers rate available risk management tools relative to one another? The responses of producers to these questions are summarized in Tables 10.1 and 10.2.

Question 1 produced the responses presented in Table 10.1. Diversification is the risk management tool used by more producers than any other tool available in California. This is not surprising in a state in which 250 commodities are produced. It does support the idea that producers operate as if they have portfolios of enterprises that can be adjusted in response to perceived changes in risk. Crop insurance, forward contracting, and government programs are all used by about half as many producers as diversification. Surprisingly, crop insurance is second overall. This implies that for some people insurance works well, but for other people it does not meet their needs. It is likely that differences in commodities being produced explain much of the difference in demand for insurance. Forward contracting is used more consistently across commodities, but contracting is required in many California crop markets, thus not all use is dependent on risk management issues. Government programs are used by varying percentages of growers in different crop markets.[1] This implies that differences in commodities being produced are important in explaining the use of risk tools. The other tool listed, hedging with futures or options, is used by a small minority of producers. The reason most often given for not using this risk management tool is its lack of availability for specific enterprises. The other tools listed in Table 10.1 were written in by respondents.

Table 10.1 California Producers' Use of Risk Management Tools in 1993

Tool	% using
Diversification	47.6
Crop insurance	24.4
Forward contract	23.4
Government program	20.0
Hedging	6.2
Labor contract	1.2
Capital	1.1
Multiple markets*	1.6
Other	6.3
None	1.9

* This includes diversifying income sources and being in multiple geographical markets for a product.

1 This applies only to voluntary programs. Obviously, mandatory programs, such as federal (or state) marketing orders, require that all growers participate.

The responses to question 2, summarized in the first column of Table 10.2, provide additional insight regarding the level of usage of the risk management tools. The first column shows the percentage of producers ranking the tool as their first (preferred) choice. Also, between 35 and 57 percent of respondents did not rank each tool (as indicated in the last column), thus indicating that many people have no experience with the tools.

Table 10.2 Producers' Preferences for Risk Management Tools

Rank:	1st	2nd	3rd	4th	5th	Unranked
			(%)			
Crop Insure	16.5	15.1	8.4	8.8	7.4	43.8
Diversify	43.8	13.0	4.2	2.6	1.1	35.3
Fwd Contract	11.4	21.6	10.9	5.1	2.8	48.2
Gvt Program	6.2	11.2	10.5	7.0	13.7	51.3
Hedging	1.8	6.2	9.5	12.1	12.8	57.6

The preferences shown in Table 10.2 are similar to the actual levels of use for the risk tools. Diversification is clearly the preferred method for dealing with risk overall. Although diversification is viewed as less of a sure thing regarding its ability to reduce risk, many producers are diversified—they believe some risk reduction is worthwhile although they cannot predict how much they are actually reducing risk. Forward contracting was the preferred tool for about one-ninth of producers because it guaranteed a reduction in price risk. The fact that hedging and participation in government programs are the preferred risk tools of few respondents is explained largely by the limited availability of these tools and the popularity of diversification.

The remainder of Table 10.2 presents the rankings given by producers in response to question 3. In general, diversification, forward contracting, and crop insurance are the highest ranked tools for managing risk (in that order, according to a weighted average of all rankings given). Clearly, government programs and hedging are not judged to be as useful in managing risk as are the other three tools. For government programs, this general attitude is supported by the results of previous studies.[2]

In general, the results imply that risk management tools may be underutilized by individual producers either because the tools are not well understood or because they provide incomplete protection from risks found in California's agriculture. This suggests that new tools for managing risk may be needed or that existing tools need to be redesigned to better suit the needs of producers in the state.[3]

Risk management tools also appear to be underutilized by a majority of California's agribusinesses. However, agribusinesses make much more use of risk tools than do producers. As shown in Table 10.3, over 46 percent of the firms surveyed listed day-to-day management, such as "knowing customer's character" or "serving customers," as a strategy for dealing with risk. Almost as many—42 percent—listed such strategies as one of their two most important means of dealing with risk. These results show that, in addition to using the tools available to deal with problems related to risk, managers also try to anticipate and avoid risky business situations (which is easier to do in agribusiness than in farming or ranching).

By far the most common strategy for managing risk by agribusinesses is using some type of insurance (used by 88 percent of the firms). However, only 27 percent of agribusinesses listed insurance as one of their two most important strategies, implying that coverage for many of the risks faced by agribusiness is limited. Diversification is the preferred strategy of over one-third of the agribusinesses interviewed, but the smallest firms have limited opportunities to diversify. Small companies were more likely to use risk-reducing inputs, but their most important strategies were usually insurance and day-to-day management. The smallest firms also appeared unable to take advantage of either government programs or market mechanisms, such as forward contracting or hedging that the larger-sized companies used.

---

[2] See Carriker *et al.*, Williams *et al.* 1990 and Williams *et al.* 1993.

[3] This is true nationally, as well. For example, in 1995, the executive director of the Iowa Farm Bureau Federation said that, as an alternative to crop insurance, farmers would like a new product modeled after the "interruption insurance" businesses can purchase to protect against loss of revenue. Also, at a 1996 regional hearing for farmers in Illinois, Indiana, Ohio and Michigan, a farm group official said, "farmers want a far more farmer-friendly (crop insurance) system." Attendees noted that a flood of new insurance policies and changes in the programs have confused farmers and insurance agents alike.

Agribusinesses are often organized as cooperatives, so any differences between cooperatives and proprietary firms concerning their perceptions and responses to risk are also of interest.[4] Cooperative officials were asked two questions on this subject. The first was " Are the risks faced and strategies used by a cooperative different from those of a proprietary firm engaged in a similar activity?" The large majority (84.6 percent) of managers said that there was no difference between the two types of businesses.

Table 10.3 California Agribusiness' Use of Risk Management Tools in 1993

Tool:	% of Producers Utilizing Tool	% of Producers Ranking Tool 1st or 2nd
Insurance	88	27
Diversification	62	37
Knowing customer	46	42
Forward contract	42	12
Government program	31	8
Hedging	12	4
Risk-reducing inputs	62	0
Other	36	0

Managers of cooperatives were next asked if they agreed with the statement " A cooperative can manage risk better than a proprietary firm because a cooperative has more complete and ready access to relevant information about its members." Again, most (73.1 percent) said no, that cooperatives did not have a significant advantage over other firms. About three-fourths of those disagreeing did so on the grounds that cooperatives do not have better access to information about their membership, while the remainder believed that cooperatives had no

---

4 America has more than 20,000 cooperatives. Some of them are huge. Farmland Industries, Inc. (based in Kansas City, Missouri), the largest cooperative enterprise in the United States, had revenues of $6.7 billion in 1994.

advantage in risk management. Perhaps the most telling argument was made by one respondent who noted that a cooperative is organized for the benefit of its membership and may increase its own risk in order to reduce the risk to producer-members. Managers who agreed with the statement noted that a cooperative structure both provides information about markets that may not be available to proprietary firms and insures input supplies.

On the surface, these results show a wide range of views in agriculture about risk, but an in-depth look reveals that farmers and ranchers should take a more active role in looking for risk solutions. To begin, there is evidence that risk tools are less understood by producers than by agribusiness managers. This is the fault of farmers and ranchers. With all the free help available from universities and local offices of government agencies, no agricultural producer has an excuse for not understanding how to use all the tools relevant to their business. Yet, there is also evidence that these tools are incomplete in their ability to manage the risks faced by producers. Risk tools available to agribusiness managers are more effective. The fault for having too few risk tools available to producers lies with both the risk industry and producers. So, farmers can try raising a ruckus about the limited risk tools available to them, but they must accept their share of the blame. If more farmers and ranchers had sought out tools for managing various risks, it would have alerted the risk industry to the need for more and better tools, making their availability more likely.

In many ways, agricultural producers have been their own worst enemy. They have spent enormous amounts of energy on complaining about their risk tools, but they were complaining to the wrong people. Instead of jawing over the fence with their neighbor, they should have been on the telephone with their insurance agent; that's what agribusiness managers do. Insurance companies have created policies covering a long list of hazards facing agribusiness, from shipwrecks to theft by bandits. In fact, the famous insurance company Lloyd's of London has issued policies at one time or another for just about every hazard known to humankind (and is near bankruptcy as a result). If farmers had spoken up to the right people, solutions may have been found. But maybe not.

Sometimes producers "bite the hand that feeds them" using and abusing risk tools. There are many well-documented cases of abuse in government programs for agriculture. Agricultural futures hedgers are also prone to become "Texas hedgers," meaning that they speculate in the markets and effectively double their level of risk instead of reducing it. Some of the lesser-known problems that exist in crop insurance illustrate the harm that a few " bad apples" can cause. The problems can be grouped into two types. First, there are problems caused by producers taking actions that *increase* risk. This type of problem is called "moral hazard". An example is the case of a farmer who seeks to get high yields by planting his entire acreage with an experimental seed that may or may not be suited to local conditions. The second type of problem is called "morale hazard." It comes from *not* taking actions that would reduce loss. A common example of this problem is a farmer who quits irrigating and tending his crop because it has already suffered a yield loss big enough to trigger an insurance indemnity payment. Producers guilty of these abuses discourage insurance companies and others in the risk industry from helping agriculture. If agriculture had demonstrated a better record concerning these problems, the risk industry might have offered new and/or better risk tools over time. Now it may be too late.

"IF YOU BUILD IT, THEY WILL COME"

The risk story told thus far in this book leads to the following conclusion: Agribusiness will get credit and will survive (outlive) farming and ranching, which are being pushed out of lenders' portfolios by increasingly unfavorable risk-return ratios. The key elements of the story are *risk*, *profit* and *credit*. If firms do not get credit, it is very difficult, if not impossible, to remain competitive in the pursuit of profits. But threats to agricultural profitability from an increasing number of risks are making lenders look for alternative investments. However, much of agribusiness will continue to grow, make money and attract lenders willing to extend all necessary credit. So, what is it that makes agribusiness special?

It is proximity to consumers. The closer a firm is to consumers in the food distribution system, the more likely that it will survive in America. Another way of putting it is, the more perishable a firm's product, the less perishable is that type of firm. It is a simple story. Some jobs can be done far from the consumer, while others must be done in a location that is near consumers because a perishable product will spoil before being consumed if it first has to be transported a great distance. Firms whose output is perishable food products must be located close to consumers. No one wants to eat a tuna fish sandwich that was made a month ago in another country. The farther a product must be transported, the longer it takes to get the product into a consumer's hand and the more opportunity there is for that product to spoil. However, if a product is not perishable but is storable instead, it can be made in locations far from consumers and not have its quality deteriorate as it is being transported.

The story of a hamburger bun illustrates why agribusiness firms generally must be located close to consumers, while farmers do not have to be close at all. To begin, a hungry American in the mood for a burger does not want to travel far to get it. If the order is a burger to go, the consumer is even more anxious that the fast food restaurant not be far from home or work or wherever the burger is to be eaten; cold burgers are not pleasant. So, fast food outlets are located as close to consumers as possible and always will be. Moving back a step, the hamburger bun used in assembling the burger at the restaurant is not baked at the fast food outlet. Buns are perishable, but not as perishable as hot burgers. Therefore, buns can be baked at central bakeries located within a short truck ride of the fast food outlets. No one wants to eat last month's bun, but most of us cannot tell whether our burger buns are fresh or a few days old. So the bun could have had a truck ride of hundreds of miles but not thousands of miles. This means that bakeries, as food processors and agribusinesses, will always be a part of America. However, moving back another step from the bakery leads to flour mills. Flour used in hamburger buns is very storable, although not perfectly so. It could be transported thousands of miles, meaning that it could easily be imported from another country. Going back another step from flour mills leads to wheat farms. Wheat is storable for years, meaning that it could be transported here via Mars if someone wanted to pay the freight bill. Thus, when an American wants a burger, he or she will get it from a local assembly plant called a fast food restaurant that uses buns that are baked in America but contain wheat that could be grown and milled into flour in another part of the world. And the bun will not be the only part of the hamburger made from imported agricultural products. Currently, the beef could be from Australia (although processed into burger form in America) and the lettuce and tomato could be from Mexico (although sliced by the local restaurant staff).[5]

---

5 The Florida Tomato Exchange filed a complaint in 1995 with the International Trade Commission accusing Mexico of dumping tomatoes on the U.S. market at prices below the cost of production. An exchange official said that the number of tomato growers in the United States has declined from 475 to fewer than 100 in the past 20 years, and Florida's share of the tomato market has dropped by 50 percent since 1993 due, in part,

Some Americans don't like the idea of getting their main meals (burgers) from imported food sources, but they really *hate* the idea of drinking foreign milk. Milk is usually the product used by agricultural advocates to argue that agriculture must exist in all regions of the world. Fresh milk—every baby's God Given Right. Or is it? Milk has been king for just about all of time. Many countries, including America, have special laws to assure that milk is available to drink anytime, anyplace, regardless of the cost. Dairy policy has given milk processors, such as butter and cheese makers, a stable supply of inputs. It has also given a lot of people stinky dairies upwind and upriver from their homes. Ask any one of the increasing number of suburban dwellers living near a dairy whether they are glad that the U.S. government subsidizes the dairy industry and they will tell you "not in my back yard." This is especially true for the people who get their drinking water from wells in dairy country. So what is going to happen in the future? Will there be dairies interspersed with the ever-growing city populations across America? Be serious. Powdered milk produced elsewhere can be used easily in virtually every situation in which raw milk is used now. Drinking fresh milk is decreasing in popularity, so fewer people have a basis for tasting the difference between raw and powdered milk. There is no reason for dairies to smell up American neighborhoods.[6] For now, there are still wide-open spaces in America that can house dairies. For example, county officials in Kansas are trying to attract California dairy operations that are finding themselves so surrounded by urban sprawl that they cannot expand. The dairy industry in Kansas has been declining and the state must import milk. (Can anyone in Kansas taste any difference between their own and "imported" milk? Of course not.) In the long run, dairies will move out of America as less-developed countries become able to produce and export milk to us at lower costs than we would have to pay for domestic milk.

The bottom line for agribusiness in the future can be summed up in a message to fast food franchisees: "If you build it, they will come."

---

to the inability of American growers to compete with the less-expensive imports from Mexico.

[6] There are other hazards from dairies that make them even less appealing as neighbors. In 1995, a third British dairy farmer died of Creutzfeldt-Jakob disease, the human equivalent of bovine spongiform encephalopathy (BSE) or "mad cow disease," doctors reported. They said that while there was no evidence that people can catch the deadly disease from cattle, the development was worrying. The 54-year-old man had been employed throughout his working life on a dairy farm on which there had been three cases of BSE.

Americans will always be in a hurry to eat, so there will always be demand for fast food. As a result, there will always be a need for the agribusinesses that support fast food outlets. Food processors, transporters, warehousers, and retailers will always be a part of the American economy. Yet, food retailers will have to adapt to Americans' passion for quick chow. Our desire for immediate gratification will make us eat out more often as our incomes grow. Fast food will become increasingly important to us. Why? Besides of the obvious reasons concerning our appetite, fast food franchises serve some important functions. When it comes to food, Americans like to know what they are going to get before it arrives. That is one of the reasons for the popularity of fast food. A person going into any of the zillions of outlets of their favorite brand of franchised fast food is sure of getting the same thing that is served at all the other outlets of the same company. Therefore, franchises are becoming a form of standardization and grading in food retailing.

Unfortunately for agricultural producers, the trend toward fast food adds to the profit pressures on farmers and ranchers. Producers are victims in the circular battle between fast food franchises and retail grocers. The story begins at the cash register. Eating out is expensive, even in the case of fast food, but retail grocery stores are not very profitable compared to other types of retailers. So, as people eat out more often, grocers see the willingness of consumers to fork out Relatively Big Bucks for burgers, etcetera, as an opportunity to improve their small profit margins. About the only way that retailers can do this is to squeeze their suppliers, and the pressure goes all the way back to producers. For example, cash hog prices were at 20-year lows in 1994 and returns for small hog producers were so far below cost that many gave up hog farming and liquidated breeding stock, according to the National Pork Producers Council (Knight-Ridder). Hog farmers were receiving about 26 percent of consumer dollars spent for pork in late 1994, well below the 38 percent received at the same time in 1993. It is a trend, the group said, that has been steepened by greed at the retail and wholesale levels. The retail share was about 54 percent in 1994, compared with 47 percent during 1993. The *Wall Street Journal* reported at the end of 1994 that, although scattered meat companies and supermarket chains were beginning to trim retail pork prices, many continued procrastinating about passing along to consumers the 33 percent drop in the price of hogs. This meant that retailers were making higher profits at the expense of both producers and consumers.

The dismal economics of food make it possible for everyone in the food distribution channel to make more money than farmers and ranchers. For example, in 1994 two rural sociologists from the University of Missouri and Iowa State University complained that farmers were getting the short end of the stick, as large food companies got a 20 percent return on their investment while even the top third of family farmers only made 3-5 percent on their investment (*Farmweek* October 5, 1994).

In the long run, retailers' efforts to increase their profitability assure that people will flock to fast food franchises. Higher retail food prices create disincentives for home cooking by making eating out relatively less expensive. Also, big franchised fast food firms can buy big quantities from suppliers, keeping their burger meal prices competitive with TV dinners and other processed foods from grocery stores. Thus, the only prolonged fighting that will go on in the $900 billion food industry will be between retailers: fast food outlets versus grocery stores, each trying to expand their "share of stomach." Agricultural producers won't like it, but they will not fight the end of farming and ranching for long. After considering the alternatives, an increasing number of people in rural regions will rather switch than fight.

DON'T CRY FOR THEE, OKLAHOMA

At present, many local areas, regions or states may seem to have nothing going for them except agriculture, but in reality many people in those areas would like something a bit more interesting. They want to switch out of agriculture, not fight its economic demise. In Oklahoma, for example, so many rural people are heading for cities that 34 of the state's 77 counties have lost population since they were formed. And most of those who switch find that there is life after agriculture. A study of former Oklahoma farm operators who exited the industry in midcareer found that the people who said they were better off outnumbered those who said that they were worse off by a four-to-one ratio (*Des Moines Register* April 24, 1995). Those people have seen the handwriting on the barn wall: "Get out of agriculture while the gettin' is good."[7] To other people, leaving agriculture sounds like heresy. The

---

[7] The story of this exodus has been told in books such as John Steinbeck's *The Grapes of Wrath* and Dan Morgan's *Rising in the West*. It is often a difficult journey, but leaving agriculture has enabled many families to march up the economic ladder. For

debate is heating up in rural regions across the country. Times are changing and so are the facts of rural life in America.

Some regions may have no choice but to leave agriculture. For example, with surface water gone from much of the semi-arid High Plains region, farmers there rely heavily on ground water for irrigation, using about 30 percent of all irrigation water pumped in the United States. Virtually all of that water comes from the Ogallala Aquifer, with minimal replenishment, resulting in rapid depletion that has lowered the water table by more than 100 feet in recent decades. As farmers continue to draw on that water source, scientists predict that some areas will dry up rendering irrigated agriculture infeasible. The dilemma threatens the livelihoods of millions of Americans and the survival of thousands of farming communities in the region. The *Washington Post* reported that hundreds of small towns in the upper Great Plains are fading away because advances in agricultural production have rendered most farm jobs unnecessary. In fact, some people advocate abandoning the region to the buffalo.

As agriculture adjusts to the increasing competitive pressures, it creates new problems for itself and rural America. One example is "megafarms," large-scale operations that are designed to cut costs as low as possible to be able to compete in world markets. However, some Ohio farmers believe that megafarms will put many of the state's 70,000 family farmers out of business because of the stiff competition. In other words, megafarms work too well: they threaten uncompetitive family farms. Environmentalists worry about the smell of megafarms and the potential for water contamination. In other words, they work well, but not in my backyard. Some rural advocates contend that megafarms destroy rural communities. "When we replace family farming operations with megafarms, rural towns will dry up and blow away," says one rural development expert (Associated Press November 28, 1994). In other words, if agriculture changes we all go to Hell in a handbasket.

There are lots of doomsayers in rural America. And if viewed from a certain perspective, there is evidence that the end is near. The *Chicago Tribune* reported in October 1994 that the population of rural towns and counties is declining as young people leave. The article said

---

example, the author's maternal grandparents left their Missouri farm and traveled a route similar to those covered by the people in the two books mentioned above. They had to work in agriculture on and off for the rest of their lives, but gradually they got the family into town and an easier life.

that some small towns survive only because of federal largesse coming from farm subsidies, although other towns will survive as supply centers for agriculture. Observers give indications in the article that the frontier is expanding in the Great Plains reclaiming abandoned farmland. Others say that the decline of rural areas is due to failure of the nonfarming sector (sure, blame everyone else).

Debate is underway as to what besides agriculture can promote the survival of these communities. Some rural residents see problems in trying to bring industries into rural areas; they mention pollution and multiculturalism (i.e. "outsiders"). For example, in 1995 some Iowans objected to a plan of Iowa State University and the USDA to build a swine research farm near a church. They believed that odors from the farm would make using the church unbearable and claimed that it could pollute a nearby creek and lake. University and government officials said that the residents had little to fear because preventing such environmental damage is one of the primary goals of the facility. Yeah, right. And if it doesn't work? The message nowadays, even from rural residents, is that when it comes to smelly agriculture, "not in my backyard." The response of Iowa's government officials was to hold the International Livestock Odor Conference. (No, it's not a joke—that's what they called it.) At the same time, Iowa legislators agreed to spend more than $9 million in research directed at environmental and odor problems caused by large-scale hog facilities. Other states are also resisting the end. North Carolina's legislature created a Swine Odor Task Force to address the growing problem of odors created by large hog farms. The task force made suggestions such as sucking the odors up a stack for dispersal over a wider area, or burning them. Sooner or later the task force is going to get serious and recommend the obvious: move the hogs before voters throw them out.

The doom-and-gloomers all too often overlook other industries that could expand. For example, a November 1994 *Wall Street Journal* article examined the impact that telecommunication is having on rural life. The article said that many rural counties *gained* population in the first two years of the 1990s, in part because advanced communications technology is helping to create jobs. In April 1995 the *Des Moines Register* weighed into the debate by reporting that, while rural counties generally had been growing again, more than half of those identified as farming counties continue to lose population. By 1996 the smallest county in Iowa had a mere 4,500 people, one-third the population it had in 1900. However, the fact that these newspapers cannot agree as to whether rural populations are decreasing or increasing shows that the picture may not be as gloomy as some people think.

But the real fear of rural advocates is that somehow the end of farming means that everyone will live in a big city. Thus, attacks are often directed at urban development of any kind. For example, a study by two farmland conservation groups concludes that farmland pays more in property taxes than it receives in services, but residential areas require more in tax-supported services than they pay in taxes. An official with the American Farmland Trust says the study indicates that farmland need not be urbanized for the sake of ensuring a community's financial stability. The study notes that farmland provides other benefits such as wetland protection and wildlife habitat. (Swamps provide these benefits, too, but that does not mean we need more of them.)

Cities are often painted in the rural press as Sodom and Gomorrah where evil lurks and nearby farmers huddle in fear of the mighty beast, "Urban Sprawl." Sometimes the urban press fights back by putting things into perspective. One example is a November 1994 *Chicago Tribune* article about a farm that survived a tornado but fell to the winds of change preceding the outward expansion of suburban Chicago. The 75-year-old farmer who was hospitalized by the tornado that destroyed all his farm buildings in 1965 sold his 80 acres in 1994 to make way for a retirement community, health-care center and shopping area. The proceeds helped him to buy a new, larger farm. So, maybe Urban Sprawl isn't such a monster after all. Few of us like the trend toward bigger cities, but in this case, Urban Sprawl made a farmer better off, not worse off. But don't tell that to most farmers; some treat the loss of each farm as a death in the family instead of as an economic development. Nevertheless, urban growth is a national fact of life.

Urbanites all over America are moving to suburban farmland. The pressure is most prevalent in the Northeast where cropland accounts for only 13 percent of total land, but it is even felt in the Corn Belt where 61 percent of land is in crops. The pressure of urban growth between 1982 and 1992 led to the loss of Michigan farmland equal to an area the size of Rhode Island, according to a report by the Michigan Society of Planning Officials (United Press International). At the same time, the average age of Michigan's farmers continued to increase, with nearly half of the state's farms in the hands of people aged 55 or older. The lost farmland represents an annual loss of between $60 million and $120 million in local farm revenue. The state's top agriculture official said, "This report clearly shows we can no longer take agriculture and farmland for granted. Something must be done, and done soon, to reverse the trends we are experiencing." What does he expect, Detroit being torn down so that a new cornfield can be planted in its place?

The same story is being played out in other states. An Iowa state official said the state must come up with a strategy to deal with urban sprawl. The *Des Moines Register* reported that Iowa has lost nearly one million acres of farmland in the last 20 years to urbanization, and the rate of loss appears to be accelerating. A study in Virginia shows that urban residents continue to sprawl into surrounding rural areas, using up farmland and leaving the city populations older and poorer. In Wisconsin, urban pressures are causing a number of city folk to seek haven in rural parts of the state. While some of them are taking up farming, most are just gobbling up farmland. As townhouses sprout where cornfields once stood and land assessments rise, families who have lived there for generations are beginning to feel as tense as their new citified neighbors.[8]

The Big Daddy of All Urban Sprawls is in California. The nation's leading agricultural state is also the most populated state, so rural-urban interface is a way of life in California. Has it brought much change? Consider this: just after World War II, Los Angeles County produced more crops than any other county in the nation. We all know that this is not true today. In the state currently, 75,000 acres are taken out of agriculture each year and put into urban use. The American Farmland Trust voiced serious concern over a California Department of Conservation report that showed urbanization of San Joaquin Valley farmland dramatically accelerating at a time when farmland conservation was slowing statewide. The rate of urbanization in the valley increased 29 percent compared to a 16 percent decline statewide from 1990 to 1992. Yet, when agricultural advocates complain, they are shouted down because agriculture is seen as part of the problem. For example, debate has become heated over the expansionist plans of Fresno, which envision a community of 1 million people in the next 25 years. One hitch is that Fresno sits on an aquifer tainted with pesticides from past farming.[9] This frightens and angers city residents. The

---

8 The Larimer County, Colorado, Commission prepared a guidebook for newcomers in rural areas. "Code of the West . . . the Realities of Rural Living" is intended to forestall complaints by newcomers on a wide range of subjects. One thing it notes is that "manure has objectionable odors."

9 A study by the University of California revealed that some 50 towns and cities, mainly in the Central Valley and Riverside County, have a serious problem with contamination of drinking water by pesticides. The main culprit was the chemical dibromochloro-

biggest loser in the plans could be the county's $3.17-billion farm economy, but no one in the city is talking about modifying plans for paving over 16,000 acres of vineyards and orchards, land that accounts for $42.2 million in gross revenues each year. Some of the best farmland in the country is disappearing because the most profitable use of that land is no longer farming.

Some states have regions that are still empty enough that officials think agriculture remains a good investment there. As noted earlier, some county officials in Kansas are trying to attract dairies from California. The dairy industry in Kansas has been declining and the state must import milk. Smaller operators opposing the migration from California are concerned that large dairies will take over. In other words, damn the torpedoes, let's live in the past! Although in this case, the small dairies' biggest threat is not from big dairies but from the economics that has caused the state's dairy industry to decline: dairies are a poor investment in Kansas. Trying to attract new dairies is like rearranging the deck chairs on the *Titanic*.

In other regions and states people have decided that, as they go through life, they do not want to stop and smell the manure. For example, in November 1994 seven counties in northwest Kansas got to choose whether they wanted a lucrative, corporate hog farm with a $1.4-million payroll to set up shop in their neighborhood. Six of the counties overwhelmingly defeated the corporate resolution, and the seventh passed it by such a slim margin that the firm decided not to set up operations there. In another example, residents in a Kentucky county were divided over whether a poultry processing plant was a good idea. The facility would provide 1,600 jobs, but many residents were worried about its potential for harming the area's water resources.

Finally, some states are beginning to see the future and trying to move forward. The *Omaha World Herald* reported in November 1994 that Nebraska planned to more than triple the amount of money it spent to make the state look good to outsiders. Part of the additional $500,000 a year would be used to help alleviate a labor shortage by making the state more attractive to workers. Nebraska's unemployment rate at the time was only 2.5 percent. The state seemed to realize that it would be smarter to switch its resources into something with a more profitable future than to fight the end of agriculture.

However, old habits are hard to break when some people have their head stuck in the sand. Ostrich, emu, deer and elk are no longer

---

propane, which is known to cause sterility in humans and is a suspected carcinogen.

considered to be wildlife by the state of Nebraska. The state had an agricultural relapse in 1995 when it followed Iowa in passing new legislation officially classifying such animals as livestock. There is a growing alternative livestock industry in both states, so they want to develop animal health regulations for alternative livestock operations and begin promoting their products to potential buyers.

Some of the attempts to stay in agriculture go past bizarre all the way to desperate. For example, a team of researchers at Savannah River Ecology Laboratory has been studying chickens foraging at the Savannah River nuclear weapons plant near Aiken. They report that raising chickens on land contaminated by radiation would be cheaper than cleaning up the sites and could provide a source of safe, inexpensive food. Yum yum, barbecued chicken without the middleman. Computer simulations developed by the scientists showed that certain types of poultry, in this case a strain of the small, domestic bantam chicken, have a high metabolism that reduces radioactivity in the birds as they grow. In this case, the early bird glows in the dark.

What can be done to replace agriculture in rural economies? The first step is to recognize the changing comparative advantage of a region. This means to look for investments for which available resources are best suited. These investments may have been in agriculture in the past, but the push-pull of risk and technology are making alternatives look better all the time. One way that these alternatives can be found is to create incentives for individual investors and provide " seed money" to get things started. One of the first steps in that direction was taken in 1994 when President Clinton announced the 105 Empowerment Zones and Enterprise Communities that were selected as part of a $3.8-billion development initiative. Three rural zones, in Kentucky, Mississippi and Texas, got up to $40 million each in grants and tax incentives. Once people look beyond agriculture, they can see the future.

The key elements in the fight to switch from agriculture to the industries of the future will remain risk, profit and credit. The trade-off between risk and profits earned will always guide investment, but the future of risk tools, credit and the rural-urban interface will shape the development of rural America. Risk tools will evolve based on the expressed demand from agribusiness (and other industries). Credit will always be a necessary input and, thus, will guide the restructuring and eventual end of traditional agriculture as it is rationed to only the strongest firms. And, finally, the people in and near America's growing cities will decide the pace and direction of rural America's transformation into a new type of lifestyle option. The end of traditional agriculture does not mean the end of rural America. The switch out of agriculture began long ago, now what remains is to end the fight and begin concentrating on what the new lifestyle will be. "If you build it, they will come."

Chapter 11

Sustainable Agriculture: Golf Courses, Nurseries and Turf Farms

I tell you turning your land into a golf course is the salvation of the farmer. That's the only thing to do with land now is just to play golf on it. Sell your land and caddie.

—Will Rogers, 1928

Agriculture will disappear from the American portfolio because it is not economically sustainable, but some small parts of the industry will survive. Truly *sustainable* agriculture in America's future will include only the very few forms of agriculture that are compatible with urban life.[1] The main entries on that list include golf courses, nurseries and turf farms.

Yes, golf courses will come to the fore. Turf grass management is one true type of sustainable agriculture because there is growing demand—120 new golf courses per year are being opened in America—and the customers are not as price sensitive as they are about traditional

---

[1] The term *sustainable agriculture* has many definitions, but Browne *et al.* (p. 102) point out that all usually include "the basic idea that agricultural resources should not be used up faster than they can be replaced." As an example, "soil erosion should not exceed the capacity for soil renewal." However, traditional definitions such as this focus on what *can* be done. This is not enough. In this chapter, a broader definition is used which focuses on what *will* be done. Just because we can manage soil erosion in an area does not mean that we will. What will be done is determined by the profitability of the action. Thus, sustainable agricultural products are those that can be produced indefinitely without exhausting available resources and that *will* be produced because of their continued profitability over time.

agricultural products. Golfers pay over $275 each to wander around on the turf at Pebble Beach for about four hours, and there is a waiting list to do it. How often do people pay farmers for the opportunity to wander around in their fields? How much do you think some city folks would pay to *avoid* having to set foot in a field?

To be sustainable, agriculture must be flexible and change with the country. It must offer products that consumers want and foreign competitors can't offer at a lower price. The competitive pressures are already building in some parts of agriculture. People in and around agriculture are looking for the Products Of The Future. Hi-tech products are starting to come out of the laboratory and into the fields. Genetically engineered tomatoes, potatoes, corn, strawberries and who knows what else will be offered to consumers.[2] These products are good ideas—they are just as edible as any other food—but their shortcoming is that they are *food* products that will still have to compete with all other food products, domestic and imported. In the marketplace food is food, a tomato is a tomato, and lots of people can grow tomatoes in their gardens. Thus, tomato prices are never going to be high enough to justify putting in 10 acres of them in the middle of New York City, or any other city for that matter. Food doesn't generate enough profit per acre to compete with alternative uses of land in an increasing number of regions.

As more commodities are forced out of the American portfolio, more people in agriculture seem to be spending more time and money trying to find new markets for old products. The desperate search for alternative uses of agricultural products may delay the end of traditional agriculture, but it will not prevent it. And desperate is the word for some of the ideas already being considered. For example, two Iowa firms won state grants in 1994 to produce experimental agricultural products. The Iowa Department of Economic Development gave

---

[2] The number of agricultural biotechnology products will increase rapidly in the next few years, but the number of competitors will hold steady or shrink, two industry leaders said (*Wall Street Journal* March 31, 1995). At that time four genetically engineered food products were on the U.S. market and seven had been cleared by the Food and Drug Administration. The industry experts predicted there would be 20 more products in the approval stage in one or two years and on the market in three of four. A few firms are working on nonfood agricultural products. For example, a new genetically engineered cotton seed impervious to insects and drought is expected to lower production costs by eliminating the need for pesticides, while also generating higher yields and a finer quality fiber. More than 110 American firms (and over 150 worldwide) are involved in agricultural biotechnology.

$100,000 to Agriboard Industries and $70,000 to Field Trials, Incorporated. Agriboard makes building material out of wheat straw and Field Trials was test-marketing technology that could turn hog waste into a usable byproduct. Oh, boy, I can't wait to get my hands on *that* byproduct. But don't "bet the farm" on it; is America really going to keep hogs around just to supply the inputs? Not in my backyard. But they don't give up in Iowa. Another firm, Iowa Select Farms, is testing a solids separator system on solid waste to reduce the odor. The system screens solids from manure and removes the moisture, salvaging a "clean," mulchlike product that can be composted, processed or easily hauled and spread as fertilizer. Although odor was supposedly almost completely absent around the facility during tests, the proof will come when the firm begins to operate at capacity. And if it doesn't work?

Yet another alternative use for a traditional agricultural product: kitty litter from wheat. The *New York Times* reported in December 1994 that a new, wheat-based kitty litter variety has been patented and is now being produced for the $700-million-a-year industry. The wheat in the litter contains enzymes that make sewage break down faster than it otherwise would; plus, the wheat neutralizes the ammonia smell that is prevalent in cat litter boxes. What a sweet idea. You start to wonder where these ideas come from: hog waste and kitty litter. It's not the kind of future that many farmers envision with pride.

However, some traditional agricultural products may have other valuable uses. Corn has been used to make ethanol for years. Also, many things can be made from soybeans: tofu and cooking oils, ink and diesel fuel, and building materials. A Minnesota company is converting soy flour and recycled newspapers into a substitute for hardwood. They hoped to be turning more than one million bushels of soybeans into the construction material they call Environ by 1997. The new company formed a farmers-only cooperative composed of members who invest in the company and promise to supply soybeans. A 1995 *Minneapolis Star Tribune* article notes that the (real or imagined) prospect of higher prices for their crops is attracting farmers to ventures such as this that convert commodities into new products.

The "biomass" industry is made up of companies banking on the notion that mines and refineries will be replaced by farms and forests as the producers of raw materials for the next century, according to an article in *Top Producer*. In it, an official with the New Uses Council says that companies are looking for a sign from Washington that products and energy made from renewable resources are important to the nation. Only then, he says, will companies take the risk of bringing products to market.3 The article says that some federal dollars are already at work in this area, and it reports on the efforts of the U.S. Department of Agriculture's Alternative Agricultural Research and Commercialization Center, as well as on efforts by the Departments of Energy and Defense. Supplying mulch to the Pentagon—now there's a sustainable future.

Some of the government projects are out of this world, literally. NASA asked the USDA for information about growing crops in gravity-free space. In 1996 they signed a five-year, $5-million contract for basic research on developing on-board gardens to provide fresh produce for astronauts and eventual space station residents. One problem to resolve, a plant physiologist says, is that a low-gravity environment "leaves plants confused" and upsets the calcium metabolism, causing deformities (United Press International). Yep, coming soon to a theater near you, *Attack of the Demented Tomato from Space*.

People in agriculture are an ingenious lot. If they cannot find a new use for an old product, they will find a new way to make an old product. For example, *Newsweek* reported that a Texas cattle rancher has equipped a portion of his herd with rainproof pagers and trained them to lead the rest of the herd back to the barn for feeding when beeped. Not to be outdone, the *Wall Street Journal* reported in May 1995 that, thanks to the work of Dutch scientists, cows can milk themselves with the help of a computer. The hi-tech bovine, wearing a computer chip in her collar for identification, approaches the machine whenever she feels the urge for milking. A robot equipped with ultrasonic sensors does the rest. The farmer is alerted by beeper if anything goes wrong. Most cows learn fairly quickly, but there are others who "just don't get it." The system is being tested for sale in America. And what might happen to all that hi-tech milk? An April 1995 *New York Times* article examined the expanding advertising campaign designed to push Cool Cow, a low-fat milk product that contains a butterfat substitute. Boy, doesn't that sound yummie?4

---

3 One example of these projects is the cooperative called Minnesota Valley Alfalfa Producers. It was formed by about 500 farmers in hopes of building a $260-million plant to produce electricity from the stems of alfalfa, their most popular forage crop for feeding cattle. Northern States Power Company, to whom the electricity would be sold, is legally required to launch a biomass project by 1998 and to have the first 50 megawatts on line by the year 2001.

4 And what do you eat with Cool Cow? How about some Lean Generation pork. A company is marketing the new English-bred NPD pig in America saying that, cut for cut,

So what can the hi-tech imaginations of American agriculture come up with in the future? Probably many ingenious products that most of us cannot imagine now. When we Americans set our minds to do something, we succeed. This does not mean that Americans will be seeing herds of robo-cows giving flavored milk anytime soon. There are limitations on our imagination this time: food products must be edible and all agricultural products must compete in world markets.

This brings us back to golf courses. No, they are not edible, but then neither do they have to compete in world markets. They serve special functions in American life and will become more important in the future. Understanding *why* golf courses will be sustainable in America's future will aid in understanding some of the weaknesses of traditional agriculture.

18-HOLE GREENBELTS

Golf courses are becoming greenbelts amidst the Urban Sprawl. They are little bits of beauty surrounded by the beasts of cities. Although for many people golf courses can be seen but not touched, the greenery is a welcome relief from the eyesores of crowded cities and suburban plastic. They are also the magnets used to draw many people into rural settings that have not yet developed into suburbs. They are the modern village green.

Japan is an example of a modern urban mess with a high demand for places to play outside—many Japanese pay Big Bucks just to belong to golf clubs. When cities swallow up all open space, any open area becomes prized. Look at New York City's Central Park. When an area is an attractive playground called a golf course, there is plenty of evidence that people will come, pay and play.

People like golf courses. Businesses like golf courses. And local governments are beginning to love golf courses. To begin, people like being surrounded by beautiful, natural settings. Golf courses aren't completely "natural," but they are close in many cases; they are clear, grassy strips of land between trees, ponds and other features of the landscape. Most of the time, very little earth has been moved to create the course (just some around the putting greens). Even public courses are kept in fairly good shape by a crew of groundskeepers. They are visually stimulating. They are emotionally soothing (assuming that you

---

the new breed contains between 35 percent and 60 percent less fat than traditional pork. "It almost looks like a health-club pig," a company executive said.

are not trying to play golf). They provide many of the same psychic benefits that parks offer.

Businesses like golf courses because they attract a steady stream of people with disposable income. Being near a golf course is good for business. Retail outlets get golfing customers; other types of businesses get a clean, quiet neighbor. All types of business get a bit of class from a nearby course.

Local governments love what golf courses can do for them. In this era, many cities cannot afford to create or maintain parks. When public money is not available to create greenery, golf courses offer a way around the problem. One approach is to shift to private ownership and/or development of green areas in cities. This can be done by letting developers put in new golf courses surrounded by residential subdivisions that pay the development costs for the course. The residents are happy with their green views and the local government is happy because it didn't have to do or pay for anything. A second approach is for the city to demand that a developer build a golf course and turn it over to the city in return for permits to build overpriced housing around the course. This is being tried with some success in states where housing prices can absorb golf course costs. Finally, if a city has a choice about how to provide green space for its residents, golf courses are a good investment. Golf courses can pay for themselves and then some, parks cannot. Rich cities (if there is such a thing these days) can afford lots of parks, but even poor cities can afford golf courses.

Taking the "user pays" approach to recreation areas (such as golf courses) leads to the realization that golf generates a better return on assets than other types of recreation areas, such as campgrounds and parks. Most public recreation areas must be subsidized by tax dollars, golf courses are an exception. Golfers addicted to their game are willing to pay the full cost of using the assets of a golf course. Few hikers or campers would be willing to pay the significantly higher fees that would be needed to keep National Parks and other campgrounds open if those facilities were not subsidized. And yet, user pays policies are becoming more common in America as government budgets get squeezed.

Finally, golf courses will become more important in America because of their potential for combining recreation and conservation functions. Across the country, golf courses serve as conservation reserves, of a sort, for plants and animals of various types. For example, delicate sand dunes along the coasts of California and South Carolina have restricted access but are enjoyed by the people passing by on the golf courses that serve to stabilize the dunes and provide habitat for wildlife. Nationwide, golf courses are often the only source of wetlands for birds and other creatures in a region. In Florida, for example, golfers at some courses have to beware of alligators (a real water hazard). Golf courses are places where natural environments can be preserved and enjoyed in a way that is economically sustainable. In the future, golf courses may become one of the few places where residents in some areas can take a walk on the wild side.

In some regions, golf courses could offer off-season urban safaris. When the weather is not conducive to golf, all kinds of activities are still possible on the links. The list can range from hiking and bird watching to fishing and hunting. Yes, even hunting has been tried. Sometimes courses are so attractive to wildlife that hunting almost becomes a necessity, but some kinks have to be sorted out first. For example, a northern Alabama golf course overrun with Canadian geese had to call off a hunt that was scheduled for January 1995. The hunt, which was supposed to chase away more than 500 geese, originally would have allowed 36 hunters a day to hide in blinds on the fairways and kill a limit of two geese each.[5] This raised protests from animals rights groups and traditional hunters so instead, the greens were treated with a special chemical to make them less appetizing to the geese. This is a rare case in which golfers don't like "birdies."

The final question regarding sustainable agriculture is, how can golf courses, nurseries, turf farms and some other agricultural-based industries become economically sustainable? In America's urban future, marketing will become even more important for agriculture.

URBAN AGRICULTURE

The few forms of agriculture that will become economically sustainable are those that understand the cliché, "if you can't beat 'em, join 'em." Traditional agriculture suffers another loss every time it competes with urban development. The dismal economic facts are on the side of cities. Therefore, sustainable agriculture must at least be *compatible* with and, better yet, *complementary* to urban development. The key to survival for producers of an agricultural product is to understand how the product can serve the needs of city folks and to use that information in getting the product to those folks.[6]

---

5 This gives new meaning to the golfing term *blind shots*.
6 The U.S. Department of Agriculture is already adopting this strategy for (their own)

Golf courses are a form of agriculture that is compatible with urban development and, most of the time, is complementary to the plans of a developer. A golf course raises the values of surrounding houses, rather than lowering them as would a hog farm or some other form of traditional agriculture. So, the number of golf courses will continue to increase with population growth and urban sprawl, whereas the number of traditional farms will decrease.[7] Unlike with farms, people want to be near a golf course and they are willing to pay more for a house if it has fairway views. In fact, golf courses are such a strong attraction to home buyers that residential developers build the course before the houses and advertise that fact. This is very evident in the expanding regions of America's Southwest. People will pay Big Bucks for a house, even if the development is miles outside of town, if there is a golf course. As a result, urban planners can use courses as a magnet to draw population growth in the desired direction.

A few other types of agriculture will also survive in America because they too are compatible with urban development. Turf farms are already becoming increasingly common. Americans are now too impatient to wait for new lawns to grow from seed, so they buy turf or sod for instant landscaping. Similarly, nurseries have always served the same purpose: to give city people plants. Both of these industries have a "rosy" future as America spreads its population out of big cities and into suburbs.

The ultimate example of this comes from Orange County, California. Despite several fruitless efforts to save agriculture there, the

---

survival. They started the Urban Resources Partnership as a way to develop urban agriculture. For example, 39 groups in Los Angeles received grants from URP totaling $500,000 for projects ranging from developing community and school gardens to habitat restoration.

7 A lot of people hate this idea. For example, the Worldwatch Institute says that golf is an increasing problem in many countries because many new courses are being built on agricultural land. A report called "Shrinking Fields" claims that hundreds of thousands of people could have been fed on crops produced on lands used for golf courses. Boy, are they missing the point! The little plots on which golf courses are built are no longer agricultural land; they have moved up the Farming Food Chain and exited agriculture when the farmer voluntarily sold to a developer.

The majority opinion is reflected in legislation proposed in 1997 in North Carolina to allow counties to protect golf courses and tourism by using zoning power to regulate large hog operations. Protesting farmers said that the bill would deny young rural families the opportunity to stay on their family farms. However, the protests were what golfers call an "unplayable lie," the state had already made its choice: golf and its related tourism pays better than hogs.

county's dwindling Valencia orange industry has withered before the advances of urbanization. Oranges are now raised on about 1,000 acres when in 1940 they covered 62,000 acres. Nursery plants have overtaken foodstuffs as Orange County's principal agricultural crop, with much of this new crop going to Las Vegas. After declining for several years, wholesale nursery sales climbed in 1994 in both Orange and Los Angeles Counties, to $128 million and $151.7 million, respectively.

Urban agriculture involves producing goods for sale to urban and suburban consumers who use the products while decorating their little piece of the American Dream. Most Americans dream at least once of owning a little house on a plot of land. The dream plots, which used to be a section (640 acres) of land, now may have been reduced to a 20-acre "ranchette," but the reality is that many Americans feel lucky if they have a reasonable-sized lot in a residential subdivision. But whatever its size, the land has to be covered by something growing. Americans do not like barren land, especially in an urban location. Many cities have ordinances requiring residents to maintain some minimum level of landscaping. So we all become weekend farmers. We till the land (plant flowers and a few trees), tend to our crops (mow the lawn) and reap our harvest (use a leaf blower to push our leaves onto our neighbor's yard). But most importantly, we do not know what we are doing, so we must go back to the local nursery often to replace the dead plants.

It's the American Way: produce goods with built-in obsolescence. It worked for other industries, so it should work for agriculture. And it is easy to do with biological products like plants. Flowers don't do real well in winter blizzards, so it is a pretty sure bet that everyone who bought flowers last year is going to need some more this year. So, agricultural producers who can identify some product that will be bought by urban and suburban consumers will have found sustainability and avoided their own obsolescence.

It's working in Florida. Obsessed hobbyists are fueling a boom in gardening, now one of the top outdoor leisure activities. Florida foliage producers sold $309.5 million in tropical plants in 1995. In the Tampa Bay area, each of the five gardening experts at the Pinellas County Extension Service answered between 50 and 100 calls a day in 1997. Business is expected to continue to grow as the population ages and empty-nest households look for new hobbies.

On the other side of the sustainability story are a lot of gentlemen farmers and urban cowboys. These are the folks trying to buck the trend. While real farmers and ranchers are being forced out of agriculture, a bunch of people employed in cities are trying to enter agriculture. In this case, "better never than late."

Many Americans have been lucky enough to acquire the ranchette of their dreams and have become "hobby farmers." These Gardeners-Gone-Mad produce small amounts of some agricultural crop that they sell in an attempt to augment their city income. Some of them actually make a net profit once in a while. Most of them are nice people, but all of them are nuts if they think that they can make Real Money in their backyards. Hobby farms will remain just what they are today: a hobby or, worse yet, a tax write-off for rich people from cities. But they are *not* sustainable. We all admire people trying to pursue the American Dream, but does the world really need another miniature winery? The marketplace repeatedly says no. The dismal economics that are driving off real farmers will always be harsher on small operators, especially part-timers. So, it is "just peachy" that lots of people want to pursue a gardening hobby, but they need to understand that when it comes to cash, it is a loser.

Recreational horse operations are no better. Few people want to be back in the saddle again, but there will always be someone who wants to ride horses.[8]   In the future, some wilderness trail rides through mountains and forests (and maybe urban golf courses) and some dude ranches will survive in certain areas. Ultimately, pony rides will not completely disappear because before they do they will be put on the Endangered Species list and become a fixture at some subsidized National Parks, but they will not be sustainable in the private sector.

Riding horses is already giving way to bikes. For example, in 1997 the Associated Press reported that a Virginia farmer wanted to open his family farm to mountain-bike riders. Without the venture, that would generate membership fees, the landowner feared his family could not afford to keep their 850-acre farm. The proposal is an example of a new set of alternative recreational uses for farmland, an option some landowners choose rather than dividing for development, according to a Charlottesville landscape architect.

---

[8] This is true not only in the West, but in the urban East as well. Connecticut is second only to Texas in horses per square mile. And the 200,000 horses in Pennsylvania pump more than $4 billion a year into the state economy, according to an expert in the state (*Patriot News*). Although they are out of the range of traditional agriculture because they are not raised for food, horses are second only in value to dairy cattle among all agricultural commodities in Pennsylvania, the expert said.

For traditional agricultural producers, the message from all of this is "do your market research." Urban consumers and foreign competitors are the reality of the market. Knowing what both groups want and what they are going to do in the future will enable producers to remain viable longer. However, viability and sustainability are two separate ideas. Viable agricultural products are profitable now, while sustainable products will remain profitable into the foreseeable future. Many farmers may get "teed off" at the prospect of having to maintain golf courses, grow flowers in plastic pots or spread sod if they want to remain in agriculture, but sustainable options will become fewer over time. Consumers won't pay more for food than the lowest foreign price and there are few alternative uses for food products. The message is, "Production agriculture is not sustainable in America."

Chapter 12

What Time Is the Last Dinner Bell?

Everyone who eats has a stake in agriculture. Americans like to eat. It is one of our favorite things to do. And as we moved up the Economic Food Chain and our agricultural population became a smaller portion of the total population, we have eaten better, not worse. In fact, as fewer and fewer Americans had to go outside to work, more and more of us had time on our hands and we used it to eat. It has become a bad habit. A December 1994 *Washington Post* article described the national trend of increasing fatness in America. The article said that 33 percent of Americans were overweight in 1994, compared to 25 percent in 1980. We are trapped, it went on to say, in a world where we don't belong; our metabolism evolved to be efficient and to store extra energy as fat for times of famine, but now food is plentiful and we do not get enough exercise. But will the good times end when farmers and ranchers disappear from the American economy? Will we all have to go outside and grow our own food again? Don't be silly.

American consumers do not have to fear the end of farming—dinner will continue to be served. We will continue to have all the food that money can buy. This means that we should fear fatness more than famine in the future. The foods available to us will continue to be plentiful and rich. America represents such a big market for most types of food that suppliers are already lined up waiting to sell us food from all over the world. There is no reason for consumers to worry about shortages, and unless one occurs they won't give it a thought. Food in America is "in sight, out of mind."

Americans will never notice as the percentage of their food that is imported rises to 100 percent. Most do not realize how much food is imported now. Occasionally, a bad grape from Chile gets a little media attention,[1] and some people in the Southwest realize that they are eating Mexican lettuce in the winter. However, most Americans are hard-pressed to name a foreign agricultural import other than French wine, and a few probably think French bread is imported. Americans just don't think much about food except to eat some every few hours.

A survey conducted in 1994 by the national 4-H and Future Farmers of America organizations indicated that Americans are not well-informed about the impact that the nation's food production industry has on our economy and our lives (*Kansas City Star*). About 75 percent of the respondents felt that they were knowledgeable about food safety and that biotechnology was acceptable in the production of food. That seems reasonable enough. On the other hand, 82 percent believed that farmers were a credible source of information on food, and only 39 percent rated the media as a credible source for food information. Boy, are consumers "out to lunch." What makes anyone think that people who spend their lives moving dirt, sticking corn seed in the ground, spreading fertilizer, driving combines through the fields, and selling their output to the local grain elevator knows anything about *food*? Farmers and ranchers are plant or animal production specialists, not nutritionists or chefs.

As little as Americans know about U.S. agriculture, we know far less about world agriculture. It is not a topic covered on television talk shows, nor is it taking center stage in school curricula. America is an urban society, so urban topics dominate our attention. Even the "farm press" rarely covers foreign agriculture unless it poses a direct threat to some American producer group. As a result, few consumers will realize that more of their food originates from foreign farms and ranches over time.

America imports much of the produce we eat now during our production off-seasons, as do most developed countries. For example, Mexico and Chile have both been major suppliers of produce to America for decades. Mexico's harvest season occurs just before the seasons in

---

[1] In 1995 the Supreme Court let stand a lower court's dismissal of a suit by Chilean grape growers who had filed for damages resulting from the 1989 scare about cyanide poisoning in imported grapes. The grape growers claimed that the U.S. Food and Drug Administration had harmed them by temporarily banning imports after a couple of grapes were found to be poisoned. The judge who dismissed the suit said that the FDA had acted within its discretion to protect the public.

Florida, Texas, Arizona and Southern California, so their produce comes to our markets before domestic output is harvested. Chile, being in the Southern Hemisphere, has seasons opposite to those in the United States enabling them to become a major source of fruits and vegetables during our winter. Shipments of Chilean fresh fruit entering through the port of Wilmington, North Carolina, increased 50 percent during 1995. The port is working with major food chains to develop the market for Chilean fruit in the state and will be expanding its marketing efforts throughout the South. Even Californians, living in the state that leads the country in fruit and vegetable production, eat fruit from Chile all winter. And for some products, America depends on imports year round. For example, bananas, sugar, coffee, and cocoa do not grow very well in North Dakota, but all are consumed there thanks to foreign suppliers.

America already depends on imports to help meet consumers' demand for many food products in addition to fruits and vegetables. For example, we have been eating beef from Australia for decades.[2] In fact, about half the beef that Australia produces comes to the United States. Argentina also sends us beef. We like fancy cheeses from Europe. We love Swiss chocolate (but no, the cocoa used to make it does not come from Switzerland, it comes from South America or Africa). And some of us are cuckoo for coconuts from tropical countries. In some cases, Americans are absolutely passionate about an import. Coffee drinkers would not give up their beverage for "all the tea in China."

Therefore, Americans are already accustomed to eating imported food, so there is no reason to expect a consumer revolt when all food is imported. Most imported food products are indistinguishable from domestic products when it comes to taste or appearance. Concerns about quality and safety are apparently being satisfied by the quality standards and inspection system already in place for imports. If more Americans were aware of the foreign origins of their food, some might be worried, but only until they discovered that they had been eating "foreign food" for years. What they didn't know didn't kill them, so why worry about it after the fact?

What Americans definitely would worry about is the price of imported food. However, there is no reason to worry about future food

---

[2] Burger King plans to increase its imports of Australian beef by the year 2000, which will consolidate its position as Australia's biggest single buyer of manufacturing beef. By 1996 Burger King was using more than 200,000 tons of imported beef annually, most of it from Australia (Knight-Ridder January 30, 1996).

prices. Prices, in absolute terms, will not change noticeably as imports replace domestic raw products. Two primary reasons are that (1) competition from various supplier-countries keeps prices from rising quickly, and (2) the farm value of food commodities is only about 24 percent of the total retail price in the United States, so even if foreign commodity prices increased dramatically, it would not raise consumer prices much. The stability of food prices in the United States is typified by the American Farm Bureau Federation's 1994 market basket survey results which showed that prices paid for 16 popular items increased only 6.6 percent in five years, less than half the annual rate of inflation in America. Also, there will be a seamless shift to imports; it is happening gradually, so if there are any price changes they will not be noticed.

The total cost of food, in relative terms, may continue to shrink as a percentage of U.S. per capita income if America is able to earn high profits from information engineering and other industries of the future. This means that even if absolute prices of imported food go up, the relative cost of food would go down as long as American incomes increase more than food prices. From 1980 to 1985, Americans spent 13 percent of their income on food, on average. Only Germany paid relatively less (12 percent) for their food during that period. By 1990, Americans were spending only 8 percent of their after-tax income on food eaten at home (which doesn't include fast food eaten out). There is no way to predict how low relative food costs can go, it depends mostly on how high incomes can climb. And American incomes in the future depend on how valuable others judge the information we engineer to be. What is certain is that food costs will remain a small share of Americans' budgets no matter where the food originates.

WHAT'S COOKING?

Cookbooks will become an endangered species. Americans will cook less because they will buy more pre-prepared foods. Yes, believe it or not, there are more TV dinners on the menu for Americans. This is possible because instant meals become relatively cheaper as incomes rise and/or technology advances. More money in the pocket has always meant less cooking for Americans. Back not too far in our history, food was the biggest expense of most working families and cooking was practically a full-time job for at least one family member; but as food became relatively less expensive our approach to cooking changed. To begin, raw commodities are the cheapest form of food, but also the form requiring the most preparation before eating (except fruits and vegetables eaten raw). As income increases, people have shown a strong willingness to pay for food items that do not require as much preparation time. In other words, they are willing to pay to have some food preparation tasks done for them. For example, people showed decades ago that they would pay for packaged cake mixes that only require stirring in a little water and maybe an egg rather than having to make the entire cake from scratch. As food technology advanced to give us frozen, dried and canned delights, food processors developed new products using those technologies. The new products continually required fewer preparation steps on the part of consumers. The original TV dinners, for example, required only that a consumer put the entire container in an oven for a relatively short time to complete the necessary cooking. Some cooking had already been done, as well as all of the gathering, cleaning, slicing, measuring and mixing of ingredients, and the placing of servings in a container that eliminated the need for dishwashing. Now even cooking the food in a conventional oven is no longer needed as microwave ovens take only moments to heat up a meal that has already been completely cooked. With the amazing variety of instant meals available today, anyone can eat like a king after pushing a button. And, incredibly, the cost of these fast foods can be about the same (especially for small families) as a meal cooked from scratch. So, who wants to cook?

The trend toward foods requiring consumers to do decreasing amounts of preparation makes information on the percentage of income spent on food deceptive; food is even cheaper than it seems.[3] The farm value of the food in the "food" that Americans buy is only about 24 percent of the price; the other 76 percent is the "marketing bill" for all the services necessary to get that item in its current form to the retail store at the time the consumer wants it. Included in that marketing bill are ever-more processing and handling costs incurred for the preparation of the product. As a result, the percentage of income spent on food has appeared to be fairly stable over the past decade even though the actual farm value of food purchased continues to decrease; it is 2.5 percent of income currently. The marketing bill absorbs consumers' willingness to spend more money on food as their incomes go up. In other words, when an American gets a raise in income he or she is willing to spend more dollars on food that is more prepared because his or her food

---

[3] Luckily, fresh fruits and some vegetables require little or no preparation, so Americans trying to eat healthier are consuming more fresh produce.

budget, as a percentage of income, has not changed and is relatively small. The consumer enjoys the convenience of the built-in cook, maid, and dishwasher that comes with every instant meal, from burgers to TV dinners.

We Americans love convenience, especially when we are hungry. We do not want to go very far to get food. As discussed earlier in this book, retail food outlets understand our impatience and locate as close to us as possible. But the highly processed foods we buy at the neighborhood grocery store do not have to originate in America. Technology has enabled us to gather ingredients for a TV dinner from anywhere, assemble and package them anywhere, and ship them to anywhere without fear of spoilage. When food is not in a fresh form, it is difficult to tell much about its origin. Who can tell how long ago a frozen dinner was made? Who knows what year the beef in a can of beef stew was born? Or where it was born? As we Americans microwave our favorite brand of evening meal, will we worry that some or all ingredients are imported? We will never notice.[4]

WHO'S IN THE KITCHEN WITH DINAH?

One group that likes to worry and will certainly worry about the end of food in America is politicians. They like worrying because it worries other people and that gets attention. And when it comes to the end of the "gravy train," politicians will squawk loudly in hopes of worrying lots of voters. The phrase "a threat to our national security" will be used in various forms. The noise level will increase noticeably. People will swoon. Headlines will be made. Careers will be altered. Agriculture will have its 15 minutes of fame and then it will go away.

It will all be much ado about nothing. American politicians do not need to fear foreign food blackmail if a mutual dependence is developed among trading nations, such as the United States and its food suppliers. Just as is the case now, the foreign countries that sell us food will not want to cut us off in the future because they will continue to depend on us to sell them many other products which, on the whole, are

---

[4] A 1995 *Wall Street Journal* article examines how America's dinner table is changing, both in the increase in the amount of food imported from other countries, and also in response to changing diets. More creative meals are noted, as are trends toward foods that are more healthful. The competitiveness of supermarkets gives consumers access to a wide variety of foods, including fresh fruit and vegetables the year 'round. The article notes increases in use of frozen entrees, rice, diet ice cream and skim milk, along with decreases in the consumption of meats, canned fruits, whole milk and beer.

more vital to their economy than bananas (or any other food) are to ours.

Mutual dependence is the ultimate result of free trade between nations. It is the highest form of economic efficiency because it enables nations to devote their resources to the products for which they have a comparative advantage, but it also means that all other products must be imported. In our case in America, we will produce unique knowledge, information, and hi-tech products in exchange for food products from less-developed nations. Our national security will not be at risk of blackmail by a cartel of banana republics, like it was during the oil crisis of the 1970s, because there will be so many countries supplying us with food that competition between them will make food embargoes impossible. Plus, America can get along quite well without any one particular food commodity by simply substituting one product for another. If there are no apples, we can eat oranges. Finally, we could survive for some time on all that stored energy that looks like fat in the mirror.

The good news is that we won't have to dip into our personal energy reserves. Networks of international trade agreements are becoming more common, increasing the degree of mutual dependence in the world. The future of such agreements got closer with the World Trade Organization (WTO), which began operating in January 1995. It provides the basis for stability and trade into the next century, according to Peter Sutherland, the first Director General of the WTO. He said that the new organization will substantially strengthen the principles of the multilateral trade system.

What politicians call a multilateral trade system is a network of mutual dependence. Gradually these networks are spreading around the globe as more countries recognize their benefits. Former GATT (General Agreement on Tariffs and Trade) director general Arthur Dunkel said that world farm trade is gradually becoming freer and fairer, but he noted that the process takes time. Unfortunately, one of the last barriers to these trading systems is the unwillingness of politicians to quit worrying and let them happen. However, economic logic eventually gets through these barriers. For example, trade for Japan and its neighbors grew twice as fast within the region as it did between that region and the United States during the first five years of the 1990s. Government officials in Japan are voicing a growing desire to play a more active role in the region. As a result, more Japanese are beginning to assert an agenda of "Asian values" that could lead to differences with the West. Yet Japan's Foreign Minister Kono said that the U.S. military

presence in the region and the region's growing economic inter-
dependence are keys to it's stability and prosperity.

Japan is leading the trend of trading for food. By 1995 Japan's
Foods Agency was importing rice from the United States, Australia and
Thailand and soybeans from China. Mutual dependence led the
European Union (EU) and Israel to sign a new association agreement
forging closer economic and political links and attempting to reduce
Israel's huge trade deficit with the EU. Among other things, the accord
grants duty-free status to 90 percent of Israeli agricultural goods, up
from 75 percent under the previous agreement. At the same time,
former foes Israel and Jordan decided to turn their swords into
plowshares and signed an accord that permitted the two countries to
begin agricultural trade. The accord gave Jordan first priority for tax-
free exports to Israel in the event that Israel imports farm produce.
Israel is able to export to Jordan all the products the Arab country
currently imports. Argentina is roaming the globe looking for trading
partners in need of food. Before winding up a four-day visit to China in
1995, Argentina's President Carlos Menem said that his country was
ready to supply wheat, rice and beef to feed China's 1.2 billion people.
Representatives of Argentina's top 18 agricultural companies traveled to
China with the president and met with officials from the Ministry of
Agriculture as well as with Chinese brewers, butchers, leather producers
and food manufacturers. South Korean and Japanese delegations also
headed to Buenos Aires to examine the prospects for importing
Argentinean beef. And Philippine president Fidel Ramos and Argentine
president Carlos Menem signed an agreement in 1995 to increase
agricultural trade between the two countries.

American agriculture has already begun developing systems of
mutual dependence which will help insure a steady supply of food
imports for the future even though the trade agreements were begun in
order to establish export markets for our current food production. For
example, DuPont Company's agricultural products unit formed an
alliance with one of India's national laboratories to develop new
chemistries to increase food production. Also, with support from U.S.
Wheat Associates (USW), flour-milling training centers have opened in
Cairo, Egypt, and Casablanca, Morocco. According to USW, although
both of those countries are large wheat importers, milling knowledge
and technology generally is not as advanced there as it is in the United
States. The USW-sponsored centers are expected to improve mill
management and increase milling efficiency and technology,

emphasizing the processing of U.S. wheat. In these cases, Americans are trading their knowledge for current access to export markets, but at the same time they are creating future suppliers for America.

A surprising side effect of trade has been the discovery that fast food is contagious. One reason for our friendly relations with Japan is that they are hooked on some of our fast food. The trend toward more easy-to-prepare foods in Japan is continuing as more women enter the workforce, more families buy microwaves and toaster ovens and more single people live alone, U.S. trade experts say (*Wall Street Journal*). During a recent slump in Japan's fast food sales, U.S. French fries were as popular as ever. America exported a record $98 million worth of frozen French fries to Japan in 1994, an increase of 12 percent from the previous year. Although tradition is still honored in meals when the occasion permits, hamburger steaks, breakfast cereal and McDonald's McNuggets are popular in Japan. The same is true in China. A 1996 survey of three Beijing schools showed that nearly all pupils knew the name McDonald's and some ate there as often as 10 times a month. As a result, China launched a campaign to promote its own fast food industry, an industry that can be traced back to 475-221 B.C.E., according to experts (Reuters July 17, 1996). Even the French are getting the fast food bug. American-style convenience foods are becoming more popular in France as the country's cuisine moves toward a convergence of traditional and contemporary dishes emphasizing freshness and health. As American fast food sweeps the globe there are a few holdouts, however. Opponents of Kentucky Fried Chicken (KFC) franchises in India say that American fast food is a bad influence on the country's economy and environment, as well as being unhealthy for consumers (picky, picky, picky). The leader of a farmer organization claims that KFC serves chicken stuffed with hormones and chemicals (welcome to modern agriculture). Despite the whiners, it seems that we all want a quick meal to-go as we negotiate our next trade.

THE CORNUCOPIA IS FULL (OF IMPORTS)

The world will be fuller of food suppliers for America in the future than it is now. Our money will attract them and our money and technology will help them to develop their ability to supply us with food. We will enjoy the benefits of our investments in foreign agricultural sectors by being able to eat as well and often as ever. We have been working hard for decades to get to this position, but now it is paying off. Future payoffs will be even better. We have trained our replacements and now we can begin leaving the job of producing food commodities to them. A Federal Reserve Bank economist said that the worldwide trend in agricultural advances means American commodities are not as important in world trade as they once were (*Omaha World Herald*). The rest of the world, he continued, is ready to step into any market void left by the United States. This is illustrated by the fact that Asia will produce almost half of the world's starch-based sweeteners by 2005, according to a British researcher. That is because the costs of wheat, corn and rice used to make the sweeteners are falling and Asia's products are already cheaper than those produced elsewhere.

America used to be called on to carry a big part of the load when it came to feeding the world, but now other countries are ready to contribute to world food markets. For example, Japan's voracious appetite for fresh vegetables is now being satisfied not only by California, but also by new suppliers such as Dole Foods in the Philippines. The company, whose pineapple sales have suffered, was rescued by the asparagus plant it developed for production in a warm climate. The company is looking for other vegetables and fruit crops to develop for the growing market in Asia.

New food exporters are busting out all over the world. Money and expertise from America and other developed countries are helping less-developed nations on every continent bring more of their resources into productive use in agriculture. For example, China's leaders expressed their hopes in 1995 that Israeli expertise will help feed China's soaring population (Reuters January 12, 1995). At the inauguration of a Sino-Israeli cooperative demonstration farm in Tongxian County east of Beijing, Chinese Minister of Agriculture Liu Jiang said that China hoped to learn more about dry-land farming and efficient agriculture. By 1997, China was exporting rice. Also, Japan is helping the United Arab Emirates, its main oil supplier in the Gulf, to develop water resources to boost agriculture. Japan is also helping Vietnam. "We believe the agricultural and rural issues confronting Vietnam today command substantially more urgency," said an official Japanese study (*Los Angeles Times*). Japan, Vietnam's largest foreign aid donor, signed a new loan agreement worth $707 million for power plants and other infrastructure projects to help Vietnam become a food supplier. By 1997, Vietnam overtook India to become Asia's second largest exporter of rice. The list of new food suppliers is diverse and surprising. Some examples follow.

Turkey inaugurated, in 1994, the first of two giant irrigation tunnels designed to boost farm exports to Middle Eastern markets. Eventually the watering of the southeastern Anatolian plains is expected to allow two harvests each year, leading to an annual $6-billion food surplus. Products will include cotton, sugar beets, tobacco, soybeans and other cash crops.

India, once a frequent recipient of American food aid, is now facing a serious shortage in food storage capacity due to increases in domestic agricultural output. In late 1994, India was seeking to reduce its overflowing food-grain stocks through exports and domestic sales. State-run agencies held record stocks of food grains—wheat, rice and coarse cereals—of nearly 40 million metric tons, up from 23 million one year earlier. The storage problem accelerated further the next spring when the 1995 wheat crop was harvested. The government had only a 22-million-metric-ton capacity in closed silos and it estimated the 1995 crop at 60.18 million tons, compared with 1994s record 59.13 million. Still, this is a nicer problem to have than those that stemmed from the food shortages of earlier decades. In 1997 India was still an active exporter. And grain is not India's only success story. In 1995, Indian sugar industry officials were urging legalization of sugar exports as a way to deal with a record crop of over 14 million tons. By the end of 1995, India, moving toward becoming a major food exporter, was pressing Japan to take its rice and fruit. It also was looking to export wheat, sugar and cotton. India and Japan have agreed to pursue trade and investment issues at future talks. And India pushed to join the Asia-Pacific Economic Cooperation group.

India's neighbor, Pakistan, also seeks to be a food supplier. The state-run Rice Export Corporation planned to export 700,000 tons of rice in fiscal year 1995-96. "We are expecting a bumper crop this year and RECP will certainly procure at least 700,000 tons for export," an official with the group said. This is quite a turnaround for a country that has so recently known hunger.

Agricultural output in Peru grew by 13.3 percent in 1994, due to higher outputs of marigold, cotton, rice and asparagus, an official report said (Reuters January 6, 1995). The Agricultural Ministry in Lima said that farm output jumped 16.4 percent during the same period while livestock production rose 6.7 percent. Also, researchers at the International Potato Center in Lima have solved some age-old problems and have come up with a way to grow tubers consistently from something they call "true seed." Thanks largely to their work, potatoes are healthier, more productive, cheaper to grow and a real hope for solving the future problems of hunger in the Third World (*Chicago Tribune*).

Elsewhere in South America, Brazil, Argentina and Bolivia are all expanding their agricultural sectors. The 100 largest agribusinesses in Brazil increased their revenues by 30.5 percent to 23 billion reais in 1994, up from 18 billion reais the previous year, according to a Brazilian research foundation. The companies' net worth increased 15.6 percent over the same period. In Argentina, the country's agriculture secretary projected that exports of its 1995-96 farm output would increase a minimum of $300 million to a possible $800 million, largely due to the increase of world prices. Argentina's beef exports increased 36 percent in 1995 to over $1 billion. And in 1996 Bolivia announced its $2.8-billion five-year strategy called the Productive Transformation of the Agricultural Sector. The plan calls for 81 percent of all public investment to be spent in rural areas and the agricultural sector (Knight-Ridder July 29, 1996).

Algeria also announced in 1996 that it planned to invest $3.8 million to develop agriculture over the next 5 years. Much of the money will be used to develop farm oases in the southern desert provinces and productive areas in the highlands.

In 1997, Egyptian President Mubarak inaugurated construction of a new canal that Egypt hopes will allow it to reclaim vast areas of agricultural land and expand the country's cultivated area by more than 6.7 percent. The canal will be fed by water taken out of Lake Nasser, the huge reservoir south of the Aswan high dam.

Zimbabwe, recovering from southern Africa's worst drought this century, reported that exports—mainly tobacco, horticultural products, textiles and minerals—grew by 27 percent in 1994 and were expected to grow by the same figure during 1995 if the weather remained favorable.

The government of South Africa earmarked 60 million rand in grants in 1995 to allow 1,300 new farmers to settle on state-owned land. Recipients of the funds would not have to repay the grants. A further 150 million rand in production credit was made available via financial intermediaries to small and beginner farmers.

Philippine President Ramos said that his country will raise its stock of cattle, hogs and chickens to meet surging demand and that the government would provide 74 billion pesos for credit support for the livestock industry. He said, "The livestock and poultry industry must be enabled to expand its export market beyond the niche market it is now limited to."

Vietnam signed an export contract in 1995 with the U.S. firm TDI to export 500,000 tons of rice to the United States. Twenty years earlier the two countries had been at war, causing much damage to Vietnam's agriculture. Now, a Vietnamese agriculture official says that the country is planning to invest $5 billion in farms, fisheries and forests by the year 2000, with about 20 percent of the funds coming from foreign sources. The government is working on new rules to clear up issues related to land use, taxes and procedures for evaluating foreign investment proposals. Agriculture accounts for 40 percent of the gross domestic product in Vietnam. Just over 100 foreign-funded projects, worth $900 million, had been licensed for the three agricultural sectors by 1995.

Even countries that have in the past been the most dependent on food imports and gifts are showing progress in developing their agricultural output. In 1994, the United Nations' Food and Agricultural Organization projected a substantial decline in food imports by six countries in the Horn of Africa due to a 34 percent increase in production of cereals. However, large-scale donor support is still needed to help victims of drought and civil strife in the region. Nevertheless, these improvements in output levels indicate that continued production gains are possible as long as the social problems are resolved so that the capital investments necessary to built up the agricultural sector can be attracted from outside sources.

Capital investment is the key to agricultural development at this time. There is tremendous potential for favorable returns on that investment, but Big Money is required in most developing countries because so much is needed to bring their agricultural sectors up to the level at which American agriculture operates. For example, China has attracted a total of $10 billion in foreign capital into its farm sector. The money has gone into nearly 4,000 projects in forests, agriculture, animal husbandry and fishing. Some of the efforts are large-scale irrigation projects that aim to raise sharply the output of grain and cotton. China's state-run newspaper said that the country's capital investment in agriculture rose over 25 percent in 1995. The increased investment was used for management of rivers, lakes and waterways, as well as for forestry and environmental projects. The government drafted new policies on agricultural investment in 1995. If successful, such projects could transform China from being a net importer to being a net exporter of agricultural products in the future.

Less-developed countries recognize their need for outside

capital to develop agriculture and other industries and are often quite willing to establish arrangements of mutual dependence. For example, Rumanian farmers sought a $600-million loan from U.S. and Swiss banks to use for purchases of farm machinery and fund growth of the animal breeding sector. Also, Hungary is hungry to enter into joint ventures with American companies to increase their domestic meat production and exports, according to that country's deputy minister of agriculture (Reuters January 17, 1995). Hungary distributed a request for tenders during President Clinton's 1994 conference on commercial opportunities in the former communist bloc, the minister said. The idea is simple and it works: America has the knowledge and the money to build modern agricultural industries in countries where such investments can bear fruit. By investing our skills and cash in those nations, we get a friendly supplier of food who will use a good deal of their earnings from food exports to buy other, high-value products from us. From that mutual dependence comes the ties that bind the tightest: economic trade based in necessity. It is a good trade for both sides.

Russia is a classic case where we can help ourselves by helping them. Russia needs a minimum of 13,000 grain combine harvesters per year for its farmers, but its equipment manufacturers managed only to produce a dozen in the first two months of 1995. That's 12 combines in two months! Also, two Russian companies that make tractors, the Kirov Factory and Rostselmash, closed late in 1995 due to a lack of cash. The Kirov Factory produced only 900 tractors during 1995, although it once produced 25,000 machines per year. Russian president Boris Yeltsin signed a decree allocating 126.5 million rubles ($28 million) to Rostselmash in an attempt to save it. The situation continues to be described as disastrous because, without domestic equipment, Russian farmers would be forced to buy foreign-made equipment, except that they have no money for it. This is typical of the opportunities available for America. We can lease or sell (with creative financing) our equipment to them or invest our know-how and a few bucks in Russian equipment companies and create an important supplier of food.[5]

---

[5] American equipment companies are strong now, but such a deal would insure them of future customers. Export sales of U.S. farm equipment have risen every year except one since 1988. Sales were $2.97 billion during 1994 and are still growing. Getting into these struggling export markets is a risk, but it could establish foreign customer loyalty, which would benefit our equipment firms with repeat business for generations. For example, in 1997 Eximbank of Kazakhstan took delivery of $114 million of grain and cotton harvesters from the U.S. firm Deere and Company. The package was financed creatively by foreign commercial banks.

America's most important trading partner, Canada, will happily continue to help feed us. Canada is unique in the developed world in that it has lots of land (it is the world's second largest country in total area) and a relatively small population, so urban sprawl will not be a threat to its agriculture. In fact, Canada is still giving much of its attention to agriculture. As a result, their potential for food exports continues to grow with new cropping developments. For example, canola has helped to revolutionize agriculture on Canada's prairies. The crop, which thrives in cool weather, is a genetically altered version of the rapeseed plant. Canola is being embraced by health food enthusiasts while its industrial uses continue to grow. Its popularity was demonstrated by the farm receipts for 1994 when, according to Canada's Agriculture Department, canola overtook wheat as the country's biggest agricultural earner (*Washington Times*). In 1994, 14.4 million acres were planted, an increase of 40 percent from 1993; the 7.39 million tons produced in 1994 was 75 percent more than the previous high. Much of canola's upsurge in popularity is due to the fact that it has the lowest saturated fat content of any oil, but canola is also used as an ingredient in cosmetics, lubricants, pharmaceuticals, inks, plasticizers and fertilizer as well as being used as a fuel additive. Developments such as this indicate that Canada may have the potential to become America's "breadbasket." Also, rapid growth in Canada's beef industry will be fueled by a 240 percent jump in exports to almost 715,000 tons per year by the year 2000, according to industry-wide projections gathered by the Canada Beef Export Federation. Therefore, Canada may provide America with hamburger and buns.

The lettuce and tomato on the burger will come from Mexico. Mexico's agricultural trade surplus rose 40 percent to over $2.4 billion in 1995, according to a report from the National Council of Agricultural Products. Coffee, cotton and tomatoes constituted nearly 75 percent of Mexico's agricultural exports. And prospects for future food exports look good. Mexico's agriculture minister said that the country planned to invest 18 billion pesos in agriculture in 1996 in an effort to increase food output and productivity, with one million acres being added to the existing five million in the national fertilization and irrigation system. Since we are their biggest customer, they will be happy to keep the produce coming.

In summary, rich folks eat all they want and America is the world's richest country, so we do not have to worry about missing any meals. We have taught others how to cook, so we can now get out of the kitchen. Foreign suppliers in increasing numbers are lined up to sell us the commodities we eat in our instant meals. The suppliers are happy to sell and we are happy to buy because we are becoming mutually dependent on each other. It is an arrangement that lets America free up resources for use in other industries as we climb up the Economic Food Chain. We will appreciate the arrangement more all the time as more Americans realize that while we are climbing we can still get a burger to go.

Chapter 13

Stop the Train,
I Want to Get Off!

What can agriculture do to stop the chain of events leading to the end of American farming and ranching? (a) Nothing. (b) Whine and fuss. (c) Broaden the public debate. Choice (a) is the correct answer. Choice (b) is what many people do when they do not like something. Choice (c) could postpone the end by raising some questions that may lead to constraints on the inevitable economics that are leading America up the Economic Food Chain. Choice (c) will be pursued by many producers, primarily because they do not like choice (a).

Our progress up the Economic Food Chain is quite apparent. A 1994 Census Bureau report said the total number of farms in America had fallen to 1,925,300, the lowest number since 1850, and dramatically less than the high of 6.8 million farms registered in 1935 (*New York Times* November 10, 1994). The report credited the diminishing numbers to more efficient farming. It said that farmers are more prosperous, but fewer people are entering the profession and the farmer population is getting older.

Many farm kids would like to stay in agriculture, but it is getting harder to do so. Despite the report showing the number of farmers dwindling to the lowest levels since before the Civil War, 63 percent of the Future Farmers of America membership surveyed at their 1994 conference in Kansas City said that they thought they would become farmers themselves. Nearly all of those headed for farming careers saw livestock production as a likely pursuit. A small number planned to grow grain. Unfortunately, as the Census Bureau reported, America's farmers are getting older, not younger. The average age of farmers was

53 in 1992, up from 50 in 1982. In the latter part of the nineteenth century, the average age was 39. Fewer young people go into farming now because of credit hassles, government rules, volatile commodity prices, and start-up costs of up to $500,000. This national trend of aging farmers worries those who see young rural people rejecting an occupation they consider to be too expensive and risky. In an evaluation of this information, an agricultural economics professor, stating the obvious, predicted that agriculture will not become a popular career again until it is profitable. Also, in the last 20 years, career opportunities have grown in agribusiness, and students with an agricultural background are not bound to live a farmer's life.

The aging face of American agriculture is being noticed. The American Bankers Association (ABA) says that agricultural bankers' primary concern is the dwindling number of Americans who are becoming farmers. The chairman of the ABA's agricultural division said, "The decades-long decline in the number of family farms has left an ominous shadow hanging over many small towns." This has led to other concerns about the long-term outlook for economic development in rural areas.

So, how can producers, bankers or anyone else pursue choice (c) and broaden the public debate? Supporters of agriculture can make Americans consider both "us" and "them"—"us" being American agriculture, and "them" the remainder of the world—by raising these questions:

1. "Will there be enough food for future generations?" and
2. "Does America have an 'obligation' to the world to preserve our agricultural capacity?"

These questions may have different answers for "us" than for "them." As the story is laid out, it becomes clear that agriculture's train is on the fast track to some other country.

CHEW THE FAT

The traditional approach taken by American farmers and ranchers whenever they need political (or financial) support is to make themselves visible so that city folks will pay attention to "us." Agricultural producers have always believed that they are special because they raise food, so simply reminding others of that fact should generate the support needed. In other words, producers and their industry representatives believe that they can win over anyone by sitting down with them to "chew the fat."

Examples of this approach are everywhere. In one case, a group called Earth Partners was formed in Champaign County, Illinois, to teach children about agriculture so that they would have accurate perceptions about farming when they became old enough to vote. "Somehow we have to educate these people who are voting on issues that affect our livelihood," the group's chairman said. The group is now developing educational curricula.

Such efforts are well meaning, but they are like trying to bail the water out of the *Titanic* using a teaspoon. They ignore some huge facts of life. First, farm kids are leaving for the city in droves, so something about agriculture is not appealing, especially for women. As women head for town, the men follow. Second, teaching city kids about dirt, manure, bugs, and toxic chemicals is not likely to win over a lot of sympathizers. The national network of 4-H clubs has done this for decades, so why would new efforts be any more successful? Finally, agriculture needs to recognize that farming and ranching is no longer viewed as the romantic and honorable lifestyle it once was portrayed to be. The American public is now aware of the social and environmental costs of agriculture, and it is increasingly unhappy about having to pay those costs. Eventually Americans may get "mad as Hell and not take it anymore."

Therefore, reality is that agricultural producers are a small minority of the population, so, while appeals to urbanites are necessary, they may not succeed. In recent years the rural-urban interface has clearly favored urban positions. For example, in California's fertile Sacramento Valley the urban population cheered the passage of legislation that established a phased-in ban on the traditional practice of burning rice straw. The urban population was tired of seeing and breathing the smoke, and they did not care if the ban made rice production less profitable. Other recent legislation in the state established noise and dust ordinances aimed at agricultural operations that find themselves too close to the sprawling cities. In many states, regulations are targeting livestock waste management, water use, chemical applications, land use and other concerns of agricultural producers. The squeeze is on.

There is a tug-of-war between urban and agricultural groups going on in many parts of America. It is unfortunate, but many urban dwellers have come to see agriculture as a competitor and, in many ways, it is. One of the biggest battles is the fight over water. For example, California water officials predict that the state will face chronic water shortages in the coming decades unless steps are taken to conserve.   A state water plan reports that by the year 2020, urban demands could increase 50 percent, while agricultural needs will increase 7 percent, and environmental projects will also require more water (*Los Angeles Times* October 2, 1995). For the short term, the plan proposed voluntary reductions in urban areas, a decrease in agricultural production and the use of water transfers.   Long-term efforts include conservation, recycling, reclamation and creation of more reservoirs. Such plans always give way to urban voter pressure in times of drought. During the state's six-year drought of the late 1980s and early 1990s, public pressure caused state water deliveries to agriculture to be cut entirely during one year. The public had been outraged to learn that, at the time, agriculture used about 85 percent of the water supplies, and the city folks demanded that people's needs come before those of plants. The message was loud and clear and the reaction of lawmakers predictable.

By 1995, a study by California's Department of Water Resources indicated that future demand by urban areas on the state's water resources would grow, while demand from agriculture would decrease. One official said that agricultural water use would decline due to loss of farmland as urban areas grew. The study noted at that time urban areas were using 11 percent of California's water resources, agriculture 42 percent and the rest was going to environmental uses. Water prospects are so bleak that some of California's southern coastal cities are looking at desalination as a way to relieve chronic water problems. By the year 2010, San Diego County, for example, will need twice the amount of water that it used in 1994. As the value of water pushes up its price in the state's evolving water market, some farmers are already giving in to the inevitable economics. In October 1995, the *Los Angeles Times* reported that after decades of fighting in California to gain and safeguard the Imperial Valley's rights to Colorado River water, a few farmers are doing something that seems foolhardy to others: they are selling a portion of the water to outsiders and letting some fields go dry and lifeless.   It comes down to this: the valley's billion-dollar farming industry does not offer as much profit per acre to some growers as they could make by selling their water.[1]

---

[1] This was clear in 1996 when the city of San Diego reached an agreement to buy several billion gallons of water from farmers in the Imperial Valley. Some farmers were concerned about the huge profits the sale earned for billionaire brothers who had bought 40,000 acres of farmland and its water rights not long before and were selling the water.

A second rural-urban battleground is in national parks and forests. No, the fight is not between Smoky the Bear and Woodsy Owl, it is between cattle ranchers and conservationists. In the West, 4,300 National Forest livestock grazing permits may not comply with federal law. The Forest Service must prepare environmental studies and receive public comment on these permits. The crisis is due to a 1994 court ruling that ordered the Bureau of Land Management to consider the environmental impact of, and public opinion on, a permit before it is issued. The ruling is under appeal, but Western courtrooms are feeling its effects as conservationists sue over grazing plans. They want public lands reserved for public use only and to end private producers benefiting from being able to graze livestock on those lands for a small fee. Some critics have called the grazing program Aid to Farmers with Dependent Cows. The cowboys bellow that increasing grazing fees gore their profits and that a ban on grazing on public lands would kill the cattle business. The public is on the conservationists' side of the debate because most people do not consider beef cattle to be "wildlife" suitable for national forests, and because they do not think it is fair for only some cattle producers to get cheap access to grazing. To defend the practice, cowboys have had to adopt "environmental" arguments, claiming that cattle grazing helps maintain some ecosystems. (For example, some ranchers offered a herd of goats to graze poison oak down as a "service" to property owners.) Imagine the irony, burgers-on-the-hoof being portrayed as an endangered species in a delicate natural environment! No wonder agriculture has so little credibility with many city folks.

The public is tired of "being fleeced." Columnist Jack Anderson wrote about the "antiquated" 1872 Mining Law and "the multibillion-dollar giveaway of mineral-rich public lands," calling it a part of a syndrome of cowboy capitalism that now reigns (*Washington Post*). For example, the Bureau of Land Management and the Forest Service currently lease 265 million acres of grazing land, yet in 1994 the federal government collected only $29 million from grazing programs that required $105 million to manage. As a result of such revelations, the urban mood is turning against agriculture. A researcher with the Cato Institute and an official with the Natural Resources Defense Council wrote that the one thing Americans want least from the Western public lands is what federal policy favors: "subsidized cows." They suggest that Congress should put grazing lands on a market footing, making ranchers and not taxpayers pay for using federal grass; bust the cowboy trust on federal lands; and authorize the Secretaries of the

Interior and Agriculture to engage an array of range-reform experiments that might better protect public lands.

A third battle, related to the second, is also in the woods. The Government Accounting Office said in 1995 that the government spent $1 billion more to log National Forests during the previous three years than the timber sales had netted the treasury (*Washington Times* October 3, 1995). The Forest Service responded that it was wrong to conclude from the GAO audit that the logging costs taxpayers money and, in fact, reported a profit from timber sales for each of the three years in question. Unfortunately, the Forest Service does not include the nearly $900-million share of the timber receipts paid to the states as a cost of the timber sale program. A Wilderness Society official said, "The timber sale program is not self-supporting." A Forest Service spokesman pointed out that the timber program provides jobs which allow the government to collect income taxes. Again, the public is on the side of conservationists because of the Forest Service's bad economics.

A fourth battle between rural and urban groups involves chemical warfare. Farmers say they need chemicals to fight off bugs and weeds. City folks are afraid that they may be the ultimate casualty. Recent developments illustrate how serious this battle has become. To begin, farmers and exporters say that lack of a substitute for methyl bromide is a serious threat to U.S. agricultural exports. The pesticide is banned from use in the United States, and although an international protocol is directed at phasing out the compound, farm experts say that the chemical is so effective that there is no incentive for developing countries to stop using it. Farmers project significant declines in crop yields without use of methyl bromide. Urban groups charge that the compound's use in agriculture has a significant effect on the environment. Opponents also charge that some farmers are often too short sighted in their use of chemicals. They point to southern Texas where malathion spraying to control boll weevils is said to have opened the door to army worms, which devoured the cotton crop at great cost to farmers and taxpayers.[2] What scares city folks most, however, are

---

2 Two USDA scientists and some cotton farmers blamed the boll weevil eradication program for also killing beneficial insects, which in turn led to a 1995 infestation of beet army worms that ate the part of the cotton plant where fibers develop (*New York Times* October 9, 1995). The USDA disputed its own scientists' report and planned a new study to determine the cause of the cotton disaster. South Texas farmers claimed that they lost almost their entire crop to the insects and the USDA paid more than $50 million in crop insurance claims.

increasing reports of chemical contamination. For example, trace amounts of common weed killers remained in the tap water of three major Iowa cities in 1995 months after the chemicals were applied on farms, according to a report by the Environmental Working Group (*Des Moines Register* September 28, 1995). Generally, they were in amounts below what the government considers to be a health hazard. But how bad is this problem really? The *Wall Street Journal* reported in September 1995 that an analysis of tree bark suggests that insecticides and fungicides have spread over the globe, often thousands of miles from where they were used, and that some chemicals sprayed decades ago are still affecting the environment. Tree bark gathered from 90 sites, from the tropics to the chilled latitudes, bears traces of chemicals related to DDT, lindane, chlordane, aldrin and 18 other pesticides or fungicides. Now that is scary.

The number of rural-urban battlefields seems to be increasing each year. Why is it that rural and urban dwellers seem to be clashing more often? It's because they are coming into contact with one another more often. It is as simple as that. Does close proximity breed contempt? Apparently so in this case. "According to Census of Agriculture data, nearly 30 percent of farms were in metropolitan areas in 1982, and an additional 32 percent of farms were in counties adjacent to metropolitan areas" (Gale and Harrington). Those numbers go up each year. As we approach the twenty-first century, most Americans do not have to travel far to get up close and personal with a farm. As a result, Americans hear or read about agriculture in their local news more often than ever before, and apparently they do not like what they are hearing. Americans often live by the credo, "what you don't know, can't hurt you," but unfortunately, they are learning more about agriculture and it sounds deadly. News reports about pollution this and toxic that easily scare most Americans, who do not really know much about agriculture. The Alar scare's effect on the apple market several years ago is just one example of how skittish city folks can be when it comes to food. They will eat just about anything if they do not know anything about it, but tell them a few facts about the production of their food and you can start a mass starvation diet.

This means that everytime farmers and ranchers try to "chew the fat" with some city folks to educate them about agriculture, the producers run the risk of having the effort backfire, causing more consumer unrest rather than less. Educating the masses is an admirable goal, but a little knowledge can be dangerous. Since there are so few

producers and so many consumers, it is impossible to expect to be able
to give all urban dwellers a sufficient *understanding* of food production
to create sufficient *appreciation* for food producers to reverse
agriculture's waning political power. A more profitable approach might
be to focus directly on trying to increase appreciation for food producers
by adopting an advertising slogan taken from the Second World War:

"*Never have so many owed so much to so few.*" —Winston Churchill

The British Prime Minister was not talking about farmers when he made
the comment, but the idea fits. If Americans thought about the bounty
on their table (without thinking about the manure pile down the road),
they might not be so anxious to see the end of agriculture in the United
States.

WHAT ABOUT THEM?

Will Americans think about "them"—the people living
elsewhere in the world both at present and in the future? There is going
to be a lot of "them." "The world's population is expected to double
from the current 5.4 billion to over 10 billion by the year 2050,
eventually stabilizing at around 11 to 12 billion or perhaps somewhat
higher" (Pinstrup-Andersen and Pandya-Lorch). The next two decades
alone will be a challenge. Farmers around the world will need "a
doubly 'Green' Revolution" to feed a fast-growing population in the
coming years, according to the chairman of the Consultative Group on
International Agricultural Research. There will be 2 billion more people
in the world to feed in 20 years, and the advances that came along with
the so-called Green Revolution of the 1960s will have to be doubled if
the world's farmers are to keep pace with the world's hungry. That is a
lot to think about.

The good news is that nearly everyone believes that world food
production can be increased enough over time to meet the needs of the
expanding population. The bad news is that there will be lots of arguing
over how to do it. Only high-yield farming and the careful use of
fertilizer and pesticide can produce enough food for a world population
expected to double by the year 2050, according to Dennis Avery,
director of the Hudson Institute's Center for Global Food Studies. On
the other end of the suggestions is a 1996 report by the United Nation's
Development Program that said governments should promote safer and
more efficient use of urban land as traditional farmland disappears under

sprawling cities (Associated Press). "Urban agriculture ranges from growing crops on rooftops to raising livestock in backyards and raising fish in ponds, streams and lagoons," the report said. "For the poorest of the poor, urban agriculture provides access to food and helps stamp out malnutrition."[3]   The best news about the arguments being thrown around is that the predictions of successful expansions in food production are supported by facts while the doomsayers deal in short-sighted fears. For example in 1996 the perennially gloomy WorldWatch Institute, noting that grain reserves were at an all-time low, worried that the world would face food shortages and steep price increases for grain. However, at the same time the UN's Food and Agriculture Organization projected that grain surpluses would continue until at least 2010 and prices would decline. Frustration over the doomsayers' ignorance of the facts led a Maryland business professor to challenge Lester Brown, the head of the WorldWatch Institute, to a $100,000 bet that WWI's predictions of impending widespread hunger and other environmental disasters are wrong (*Washington Times* January 30, 1996).   The professor said that every measure of material human welfare in the United States and the world had improved rather than deteriorated.   He noted that in the 30 years since WWI's first prediction, world food production had doubled and real food prices had declined.

At present, food distribution is the problem, not food production. Pinstrup-Andersen and Pandya-Lorch report that "globally, about 2,700 calories are available per person per day, considerably exceeding minimum requirements."   Yet, almost one-fifth of the population in the developing world goes hungry because the people are too poor to buy all the food they need. This situation is improving, and it will continue to do so as developing countries move up the Economic Food Chain. However, the rate of improvement will be a distribution problem more than a production problem. If the money earned from increases in food production in the future reaches the poorer people in developing nations, hunger will be reduced.

For America, the first question remains, "Will there be enough food for future generations?"   The answer depends on who you are talking about and on America's position in the "King of the Hill" game of the world economy. The King of the Hill will be the first country(s) to reach the top of the Economic Food Chain.   Just like in the kid's

---

[3] This is a far cry from the urban agriculture in America. In less-developed countries, urban agriculture is a necessary supplement to the food supply available to many people. In America, urban agriculture is decorative.

game, the King(s) can push others back as they try to reach the top level, assuring the King's position for a longer period. One result of this economic hierarchy is that poorer countries suffer the brunt of world food shortages, not the King(s). America is the leader in the fight to reach the top of the Hill, so we will have access to all the food we can eat for generations to come whether or not we grow anything. It is future generations in the poorest countries that are at risk if the world's food production does not keep pace with population growth.

At present, it appears that the world has sufficient resources that can be developed to meet food needs for the long run. But appearances can be deceiving. So the second question facing America is, "Do we have an obligation to the world to preserve our agricultural capacity?" Our land will not be needed to feed us, but it may or may not be needed to feed others.

If America answers, "Yes, we do have an obligation," it creates a constraint on our economic development up the Economic Food Chain. Any constraint threatens our future prospects for becoming the King of the Hill. If we do not invest our land and other resources in their highest and best use, our economic growth will be slowed down and someone else, more willing to do what it takes to get to the top, might pass us. Americans are smart enough and selfish enough to realize that being the King is more fun than being anything less. Thus, America will answer no to any such obligation because we plan on being the well-fed King.

Legislated land-use constraints could, by definition, keep land in agriculture. America is full of examples of laws preventing natural economic evolution from occurring and creating little Ag Zones where land is kept in agricultural production. One of the more bizarre cases is that of the dairy reserve in Riverside County, California. It is a 20-square-mile district in which only dairies are allowed to operate, but it is completely surrounded by expensive houses, shopping centers and freeways. What is the point of trying to keep that particular piece of real estate covered in manure?

Oddly enough, there are also government programs designed to take land out of agricultural production. To many American producers, this is the root of most evils. For example, a *New York Times* (October 30, 1994) columnist said that American farmers would see their share of the global market shrink, with or without the GATT accord,[4] because of

---

[4] GATT is the General Agreement on Tariffs and Trade. It is a world trade agreement that seeks to make trade more free of barriers between participating countries. A new

misguided domestic policies that idle land. The USDA's acreage-reduction program and Conservation Reserve Program (CRP) were the two main culprits named in the article. Both programs pay farmers for *not* producing anything on certain land parcels.[5] The columnist cited a study indicating that the return of 38 million idle farm acres to production would raise farm income $8 billion ($4 billion net). Unfortunately, the columnist and the study he cited both ignore the fact that the world is not suffering a food shortage, thus 38 million acres of additional American output would just drive prices down for all producers causing economic hardships for many. For this reason, the USDA projected that about 32-33 million acres will remain in the CRP through the year 2000, down from the 1994 enrollment of 36.5 million, under its plan to extend expiring contracts for 10 years. Also, the USDA announced that CRP contracts will be extended and modified and new acres will be enrolled, as the program becomes "more environmentally sensitive." These actions will enable the USDA to maintain substantial CRP participation and target the CRP to achieve enhanced environmental and conservation benefits. Thus, both economic and environmental goals are being pursued now.[6] This is quite a change from the advice that farmers got in the 1950s and 1960s, when the USDA told them to "plant fencerow to fencerow."

---

round of GATT talks are undertaken every five (or so) years to update world markets for all types of products, including agricultural goods.

5 Some farmers have gotten very good at *not* producing. There are lots of stories of successful unproducers. One tells of a farmer that was near to losing his farm when he decided to quit growing anything. The money began rolling in from the Conservation Reserve Program. Things got even better when the unproducer found that he could use his idle farmland as a hunting range and charge rich city folks Big Bucks to come and kill wildlife there. He is now one of the wealthier people in the county and still a happy unproducer.

6 There certainly is no agreement on the value of these programs. A 1995 study by the Food and Agricultural Policy Research Institute (FAPRI) says that eliminating two cotton and grain set-aside programs could save $1.5 billion over nine years. FAPRI's study indicates that the move would "also reduce net farm income slightly" and eliminate the disaster safety net many farmers rely on. Critics of set-asides claim that the programs hurt farmers by limiting output and income. They say the emergence of the world market has made obsolete the practice of bolstering market prices by preventing crop surpluses. The bulk of the 41 million acres of land held out of production in the United States in 1995-96 were in the Conservation Reserve Program. Some farm groups (rice and cotton) claim that the system has worked well, and the National Association of Wheat Growers says that relying on export sales for huge crops was bogus economic theory. USDA's chief economist said that set-asides may continue to be effective in restoring markets that get badly out of balance, but, he concluded, the usefulness of such programs becomes less clear as trade agreements open new markets.

Some city folks like the Conservation Reserve Program despite its annual cost of $1.8 billion. A *Wall Street Journal* columnist outlined, in a February 1995 article, how much the CRP has benefited wildlife habitat and the hunters that enjoy recreating in it. A biologist with the Wildlife Management Institute said, "There would be a rampage at the thought of losing CRP" if people knew of the benefits they were getting compared to what is spent on general crop subsidies. In other words, farmers are being paid for converting their land into hunting clubs and other forms of playgrounds.

In summary, yes, land can be constrained for agricultural use only, but at who's expense? The land owners'? The public's? And what would be accomplished? Aesthetics? The maintenance of living history? The facilitation of hobbies? The questions are many, and even farmers are not in agreement on the answers. The debate over farmland preservation versus property rights is raging across the country. Some farmers want to be able to do with their land as they see fit; others argue that farmland should be preserved to maintain production agriculture, open space and a balanced economy.

Most farmers do not want their land restricted to agricultural use only because that lowers their land values. In California, for example, the state passed the Williamson Act more than a decade ago to give participating producers lower property tax rates, but a small percentage of eligible land is covered because the program requires keeping the land in agricultural production for 10 years. Many nonparticipants want to be free to sell their land to real estate developers "when the city grows out to meet us." For most farmers and ranchers, their retirement depends upon being able to sell all or part of their land for Big Bucks and everyone knows that property sold as farmland gets a much lower price per acre than land that will be developed into some commercial or residential use. Therefore, laws that restrict land to agricultural use directly reduce the net worth of the individual owners involved. Those people ask, Why me?

Farmers in favor of preserving farmland don't want their net worth reduced either. They believe that they should be paid the full market value for their land when it is restricted to agriculture. That means they want taxpayers to "buy" the land from them. This is also an issue with landowners subject to environmental restrictions. For example, voters in Arizona intent on protecting their private property from government regulators squared off against environmental activists as they voted on Proposition 300 in 1994. Proposition 300 would have directed state agencies to analyze how new regulations would affect the value of private property and determine whether and how much citizens should be compensated for their losses. The proposition was defeated, but the battle goes on. In 1995, Washington State voters were faced with Referendum 48. If the measure had been approved, the state's taxpayers could have been hit with bills of up to $11 billion for reimbursing property owners for restrictions put on their lands. The issue will keep coming up as long as individual farmers (or others) face economic losses from government restrictions.

How will the struggles over agricultural land end? Economics will rule and the market will allocate land to its highest and best use. What does that mean? The story goes something like this: Preservationists see the American Midwest as a "green belt" which is narrowing over time. They want it saved for a variety of reasons. But the question to ask them is, "Who would take care of the farmland if it were saved?" Sure, a few high school kids in Future Farmers of America clubs say that they want a farming career, but when they get old enough to face the music, they are voting with their feet; they are heading for the city, where the money is. So, no one can afford to become a farmer, and existing farmers want to sell their land at nonagricultural prices. That means the land will eventually find its way into nonagricultural uses. Conservationists, meanwhile, also want land to go into nonagricultural uses like parks, wetlands, and wilderness areas. This requires tax dollars to acquire the land. The federal and state governments are trying to cut their budgets, so not all land acquisitions can be funded. Since there are fewer protectionist farmers than there are users of parks and the like, whatever public money is available for acquisition of land will go to conservation causes, not to preserving farmland. That is how voters want it now, so future farmers have little hope of being bought out by Uncle Sam; if they want the Big Bucks, they will have to sell to private developers.[7]

So, will Americans think about "them"? We will think about others, but we will act in our own best interest. When push comes to shove, Americans will fight to be the King of the Hill. It's the American

---

[7] There are rare private investors who would prefer to conserve land rather than develop it. For example, in an effort to preserve the nation's tall-grass prairie, Fort Worth millionaire Ed Bass paid a private conservation group $2 million for grazing rights on almost 11,000 acres in Kansas. He also contributed $1 million to the National Park Trust's campaign to create a national park that would include the property, considered to be one of the largest tracts of pristine prairie left in America.

Way. We will not take extraordinary steps to preserve our agricultural capacity as the market moves the resources into other, more profitable, industries. We will make the best investments we can to benefit ourselves. However, many of our investments will benefit "them" as well.

IS FOOD PRODUCTION A NECESSITY?

At this point it is useful to remember assumption number one in this book: "Americans will continue to eat at least their share." But if we want to eat, isn't food production a necessity? Only if no one else will sell food to us. We don't have to produce commodities because we expect to be the King of the Hill. From our vantage point on top of the economic heap we will be able to buy whatever we want to eat. Less-developed countries must sell food to America and other wealthy countries to further their own economic development. So, we will be "fat and sassy."

But what about wars or economic disputes that could cut off our food supplies? Would America be at risk of food blackmail if all our raw commodities were imports? No way. Being the King means that you can hurt others more than they can hurt you. But more important, most of the world has learned the Great Lesson Of The Twentieth Century: mutually dependent nations do not fight. America has understood this for decades and will reap the rewards of our past efforts to help others, including former foes. For example, America and Russia will continue to be peaceful trading partners as they switch roles. In the past we sent food to Russia, even during the Cold War. The mutual dependence that developed ("us" needing a market for our surplus production and "them" needing the food to cover the shortfalls from their inefficient system) may have prevented the political war from heating up. In the future they will send us food in exchange for the technical information we send them. We will help them improve their ability to produce food and other goods.[8] There is already evidence that the role reversal is coming. A 1994 study by the International Food Policy Research Institute (IFPRI) said that Russia and Eastern Europe

---

[8] An official with the U.S. Citizens Network for Foreign Affairs said that the number of U.S. business ventures in Russia, Ukraine and Kazakhstan grew to at least 20 by 1997. Also, international officials plan to help the Ukraine to develop a legal framework for privatization, the transfer of firms in the farm sector to private hands, and to accelerate land privatization.

can go from being chronic food importers to being exporters of about 30 million metric tons per year in the next decade if economic reforms are successful. The IFPRI study indicated that this would cut world grain prices by 20 percent, hitting Third World farmers and American, Canadian and Australian exports. So, we will be able to buy food from foreign sources and possibly spend less for it than the amount we currently pay to our domestic producers.

Other old foes will also become sources of food for America. Vietnam received 1,000 pregnant dairy cows (the "herd shot round the world") in a deal negotiated during Washington Governor Mike Lowry's 1995 trade sortie. Also, Vietnam was the world's third largest rice exporter after Thailand and the United States in 1994 (and second largest by 1996), according to the official Vietnam News Agency. To achieve the rice production target of 25-26 million tons by the year 2000, yields will need to increase to 4-4.5 tons per hectare through intensive farming, the agency said. In 1995, Vietnam banned the conversion of rice fields to industrial use to maximize rice production. During the same period, China's exports of rice increased about 23 percent in 1994. That country also achieved a record grain harvest of about 460 million tons in 1995, up from 444.5 million tons in 1994, and remained a net grain exporter in 1995 and 1996 despite shortages of some grains at home. This indicates China's dependence on export sales and demonstrates the importance that they will place on customers such as America. Future export prospects are being enhanced by technical advances. In 1995, a Chinese agriculture official said that they have developed a new variety of spring wheat that will boost yield by as much as 36 percent.

China is typical of developing nations that are recognizing the importance of their agricultural exports in funding their climb up the Economic Food Chain. China's Communist Party leaders finalized a five-year economic blueprint in 1995 which said that agriculture will take priority. "We must earnestly place top priority on agriculture in the development of the national economy," the 301-member Central Committee said in a statement (Bloomberg). An alarming loss of arable land to massive industrial development prompted China's minister of agriculture to call for more effective measures of protecting farmland and increasing crop yields. In response, the Chinese government issued a plan in 1995 aimed at limiting the loss of farmland to so-called development zones. Also, in 1995, the government earmarked some $4.1 billion in loans for important food-growing projects in a bid to increase production and efficiency. The minister said that increasing the supply of cultivated land was the first step in helping China reach its production goals for grain and cotton. He also said the agricultural department should improve its environmental monitoring system at all levels and pay close attention to control of pollution in rural areas. Even in developing countries the food production-environmental pollution battle is being fought. The difference is that in developing nations economic necessity still gives an edge to food production, the reverse of the situation in wealthy countries.

Many poor countries will shift food production into high gear as soon as trade opportunities appear. For example, Burma and Cambodia will become Asia's top rice suppliers when the full impact of the new GATT accord takes hold, perhaps in a decade, according to a researcher with the International Rice Research Institute. He said as other countries' investments move away from agriculture toward industry because of the influence of the GATT accord, Cambodia and Burma will supply 10 million tons of rice to Asia each year by 2005.

Wealthy countries around the world are making political alliances to insure future food supplies as their resources are shifted out of agriculture. For example, Britain will redouble efforts to reform the Common Agricultural Policy in preparation for the expansion of the European Union eastward, according to the United Kingdom's Agriculture Minister William Waldegrave. He told the 1994 annual conference of Britain's Conservative Party that costly food mountains would reappear if the potentially high-producing nations of central and Eastern Europe joined the European Union.[9] However, the prospect of being replaced by producers to the east is not popular with British producers. British farmers fear an exodus from the land as cuts in subsidies begin to kick in under the GATT agreement. The number of farmers in Britain is dwindling; the average age of farmers is already 55, and thousands more farmers are expected to leave the land in the coming years. The handwriting is on walls all over the wealthy part of the world.

Joining trade blocks is becoming a popular move for

---

[9] By 1995, estimates indicated that extending current farm subsidies to 10 eastern European countries that are on track to join the European Union will add 12 billion ecus ($15.8 billion) to the annual budget by the year 2010, according to a report by the EU Commission. Even if the 15 current member states were willing to pick up the bill, extending the Common Agricultural Policy to the new democracies would simply create a new class of subsidy-rich farmers and lead to a massive surge in food prices paid by consumers, the report warns.

governments, but the effect of these alliances on countries' agricultural sectors depends on where they are on the Economic Food Chain. Norwegian farmers fear that their rural roots will be shaken loose if Norway joins the European Union. They correctly believe that many farmers will be forced off the land by lower EU prices and imports of cheap food. Norway's 70,000 farmers are among the most subsidized in the world because their resources are not well-suited to agriculture compared to some other countries. On the other hand, the results of bilateral negotiations accompanying the talks on the GATT accord will make it easier for Argentina to export its beef and peanuts to the United States. Argentine resources are suited to agriculture, so they can successfully compete in world food markets. As the subsidies and trade barriers protecting farmers in wealthy countries from having to compete with farmers in developing countries come down, cheaper sources of food become available to consumers and market partnerships (called "market integration") become possible.[10]

Trade agreements between countries are just the first step in insuring future food supplies. The second, and more binding, step is the vertical market integration (formation of market partnerships) that will occur across international boundaries when firms feel that political and/or military disputes between the trading nations are not likely. Food processors and other types of agribusiness will have to integrate backwards (have partnerships with producers) to insure access to input supplies, especially raw commodities. For example, the American makers of TV dinners will need to insure sources of supplies for the meat, vegetables, fruits and grains used to make their final product. These sources will be in other countries, thus food supplies will be secured for American consumers by the "middlemen" that farmers have so often criticized. These "strategic alliances" will keep the American gravy train rolling.

---

10 Trade blocks are busting out all over the globe. For example, in 1995 Chile's president said that he was strongly committed to creating a hemispheric free-trade zone by 2006. Member states of the South Asian Association for Regional Cooperation—India, Pakistan, Bangladesh, Sri Lanka, Nepal, Bhutan and the Maldives—agreed to form a preferential free-trade zone and establish a special development fund. Also, economic ministers from the six-member Association of Southeast Asian Nations (ASEAN) promised to speed up industrial cooperation and eliminate barriers to trade in the region. The announcement came at the end of a meeting in Thailand to review implementation of the ASEAN Free Trade Area, scheduled to come into effect by the year 2003. The ministers, however, were stymied in trimming a list of unprocessed agricultural products. ASEAN officials said they were toiling to remove more than 2,500 products currently covered by tariff barriers.

The international mutual dependence needed to reduce conflict and to enable America (and other wealthy nations) to rely on other, less-developed nations for commodity inputs will be created by this integration of foreign farmers and American agribusiness firms. Farmers in developing nations will become dependent on the market offered by the American firms for their income and economic stability. To insure the stability of their suppliers, the American firms must share their profits with the foreign farmers producing the raw inputs for the food processing sector. American agribusinesses will achieve the necessary integration (market partnerships) by using both ownership and contracting methods to create strategic alliances. First, American firms will continue the current trend of buying foreign agribusinesses through direct foreign investment. Then, those American-owned agribusinesses in foreign countries will contract with local farmers and ranchers to supply the raw agricultural commodities needed to keep up with America's appetite. This process is already underway. Ning and Reed report that "the growth rate of foreign affiliates' sales was 260 percent higher than the growth in U.S. exports" from 1985 to 1990. In other words, American firms that own companies in foreign countries are seeing the sales of those foreign companies grow faster than their own export sales out of America. "Going global" by investing directly in foreign firms is one of the most popular business strategies of American companies. One reason for this is that buying a firm located in a foreign country allows the American owner to dodge trade barriers set up by the host country. Ultimately, it means that American agribusinesses will spread over the globe, finding producers who are willing to take Top Dollar to sell their commodities to local outlets of those firms. The economic needs of both the foreign farmers and the American agribusiness firms will create a strong network of economic partnerships, insuring a steady flow of imported food to America. Thus, agribusiness firms are increasingly becoming examples of a "global web" and their products are "international composites."

Examples of American firms' efforts to develop global webs are numerous. Recent cases are typified by Cargill Incorporated's plans to invest some $1.5 billion over 10 years mainly in grains and oilseeds in Asia. The focus of the investment will be in oilseeds processing, the animal and poultry sectors and Cargill's trading businesses in some areas, the top official of the firm's Asian unit said in 1995. Also, a number of large and premium U.S. winemakers are investing in Chilean vineyards. Chilean wine sales to the United States grew 20 percent, to

$40 million in 1995, and are expected to continue growing in the future. And in 1996, U.S. Secretary of Agriculture Glickman and his Indian counterpart signed an agreement for cooperation between agricultural scientists and research institutions of the two countries. He noted India's growing role in world trade, and the two agricultural leaders discussed ways to increase U.S. imports of farm goods from India.

Developing these international market partnerships is such a good idea that other countries are doing it just as much as America. Europe has been doing it for ages. Even Australian food firms are investing directly in the Egyptian and Asian food processing industries to get around import barriers on processed foods. It isn't a new idea; Japan has been using it for decades to gain access to lots of international markets, such as the American car market. One example of these agreements is provided by an Australian company that signed a 50-year joint venture with Beijing General Corporation of Agriculture Industry and Commerce (BIAC) to supply live cattle to establish China's first large-scale cattle breeding and research station. BIAC is already a joint-venture partner with other firms, such as McDonalds, which is estimated to require up to 500,000 head of cattle to meet its demand in China within the next five years.

While American agribusinesses are waiting for our transition from food exporter to food importer, they are establishing market partnerships and polishing the trade routes using exports. Thus, it will be an easy switch to funnel the imports here in the future: the contacts will be established, the transportation facilities in place, and the people familiar with each other. As the *Los Angeles Times* reported in 1995, a number of trade experts say that American exports are strong and about to boom. One of the sectors that is leading the way is the American food processing industry. One study found this sector to be three times as productive as Japan's even though Japan's employed nearly as many workers as America's sector. "We are light years ahead of the foreign competition," said one food industry analyst. So, it is the often-maligned middlemen who are riding to the rescue and insuring that dinner in America will continue to be served.

WHEN PIGS FLY

The intermediate step between the traditional "free-range" agriculture that we still see now and the future's network of integrated international firms is what is being called the "industrialization" of agriculture. It is not a step that many family farmers want to see, but it is already occurring in some commodity sectors. The best current example is the American hog industry.

At the end of 1994, U.S. Department of Agriculture numbers showed increasing concentration in the American hog industry; the number of hog operations declined 7 percent from 1993 (13 percent from 1992). Two percent of the operations contained 37 percent of America's hog inventory. The trend was also toward "mega farms" and locations farther from populated areas. The High Plains region of the Southwest was becoming a magnet for massive hog farms, mainly because it is high, dry and sparsely populated. Premium Standard Farms planned to have the largest hog farm in America by building a $200-million expansion in the region in 1996. Also, the Seaboard Corporation plans to invest $500 million in the region to establish a hog operation, including a $55-million slaughter facility. Experts say that the industrialization of the hog business bears some similarity to what happened to the chicken business 30-40 years ago. The good news is better pork for consumers; the bad news is the competition faced by small producers.

The real bad news for agriculture is that this type of industrialization has some built-in problems that will eventually kill it. One way of explaining it is to ask, Would you want to live next door to one of these mega hog farms? No one does, of course, so rural residents are fighting them with every weapon available. Various strategies are being tried by numerous groups. For example, a coalition of small farmers, animal rights activists and other groups formed a steering committee to stop corporate hog and poultry farms from expanding in Ohio. At present, zoning is the main strategy. While zoning won't stop the big hog operations, critics are saying that it may at least give them the power to control construction of the sewage lagoons that foul the air and water.[11] They face a tough fight, however, because rural residents fear that the same rules used against the big hog farms could eventually be used against them. As a result, zoning has had some successes and some failed attempts to restrict hog farming in the Midwest.

Governor Carnahan, of Missouri, and others called in 1995 for

---

[11] The High Plains area that stretches west from a line halfway across Nebraska to the Rockies used to be known as the Great American Desert until the Ogallala Aquifer was discovered and tapped. The waters of this aquifer are being drawn down at an alarming rate. If large-scale hog production continues to move west, as seems to be the trend, more stress will be placed on the aquifer. The High Plains area might be able to compete for a while with Iowa's renewable water resources, but this could eventually spell disaster for the High Plains' ecological future.

tougher environmental supervision of large hog farms in response to the seventh manure spill in a month, which killed fish in the state's streams. Carnahan had welcomed development of factory farms in the state earlier, yet a spokesperson said that the governor supports economic development but not at the cost of the environment. At the same time, spills into Iowa waterways were creating such a public outcry that at least half a dozen Iowa counties passed nonbinding resolutions calling for a halt to the construction of livestock facilities, following Humboldt County's lead. Unfortunately, the Iowa Supreme Court said that counties cannot use zoning to restrict large hog operations. Those legal battles continue. Similar fights rage in places like North Carolina and Kentucky.

Are hogs really that bad? A news service reported that fumes from the waste of 72 pigs flying from Britain to South Africa triggered the plane's fire alarm system and forced an emergency landing. Fifteen of the animals were asphyxiated by the halon gas released as part of the plane's automatic fire extinguishing system. Any more questions?

The hog industry's optimism about the prospects for megafarms is typical for agricultural producers. The National Pork Producers Council expects the pork industry's future to be "phenomenal" as economic and political stability grows in the developing world and their demand for meat increases. The industry is working with low prices and record production to package and process meat cuts especially for overseas buyers. Unfortunately, they do not want to see the handwriting on the barn wall.

In the future, the "overseas buyers" will be Americans because the hog farms and many of the processing plants will be in foreign countries. Industrialized agriculture is efficient, but it is also smelly, ugly and potentially polluting. So, Americans will eventually say, "not in my backyard" to hogs and all other types of agriculture. The city folks will go beyond zoning to outright bans on many agricultural industries, just like many people living next to nuclear power plants did in the panic after Three Mile Island.12 But it will not be zoning, bans or

---

12 Across America people are fighting back against the "hog wild" growth of intensive livestock operations. A 1995 *Des Moines Register* editorial said that 19 people had been killed in Iowa or near its borders in recent years by the concentrated fumes from hog manure. In 1996 the Iowa Supreme Court, calling a Buena Vista County hog lot a "permanent nuisance," cleared the way for neighbors to collect damages because of pungent odors. The high court said suggestions that new technology can solve odor problems at hog lots is "wishful thinking" and sent the case back to a lower court to award "past, present and future damages" to neighbors. By 1997 some farm residents of

any other type of restrictions on land use that kills off agricultural production in America. It will be economic realities. For example, in May 1995, Premium Standard Farms suspended its huge expansion in the Texas Panhandle due to low hog prices. In July 1996, they filed for Chapter 11 bankruptcy protection. Eventually all dreamers come back to earth. One by one, individual farmers and ranchers will be faced with the choice of losing money in agriculture, converting their land to some more valuable use or selling the land to someone else who will develop it in some way. As each of these individuals makes his or her decision to take land out of agriculture, the economic noose becomes tighter around the necks of remaining producers, thus making it more certain that current survivors will eventually be faced with the same decision. One by one, American farms and ranches are climbing aboard the express train to some other country that wants them more than Americans do. It is a one-way trip into a very different world, but only farmers and ranchers will miss the old world; American consumers will be too busy eating to notice.

Franklin County, Iowa, formed a new town to stop development of a large hog farm. They cited health and safety factors as motivation for their actions and they wanted local control over what happens in the rural area. In Kansas, people were shocked to learn that a Seaboard Corporation facility will produce as much sewage as half the state's population. In North Carolina, inspections of the state's 4,606 animal waste lagoons found serious violations at 200 sites. Investigators found that 3 percent of the state's 3,535 hog farms were in violation of state water quality regulations, compared to 7 percent of the cattle farms and 10 percent of the poultry farms. Also, researchers at Clemson University found that more than half of the lagoons they surveyed in South Carolina leaked animal waste into areas with subsurface streams. People are getting "mad as Hell and they're not going to take it anymore."

Chapter 14

Guns for Hire

In the future, American universities will continue to serve as a catalyst for international economic development by educating the population, but agricultural research for America will focus on agribusiness and the environment, rather than on farming and ranching. This change in focus is already occurring and has important implications for everyone involved. The reason for this change is that government subsidies for agricultural research will dry up as food production disappears. This will leave a lot of the academic gunslingers currently working in America's land grant universities without a "meal ticket." These research guns for hire will be forced to take what they can get and this is bad news for agriculture.

When academics are forced to beg for their dinner, anything can happen. Researchers in search of grant money often adopt an approach characterized by a line from the 1960s rock band The Doors, "Hello, I love you, won't you tell me your name?" They will take crumbs, but they like bigger money if they can get it. As a result, researchers go where the money is.

This means that over time private industry money will have an increasing role in directing the research agenda of agricultural college faculty, except for those "managing Mother Nature" for the public sector. In other words, private money will support research on agribusiness topics and whatever public money still goes to agricultural colleges in the future will support resource and/or environmental research. This represents quite a change from having the primary focus be on agricultural production research, as it has been for over 100 years.

In the long history of agricultural research, research taking place in universities has, in general, been good for agriculture. Research advances have greatly increased American agricultural productivity, representing more than 80 percent of agriculture's economic growth since World War II. Now American farmers are quantifiably the best. The global strength and efficiency of American agriculture is in the numbers, according to figures compiled by the National Cattlemen's Association. The United States has just 0.3 percent of the world's farm labor force, but American farms produce 22 percent of the world's beef and large shares of other commodities. Unfortunately, some university research agendas "run around like a chicken with its head cut off," leading to some strange projects. Just a few examples follow.

Utah State University scientists are testing a new device to measure methane gas production by cows. The researchers claim that the more-precise measurements should enable them to determine if methane gas production by cows truly has an important impact on atmospheric conditions. Measuring cow exhaust?!

A Purdue University geneticist has been working to breed a kinder, gentler chicken that is less aggressive in order to reduce mortality in flocks and save farmers (and chickens) from practices such as grinding down beaks. Animal rights activists criticized his approach, saying all that is needed is more humane housing for the birds. The researcher says that the chickens he has developed can save the industry millions in reduced mortality and increased egg production. Maybe friendly chickens will replace pigs as the next urban pet fad?

Texas Tech University, looking for ways to help Texas farmers find new markets for their cotton crops, is experimenting with grinding cottonseed into a flour that can be eaten by both livestock and people. But there is a problem: Cotton plants naturally produce gossypol, an insecticide that, while not lethal, will make humans and animals sick. The head of the project is working on a cost-effective method—called supercritical fluid extraction—for removing gossypol with propane and carbon dioxide. Yum yum. So, who wants to be the official cotton taster for this project? No, this isn't cotton candy.

Scientists at the University of Florida said in 1994 that they had genetically engineered lettuce that could relieve farmers of the costly, labor-intensive task of hoeing by hand. The new variety is resistant to herbicides and would allow farmers to use chemicals rather than weeding manually. While scientists have engineered and field-tested other crops with herbicide resistance, this is the first time they have done so with a leafy vegetable. The researchers said that their work could have a major impact on other vegetables as well. Oh boy, they have figured out how to put *more* chemicals onto our food! Is this progress?

A Cornell University scientist has discovered the chemicals that a cockroach and a beetle use to trigger reproduction. Use of the chemicals to mess up the bugs' love life can help farmers spray at the most effective time and reduce the use of pesticides. Also, these compounds can now be used with or without poisonous chemicals. Therefore, farmers can now choose whether they want to poison the bugs or just let them die a lonely, celibate death.

Are Americans glad to have their tax dollars go to public university research projects like these? Are you kidding? The more that urban Americans learn about agriculture the more they are demanding an end to the "pork barrel" subsidies. Urban consumers do not understand the connection between some research efforts and the food they eat. They don't care if somebody wants to measure cow fumes, just as long as they don't have to pay for it (or smell it).

Therefore, if American production agriculture (as opposed to agribusiness) wants to prolong its life through continued growth in productivity, it needs to use its money to support and direct university research on applied topics or that research will fade with government budgets. This is not going to be easy for farmers and ranchers because they will be competing with agribusiness for the best hired guns. Producer groups have contributed to university research in the past, but the level of their funding has been "chicken feed."[1] Agribusiness started funding research much later in American history, but their grants now amount to "small potatoes." In Agricultural Math:

small potatoes > chicken feed.

Therefore, agribusiness is winning the bidding war for the best university gunslingers. Agricultural producer groups are at a disadvantage in this war because the dismal economics makes the process of getting contributions from individual producers like "squeezing blood from a turnip." As a result, American agricultural production research will eventually fade to whatever level foreign governments are willing to

---

[1] For example, Iowa's pork, corn and soybean associations said that they plan to contribute $1.7 million to Iowa State University for additional research into solving odor problems related to livestock waste. ISU now spends $4 million annually on this type of research.

fund, adding to the pressure pulling farmers and ranchers out of agriculture.

TOMATOES ON THE NORTH POLE

In the battle for the ever scarce research dollars, the overcrowded list of land grant universities must be careful to give agriculture what it *needs*, not just what it *wants*. If universities focus on needs, it will increasingly be bad news for individual agricultural "clients" because what they need is to hear the sad truth. Agriculture colleges within these universities have long viewed farmers and ranchers (rather than the entire population) as their clientele and, therefore, have strived to make producers happy. However, this has led to some big problems, a few of which are making the exit from agriculture more painful for producers than it should be.

Many problems begin with agriculture colleges pandering to the wishes of producers. Producers want to stay in agriculture, so faculty members develop education and research programs aimed at that goal, without questioning whether or not the goal is realistic. For example, Iowa State University started the new Ag-Link College-to-Farm Transition Program in 1995 as part of its Beginning Farmer Center. Farmers had complained that a number of family farming operations go under when they try to bring in another member of the family, and the Ag-Link Program is designed to smooth the transition. This amounts to trying to hide the handwriting on the barn wall. The education program may be fun and popular, but it cannot change the fact that you cannot feed four at a trough built for one.

An example of a research program that will make farmers happy for a while but will not solve their bigger problem is the case of a Clemson University scientist who has developed a tobacco strain that is less tasty to budworms. The plant was developed over 25 years through conventional breeding techniques. The budworm problem may be important to tobacco farmers, but a quarter of a century is a long time to work on a product with such a questionable future. If those 25 years had been spent developing alternative products that could replace tobacco, a lot of tobacco farmers and consumers would be better off today.[2]

Perhaps one of the most revealing cases of agriculture college

---

[2] A 1995 study of tobacco farmers found that many have a strong and continuing economic dependence on the crop, but the younger and more-educated among them were more eager to supplement tobacco income with other crops and were more concerned about the long-term uncertainties of tobacco farming (*Lexington Herald-Leader*).

pandering "going wrong" led to the Second Shootout at the OK Corral. The story begins during the mid-1980s in Cochise County in Arizona's southeast corner. Cotton had been King in the area for decades, but the dismal market of that period had forced many producers to look frantically for alternative crops. They had turned to the agriculture college of the University of Arizona for help in their search. Unfortunately, the producers had contacted the Crops Department first. There a Cooperative Extension Specialist reassured them that he had just the solution for their problem: sweet corn. He organized numerous producers in the region into a large-scale effort to grow sweet corn in place of cotton. Sweet corn had never before been grown in the region, but the Crop Specialist assured the growers that his research indicated that it would do just fine. He was right. A year later the growers harvested some of the best-tasting sweet corn any of them had ever experienced. It was delicious. It also yielded a good quantity per acre. When the growers started to sell their sweet corn they got good prices for it, compared to sweet corn grown in other states. Yes, the growers thought that life was sweet.

Another year later, at the second annual (and final) sweet corn project meeting, the shootout began. The meeting room on the University campus was full of growers that had come to hear the research results and the Dean of the Agriculture College had dropped in to listen. As the Crop Specialist, being the project leader, started the meeting he focused on the yield results and other technical aspects of the sweet corn production process. Some of the growers asked questions and expressed satisfaction with the production data being reported. But after sitting quietly for an hour, the Cooperative Extension Economist who ran the university's crop budget program could listen no longer. He was less than a year from retirement so he was fearless. He politely drew the attention of everyone at the meeting to the few questions that had been asked by some growers who were concerned with their apparent economic losses on the sweet corn. He wondered why the Crop Specialist had sidestepped the questions. The economist smiled as he distributed a budget he had recently generated for the Cochise County sweet corn. He made note of the fact that neither he, nor any other economist, had been asked to join the project and that he was attending the meeting only at the direct request of the Dean. The room had become absolutely quiet by the time the economist looked the Crop Specialist in the eye and said to everyone, "This sample budget shows that none of you should have planted any sweet corn in Cochise

County." He went on to explain that he did not expect any sweet corn to be grown in the county the next year. He was right in that forecast. As the stunned audience looked at the budget, the senior economist explained that the average elevation of cropland in Cochise County was nearly 4,000 feet above sea level. This meant that the electrical costs of pumping irrigation water up to that elevation from far below the desert was, by itself, more than the *total sales revenues* collected by growers for their sweet corn! He concluded by saying that it was absolutely impossible to make a profit growing sweet corn in the county, a fact that anyone would have quickly seen if they had done any budget analysis. As the realization sank in that such a budget could have been estimated before the first ear of corn had been planted, the fireworks began.

The Sweet Corn Fiasco seriously damaged the university's reputation and cost a lot of farmers Big Bucks. Farmers' optimism and unwillingness to leave agriculture when the exit sign first comes into view always cost them Big Bucks. They *want* universities to help them stay on the land, but it often is not what they *need*. By not helping them to see the truth, the university hurt the very people that it considered to be its clientele. The gunslinger (Crop Specialist) had shot himself, and the university, in the foot.

Yes, tomatoes *can* be grown at the North Pole, but that does not mean that they *should* be grown there. Universities are intended to be places where possibilities are explored. However, agriculture colleges need to face realities as well. Yes, food can be grown in all 50 American states, but trying to maintain that production just for the sake of possibilities is not realistic.

EDUCATION FOOD CHAIN

What if they had an agriculture college and no one came? Many institutions are fast approaching this crisis. The dwindling number of people in farming and ranching represents a dwindling clientele for agriculture colleges, and those institutions are scrambling to avoid the inevitable. In the Education Food Chain there is a hierarchy, just like in all food chains. Those at the bottom of the chain will be the first to go, while those at the top will survive longer. In the case of agriculture, teaching colleges will go first, followed by research colleges.

The erosion of this educational infrastructure for agriculture is important because it will influence the speed at which American farming and ranching disappear. Education improves the quality, or value of work done by people, which means that it raises their productivity.[3] Had it not been for the improved quality of labor (and other inputs) in American agriculture, the sector's economic growth since World War II would have been *negative*. Obviously, negative growth would have meant that agriculture was becoming less competitive over time and more producers would have been forced out of business much sooner. Simply stated, educated farmers are more likely to succeed than uneducated farmers, so having fewer agriculture colleges will lead to a less competitive agricultural sector. The colleges are definitely shrinking, so American agriculture will definitely follow.

The situation facing many teaching colleges of agriculture is typified by that facing California State Polytechnic University, Pomona. It is located in the eastern part of the Los Angeles metropolitan area in a region that was rural when the university was founded. It is one of four state teaching universities that have agriculture colleges.[4] By the 1990s, there was no agriculture anywhere near the campus because the region was completely covered by urban sprawl. Enrollment in the agriculture college had been sliding for a couple of decades and the faculty was being shrunk intentionally through attrition. The university was constantly pressuring the agriculture college to reverse the downward enrollment trend or lose its resources. By 1995, the college had transformed itself, for all intents and purposes, into a training facility for foreign students. Since there was no agriculture in that part of the state from which to draw domestic students, the college actively looked overseas. The curriculum had been depleted by lower faculty numbers and twisted into a constantly changing collection of courses designed for the specific needs of foreign "clients." It is currently a college of agriculture in name only. The remaining faculty wait nervously to see if the university is going to keep up the illusion of having an agriculture

---

[3] One example of this is "precision-farming" technology, with its reliance on computers and satellite signals, which is being used on huge farms in the Midwest and is being adapted for use in the South, where fields are smaller and crop varieties are greater. University of Georgia scientists will test precision-farming equipment throughout South Georgia in wheat, rye, canola, cotton and peanut fields. Equipment designed for the smaller fields should be commercially available in a few years.

[4] The others are Cal State-Fresno, Cal State-Chico, and Cal Poly-San Luis Obispo. Cal Poly-San Luis Obispo is larger than the other three combined due to its longer history and rural-coastal location. Teaching universities are those in which all faculty members are hired to teach full time. Research universities hire faculty to do research and teach. In California, the public research universities with agriculture colleges are the University of California campuses at Davis, Berkeley and Riverside.

college long enough for them to reach retirement. In the meantime, those faculty trained in agricultural disciplines teach new courses related to foreign agriculture and development: subjects that they know little more about than what they get from the textbooks they read just ahead of their students. It is an uncomfortable situation for everyone involved. They all know that the college must be shut down so that the university can use the facilities for something else, but no one wants to pull the plug.

Just like weak teaching colleges that are "dying on the vine," weaker agricultural research colleges will be "weeded out" first. As American agriculture disappears, strong agricultural research colleges will survive due to foreign support. Universities with agricultural colleges that are not both well established and well known overseas will see those colleges wither away as domestic funding dries up.[5] For example, in 1997 University of Wyoming trustees eliminated 11 academic programs, including bachelor programs for food science and vocational agriculture. The End is coming.

In the future, scientists and universities in America, Western Europe and, to a lesser extent, Japan, will be paid by foreign sources to do agricultural production research and to teach others how to do it. These rich countries already have the technology, which developing nations should not try to reinvent. We also have a stake in the continued advancement of foreign agriculture because it will be supplying our raw food products. As a result, mutual dependence will develop between American agriculture colleges and foreign agricultural sectors. They will need our know-how and their students and research grants will provide some justification for the continued existence of American agriculture colleges. Of course, in the future fewer hired guns will be needed to service the needs of world agriculture, so there will be a continuous shootout between American research universities over the

---

[5] DuPont Company and Cargill Inc. are among the agricultural corporations that are increasing their presence on college campuses and encouraging universities to introduce the subjects of agriculture, including agri-economics, agribusiness, genetics and biotechnology. But they are having a tough time because many students from urban areas, including minority students, think of jobs in agriculture as harvesting crops and milking cows. As a result, Michael Martin, the dean at the University of Minnesota's College of Agriculture, wants to make the school more relevant to urban residents who associate the St. Paul campus with cows and corn. He envisions the college providing research and programs that would influence what people eat and how consumers shop and explain how plants and chemicals affect the environment in cities as well as on farms.

limited funds that will be available. Teaching agriculture colleges will not be able to compete with research colleges (which also teach), so eventually just a small network of agricultural research programs will remain in America. The American gunslingers will research the foreign agriculture problems (which are the same problems we faced in the past) and teach foreign graduate students how to run undergraduate programs in agriculture once they return home. This has been happening for decades, but the difference is that in the future it will be a full-time job for a few, strong American agriculture colleges instead of the part-time job currently held by colleges in all 50 states.

Universities are diversified institutions, so the demise of one part of their portfolio, the agriculture college, will not ruin them. However, the loss of the local agriculture college will be a blow to agricultural producers in the area or state. This is an important part of American agriculture's downward spiral: fewer producers mean fewer students for agriculture colleges, thus the colleges shrink and the assistance they offer to the productivity of producers decreases, causing more producers to become uncompetitive and be forced out of agriculture.

Some realities are tough to take, but for agriculture colleges, academic gunslingers and producers there are "cherries" and "lemons." In the harsh realities of Agricultural Math:

$$cherries > lemons$$

so the lemons get squeezed first. It is not always a pretty sight, but it is part of life. The only defense that American producers and most agriculture colleges have against being squeezed out of existence is to develop stronger ties of mutual dependence between the two groups. Producers could help direct agriculture colleges and their research gunslingers away from cow exhaust and, in turn, the hired guns could help fend off farmers' and ranchers' economic necessity to leave agriculture. It is too late to avoid The End in the long run, but working together more closely can make the short run last longer and be less painful for everyone.

Chapter 15

Is the Sky Falling?

The end of the world (or the United States) is *not* coming with the end of American farming. This is not a "Chicken Little" story. Much to the dismay of agricultural advocates, America no longer has a rural population and, thus, most Americans could not care less if farming and ranching disappears, just as long as they get their burgers and fries. America will waddle on. Our economy no longer needs agriculture and is rapidly outgrowing it. Our voters support urban positions over rural interests. Our taxpayers are tired of paying subsidies to farmers while surplus food sits in subsidized storage facilities. Our suburbanites are fed up with the odors, dust and toxins from the old farm down the road. No one is buying the farmer's sob story anymore. Instead they are buying imported food.

In reaction to all of this, Defenders Of The Farm sound the alarm about the disappearing lifestyle of the family farm. They argue that such a loss would somehow reduce the quality of American culture, so the institution of family farming must be saved. Have you ever heard anything so "lame"? Every country on Earth was originally populated by farmers, so why do American farmers think they are special? American culture is no longer rural. Just like other rich countries, America has created alternate lifestyle choices in and around cities and the population has "flocked" to them. Furthermore, in this stage of our economic development, America offers varied rural lifestyle choices. Family farming is *not* the only form of rural living available to the American population. People can live near cities and still have the ranchette of their dreams. As America develops further, information engineering and other new industries will enable a return to a rural lifestyle for many people if they desire it. It is already happening.

The fact that America was once populated by a lot of farmers does not justify remaining so. We also rode in stagecoaches as a form of mass transit once, but that has not prevented us from moving on to more efficient methods of getting around. We grew up.

Part of the attachment to family farming comes from the "small is better" bias held by many Americans. There may or may not be some truth to this notion elsewhere in the economy, but it no longer applies to farming and ranching. In the 1970s, Jim Hightower and others popularized this bias even though the economics of agriculture were already clearly pushing farmers to expand. He told a good story and won our sympathy.[1] Today, Hightower's hypothesis appears naive and outdated because the world's agricultural markets are increasingly integrated, thus competitive, requiring that producers expand in scale to gain cost economies and to profitably add value.[2] Today, the only people who argue in favor of "saving the family farm" are former or current family farmers who have been or are being pushed out of business because they cannot compete with their larger neighbors. Small, mom and pop operations cannot compete with larger firms, thus family farms have become an expensive lifestyle that America cannot afford; it is an inefficient use of resources that is becoming a hobby that leads to bankruptcy.

Large-scale American farms and ranches will outlive family farms, but they will not survive indefinitely. Those big fish will feed on the little fish, but eventually they will fall prey to leaner, meaner foreign fish. The high costs of producing food in America, compared to the costs in poorer countries, are pushing American producers out of

---

[1] The author read Hightower's book, *Eat Your Heart Out*, which argued in favor of small farms, at that time and it remains a favorite. Apparently, many people liked the story because Hightower later became Texas' Commissioner of Agriculture.

[2] A University of Illinois rural sociologist has found a pattern of "fragmentation" in farming in Illinois and other Midwestern states that he says is usually associated with developing countries (*Chicago Tribune*). Fragmentation farming means that many farmers are each working, not a single piece of land, but several separate parcels, which may be several miles apart. Only 10 percent of the farmers that the sociologist surveyed are farming one piece of land, the remainder are farming an average of 8.4 parcels. Problems associated with this farm structure include transportation of equipment and the inefficient use of time. "Fragmentation is one of those phenomenon that is widely observed yet we don't know much about the extent of it or what its implications are," the researcher said. However, it is clearly a result of farmers trying to expand the size of their operations.

business as foreign competitors develop enough to serve the same markets. Foreign firms with lower cost levels will increasingly be able to underbid American producers. As a result, American agricultural firms will lose their profitability and be forced to shift into some other industry with better prospects. This is not a bad thing. This is life in a competitive world.

"THE ONLY THING WE HAVE TO FEAR IS FEAR ITSELF"

When President Franklin Roosevelt said, in 1933, "The only thing we have to fear is fear itself," America was in the Depression and facing an uncertain future. The country was about to take some steps up the Economic Food Chain. The number of farms in America was at the all-time high of over six million and our base manufacturing industries were just beginning to dominate our economy. Our hi-tech manufacturing industries were still decades away, as television and atomic energy were still just lab experiments. But we were on the move. A dramatic shift in resources from lower stages of the Food Chain to higher stages was occurring. The same is true today. America is making another step up the Food Chain, and it is making a lot of people nervous; for the first time in our history, the step involves leaving a large industry behind.

Some people worry that leaving agriculture behind and shifting to imported commodities may cause Americans to miss a meal or two, but this argument is "hard to swallow" considering the facts. We have been importing an increasing amount of food for years and our waistlines are growing, not shrinking. Americans are getting heavier, according to a 1995 Harris poll that shows nearly three in four are overweight. Of the 1,250 Americans age 25 and older who were surveyed, the poll found that 58 percent were overweight in 1983, 64 percent in 1990 and 69 percent in 1994. Other studies show that the average American has gained 8 pounds in the past decade.

The alarmists are starting to worry about the future, but their view is limited and isolationist. For example, according to a panel of "experts" at the 1995 national meeting of the American Association for the Advancement of Science, energy shortages, exhausted land, scarce water and a doubling in population will combine to radically change the American diet by the year 2050. The panel said that American lands are already pushed nearly to the limit of production and that crop yield increases are not going to keep up with population growth. These experts predicted that by the year 2050, arable American farmland would decrease to 290 million acres from the present 470 million. They also said that water will become less available for agriculture, forcing a shift of farmers to regions where rainfall is plentiful, and that the United States will cease to be a food exporter. The new diet, they said, will have less meat and dairy products, more grains and beans and a sparser variety of vegetables. They concluded that, by then, Americans could be spending up to half their income on food instead of the present 13 percent. The shortcoming of all these predictions is that they ignore food imports. The experts suffer from the "America must be self-feeding" bias. It is time for these people to "wake up and smell the (imported) coffee". America has not been completely self-sufficient in our food supplies since the days of the Boston Tea Party. Our imports of food commodities have increased constantly and will continue to do so.

But some people fear agriculture's loss of economic importance. They try to deny it, but the decline of agriculture is a national phenomenon. Even in the Midwest, where agribusiness remains a powerful economic force, manufacturing is the main engine of the region's economic boom. Figures on farming's recent success hide a problem: farmers themselves did not fare so well because the ratio of prices they received to prices they paid is at an all-time low. Agriculture's poor profitability is its downfall. There is no plot against farmers. No one is doing anything to purposely hurt agriculture. Agriculture in America is simply losing its economic competitiveness as other industries develop and offer investors a better return.

So, what do farmers—the group with the biggest investment in agriculture—want? Surprisingly, many want the government to quit "helping" them. A survey conducted in 1994 by the National Public Policy Education Committee of some 10,000 farmers in 15 leading farm states asked questions about a number of USDA's missions. Concerning farm program issues, 41 percent of all respondents want to phase out gradually all federal commodity programs, including price-support loans, cash deficiency payments and federally subsidized storage. About a third of the respondents want to keep the present programs. The youngest, oldest and largest farmers were most supportive of the status quo. These results reveal who is getting the federal cash presently: the youngest, oldest and largest farmers.[3] They also reveal who is not benefiting from federal farm programs: most farmers. Clearly, farm

---

[3] It is difficult to understand why the largest farmers are getting any handouts, but they are getting plenty. Therefore, farm programs are not really intended to help needy farms, instead, they benefit all participants in specific commodity markets, regardless of need.

programs are not improving the profitability of agriculture as an industry, they just improve the bank accounts of selected people.[4] And, unfortunately, many of those lucky people are not farmers or ranchers.

During the bickering over the 1995 Farm Bill, it was discovered that being a farmer was not a prerequisite for getting federal handouts. Since 1985, the federal government has handed over $1.3 billion in agriculture subsidy payments to residents of the nation's 50 largest cities, according to the Environmental Working Group's analysis of USDA records (*Kansas City Star*). The group said that analysis shows that about $130 million a year in farm supports goes to 74,000 people or businesses in big cities. The study questions whether it is good policy to pay subsidies to land speculators. The group's president said that he had no problem with urban residents' investing in farmland but asks, "Why on earth should taxpayers be involved in the arrangement?" The study was limited to 50 urban areas and did not analyze payments to suburbs, so its estimates are conservative. The study claims that a basic flaw in the farm program is that farm payments tend to be based on land ownership, not land stewardship. For example, the largest Kansas City recipient was a real estate investment group. Apparently the surest bet in agriculture is "farming the system."

With revelations like these, no wonder marginal farming operations are nervous about the future. The "system" is about to wean them from federal cash. In 1995, rural commentator George Anthan said that the nation's agricultural economy was headed "into a financially uncertain period" as farm program cuts seemed inevitable and farmers' net cash income was falling to the lowest levels since the deep recession of the mid-1980s. He pointed out that USDA economists acknowledged that the combination of higher debt and lower incomes will result in some farmers having "difficulty in meeting their debt service requirements," leading to more farmers going out of business.[5] Loss of subsidies would have a greater relative effect on small farms than on large operations, according to the USDA economists. The biggest impact of a loss of federal subsidies would be in the Corn Belt and the

---

4 Amendments to New Jersey's 1964 farmland assessment law proposed giving tax breaks for land used for boarding, training or rehabilitating livestock, including horses. Sponsors of the legislation wanted to help the ailing horse industry; critics said the proposals did more to help the wealthy than to preserve farmland.
5 A lot of unprofitable businesses will have to face the funeral music. For example, price supports for mohair disappeared in 1995 saving taxpayers more than $50 million per year. As a result, the goat ranchers of Texas, despite producing more than 90 percent of the nation's mohair, may find themselves the last of a dying breed.

Northern Plains, which together get half of federal outlays. But this weaning process is a good thing. Good farmers want bad farmers out of the way. That is why so many farmers want an end to government meddling.

The picture is so clear that even the government can see it. The number of American farms is shrinking, but those that remain are more productive. In 1994 Department of Agriculture economists described this as a long-term structural trend that is likely to continue into the next century. No kidding! Farm numbers have only been declining for over 60 years; how long before you get the message?! The economists report that the decline in the number of farms continued steadily into the early 1990s, at a rate similar to that of the mid-1980s. Census of Agriculture figures showed a total of 1.93 million farms in America in 1992, down from 2.7 million in 1969 and 2.09 million in 1987, a drop of about 33,000 farms per year. If the pattern holds, the number will fall to 1.73 million in 1997 and to 1.54 million by 2002, according to the USDA. The net loss would grow to about 38,000 farms per year between 1992 and 1997 and to around 39,000 between 1997 and 2002 and then begin to slow, the figures show.

Is this decline in farm numbers something to fear? No, it is an improvement in the efficiency of America's economy. Is it a scary thing? Yes, it is very traumatic for those farmers and ranchers facing the end of their small businesses. Is the demise of a family farm any more important than the end of a family business of some other sort? Of course not; all small businesses are important to their owners, but insignificant to the economy. Is America going to be all right? Yes, we are still climbing up the Economic Food Chain and we are still the closest to being the King of the Hill.

THERE ARE NO PREREQUISITES FOR COMPLAINING

To protest against a "symbol of what's going wrong in rural America," entertainer Willie Nelson appeared at a 1995 rally against construction of a large hog-production facility near Unionville, Missouri (*Des Moines Register* March 15, 1995). "Factory farms are threatening rural communities," Nelson said when he announced that he would join residents of Putnam County in their fight against Premium Standard Farms. What is wrong with this picture: Willie Nelson, organizer of Farm Aid fundraisers, protesting *against* a farm?[6]

---

6   Farm Aid supporters are having difficulty keeping the spotlight focused on their

The fight over big pigpens typifies the current situation in American agriculture. It is a rural versus urban clash. It is a producer versus environmentalist clash. It is a big versus little clash. It is a public versus private clash. It is a clash between fact and opinion.

A *Des Moines Register* columnist said that rural residents in Iowa object to a large hog operation in their midst, as the changing wind direction affects their rights to fresh air. She said that the state has given the firm "corporate welfare" and fears that it will come at the expense of Iowa's environment. She supports continued pork production by individual (small) producers in Iowa.

An agricultural consultant responded by saying that no one likes the odor of large hog operations, including the hogs themselves. He said the hogs do poorly and, in the long run, the market will solve the hog odor problem. (This implies that large hog operations may fail.) He said that there is demand for pork now, and Iowa has the corn to feed them. (This implies that the farm should go ahead anyway.)[7] He claimed that agricultural engineers have solved livestock waste problems. (This implies that no one will die right away, so the city should let the farm proceed.) Finally, he called the discussion of corporate versus family farms a "distraction," noting that average producers have not been efficient and the blame for the entry of large operations falls on the traditional producers as much as anyone. He noted that Iowa was set to lose about half of its hog operations in the 1990s and the present poor pork market will speed up that exodus. So, in total, he argued against and for the hog operation, brushed health concerns aside, and blamed the problem on the small farmers whose economic survival will be threatened by the large operation.

The complaining, arguing and finger pointing goes on and on. Anyone can join in; having all the facts is not required. Having only a few facts is common and confusion caused by the facts is rampant. It is a very complicated story to most people, so they tend to select the facts that they can understand and run with them.

For example, in a 1995 *Progressive Farmer* article, an agri-

---

efforts 10 years after the first concert, for which 100 performers volunteered and which raised $9 million. The 10th anniversary concert featured seven performers; ticket sales raised $587,500 for grants to rural groups, more than the amount raised at any of the previous three concerts. Farm Aid mainstay Willie Nelson says that he works to ensure that "someday family farmers won't be an endangered species."

7 This is the "damn the torpedoes, full speed ahead" approach. It is a version of the "we *can* grow tomatoes on the North Pole, so let's do it" philosophy common in agriculture.

business official expressed his opinions on how the "industrialization of agriculture" will lead to significant shifts in food policy, farm policy and rural development. He doesn't mean more corporate agriculture (heavens no, not *that*), but rather farmers using financial management and contracting to keep themselves competitive.[8] He sees farmers finding special market niches, alternative products and off-farm income to survive. He expects tomorrow's farmers to employ new technology more rapidly and be less capital-limited. He also expects farmers to organize with like-minded people to protect agriculture's interests. These "bold" predictions for the future simply describe things that have been happening for decades. They also indicate that many people in agriculture "cannot see the forest through the trees." Maybe they just do not *want* to see the red ink on the barn wall, but the ink is there telling the most important part of the story.

Even when a Defender Of The Farm sees some of the dismal economic facts that tell the story of American agriculture's doom, they spend so much time complaining that they miss the point. For example, two rural sociologists, from the University of Missouri and Iowa State University, said that farmers raising commodities are "getting the short end of the stick." Large food companies are getting a 20 percent return on their investment, but even the top third of family farmers only make 3-5 percent on their investment. The decline in family farms, the sociologists said, goes beyond agriculture and is really a question about the food system and the socio-economic fabric of rural America. "Will consumers," they asked, "have a better quality, more available, more wholesome food system under a corporate, integrated model than what they've enjoyed under the family farm?" The sociologists are so busy worrying about the institution of family farming that they ignore the bottom line: there is no "rural America" any more and the people trying to hang on to the outdated version of farming are simply holding onto a bad investment. No amount of complaining is going to change the economic facts.

---

8 A February 1995 *New York Times* article examines the trend toward crop contracts as part of a shift toward industrialized farming and specialized farming to meet specific markets. The article notes the potential for making more money by growing specialty crops. Some criticize industrialization of farming and point to the hog industry as an example of how drastic the changes can be. The president of the American Farm Bureau Federation says that the goal "is no longer to sell what we can produce, but to produce what we can sell."

THE LAST ROUNDUP

American agriculture is heading for the last roundup. Our rural countryside, both the beautiful and the "visually challenged," is heading into the final stage of its economic development. As we look out across that countryside, many of us will find it impossible to imagine our country without farms and ranches. Especially at this point in our history, when American agriculture leads the world in almost every way, it is startling to think that we will not need farmers or ranchers for much longer. But it is true.

To understand and appreciate the changes, we need to place farming into context. We need to strip away the romance and nostalgia surrounding agriculture and see it for what it is: a business.[9] It is a type of business that has limited potential for long-run profits because of its competitive nature. The whole world can "do it." In America, the cost of doing it has risen to the point where it is not very profitable compared to alternative types of businesses. Thus, the people, money and other resources invested in agriculture currently will be forced to leave for "greener pastures."

In the transition, America's green pastures are going to have a bumpy ride. Prices of farmland increased 6.4 percent nationally in 1994 and increased again in 1995 and 1996. An economist in Ohio said that the price protection provided by federal farm subsidies, combined with high production, has farmers feeling good. Demand for farmland is high, with urban dwellers contributing to the price pressures because of desires to escape the cities. Unfortunately, demand from city folks will grow slower than the rate at which farm subsidies will be reduced in this era of tight budgets. Less cash income (or subsidy payments) from farming makes farmland less valuable. For example, land values in Kansas could plummet 53 percent if Congress completely eliminates farm subsidy programs, according to an official with the Kansas Wheat Growers Association (*Wichita Eagle*).[10] Citing a Kansas State University study, the official told a Senate committee that even a 30 percent cut in the programs could reduce the state's land values by 9

---

[9] Urbanites have always had romantic notions about rural life and work, idealizing jobs like cattle ranching because it might put them in closer touch with nature. Dispelling that myth, a *Wall Street Journal* article took a look at a Montana cattle ranch manager. He spends most of his time behind a computer or on the telephone in his office.

[10] If this estimate is accurate, farming in Kansas is a ridiculously bad investment for America. It means that the only thing the land is good for is growing subsidized crops, which America doesn't need.

percent. He said that small towns and rural communities would be hurt.
In the long run, however, city folks will ride to the rescue. A growing
number of Americans are using telecommunications to bring their high-
salaried, urban jobs into rural America. In one example, using a Small
Business Administration grant of $680,000, a Nebraska business
developer set up two telebusiness centers with the aim of ending the
exodus of rural Americans from the region.

It is ironic that many farmers and ranchers retiring in the future
will be thankful for the flood of city folks into rural America. At the end
of a farmer's career, virtually all of the money he or she has been able to
accumulate is in the form of farmland. Thus, the farmer needs to sell to
get the money into a spendable form. If it were not for buyers from the
city, many farmers would not get anything near the price they expect for
their land.

That irony is lost on many Defenders Of The Farm. Several
groups, such as the American Farmland Trust (AFT), still strive to
preserve the nation's farmland. They hate the fact that the United States
is losing at least 1.4 million acres of farmland per year to development.
AFT says that, more important than the acreage figure, much of the land
being lost tends to be the most productive and nearest to consumers.
Boy, there's a shocker: land closest to consumers is consumed first!
With a keen eye for facts like that, no wonder Defenders Of The Farm
have had to give up trying to beat 'em and have joined 'em in many
cases. For example, in some places where the economic pressure to
develop farmland is strong, the AFT has created a "Purchase of
Development Rights" program to help farmers reap some of the
development value of their land without selling to developers. In other
words, when the value of land is too high to justify farming it, AFT will
buy it at market prices so the land can sit idle instead of being developed
into something useful. This is an example of shooting yourself in the
foot. Nevertheless, the AFT is hoping to raise $38 million for their
campaign to save farmland. It must be nice to have so much money that
you can afford to give it away in big pieces.

People on the other side of the fight over land haven't exactly
got the story figured out either. In 1995, a *Des Moines Register*
columnist argued against sweeping laws to protect prime agricultural
land. He noted that although "vanishing croplands" has always been a
popular headline, we are paying farmers to take land *out* of cultivation.
He said that residential developments like the one he lives in near Des
Moines have resulted in "urban forests" that support a wide variety of

wildlife. Who would have believed it years ago—someone in Iowa defending urban sprawl because it was a source of wildlife habitat? Can there now be any doubt that The End is near?

It seems that no matter how close the exit sign is, some people refuse to see it. In American agriculture, some folks will go down swinging. They are willing to shoot themselves in the foot in an effort to resist the inevitable. A classic example of this comes from reports that retiring farmers are passing their livelihoods on to young enthusiasts through a growing number of programs that match retiring farmers with younger ones in order to keep alive a family farm and a way of life. The idea of "matching services" was developed in 1990 by a think tank in Nebraska and has spread to more than a dozen states across the country. Yet, all analysts agree that these programs are not going to change the face of agriculture because most farmers will always choose to sell out rather than commit several years to a transaction that requires working closely with a stranger. However, the motivation to use these programs is not money, says one proponent. Therefore, participants must be either (1) independently wealthy, or (2) crazy. Since very few people in American agriculture fit either of these two categories, these well-meaning programs are doomed to fail.

The good sense and bad bank balances of American farmers and ranchers will win out over their hopes and dreams. As farms in Montgomery County, Maryland; Fresno County, California; and everywhere else in America continue to be shoved to the outer reaches of the county, and the urban sprawl continues to spawn new regulations with which to check growth, farm families are having a hard time figuring out how to fit in and maintain their way of life. They *want* to maintain something that they enjoy and do well, but they are bright people with families to protect, so they must do the prudent thing. As painful as it might be, the prudent thing is to manage their portfolio of assets with their head, not their heart.

As a nation, America must do the same. We can still listen to country music, but we have to drive our pickups into town. We must learn to let go of farming and ranching. In the short run, this means eliminating the subsidies that delay the inevitable development of our nation out of agriculture and into more profitable industries. In the long run, this means becoming citizens of the world, dependent on others for our food commodities while we produce the marvels and the know-how for the future. We have to do these things to become King of the Hill. It will be difficult for some of us to make this climb, but as a nation we have shown that we can do anything to which we set our mind. The first step is to accept that farming, although it enabled us to move into our dynamic future, is part of our proud past. Job well done.

Partial Glossary of American Food/Agricultural Clichés, Colloquialisms, Sayings, Etc.

All the tea in China: A very large amount of a valuable substance, great wealth.

Apple of his eye: His favorite person, creature or thing.

At the feed trough: Consuming large quantities, piglike.

Awkward as a hog on ice: Ungraceful.

Bananas: Wild, crazy.

Bean counter: Someone paying close attention to detail.

Bear fruit: Produce a useful output.

Beating a dead horse: Wasting time on a fully resolved issue.

Beef up: Increase in size, bulk.

Being fleeced: Being robbed of something of value.

Bite the hand that feeds them: Hurt the person or organization that supplies necessary income, food or other support.

Black sheep: A rebellious nonconformist.

Bologna: Not real or true.

Bought the farm: Died, or was cheated.

Bread: Money.

Bread and butter: Staple or main source of success or income.

Bring home the bacon: Earn or win money, food or something else of value.

Bucket fed: Received special treatment.

Bull: Untrue or of no value.

Bulls and bears make money, hogs get slaughtered: Greed leads to destruction. (A phrase from stock and futures markets.)

Cackling like a bunch of hens: Talking continuously and simultaneously, chattering with great volume and little content.

Cake walk: An easy task.

Cash cow: A product or service that provides lots of revenue with little effort.

Cat's meow: The best of something.

Cheesy: Tacky, low quality.

Cherry: An item that is like new and very attractive.

Chew the fat: Discuss something at length.

Chicken feed: A very small amount of money.

Chicken out: Decide not to do something due to fear.

Chicken scratchings: Unreadable handwriting.

Cold turkey: Quitting instantly.

Cool as a cucumber: Calm, not nervous.

Comparing apples and oranges: Comparing dissimilar things or concepts.

Corny: Funny in a nonwitty way.

Cow is out of the barn, The: The idea is no longer a secret.

Cream of the crop: The best of a group.

Cream rises to the top, The: The best people or ideas eventually succeed.

Crummy: Low quality.

Don't bet the farm on it: A proposition has a low probability of success.

Don't count your chickens before they hatch: Do not anticipate a favorable outcome.

Don't cry over spilled milk: Sorrow will not improve the situation.

Don't look a gift horse in the mouth: Accept unexpected good fortune without reservations.

Don't put all of your eggs in one basket: Do not risk much on a single proposition or project.

Dying on the vine: Never having a chance to prosper or develop.

Early bird catches the worm, The: One who starts first and works hardest will be successful.

Easy pickin's: An easy job, or something that's easily accessible.

Farmed out: Delegated or assigned to someone else.

Fat and sassy: Satisfied, happy.

Feeding at the trough: Consuming large amounts.

Flew the coop: Left hastily, departed from home, moved out.

From the horse's mouth: Direct from the source.

Fruitcake: A person considered to be completely mentally unstable. (*See* nut *and* vegetable)

Fruitless: Unsuccessful, unproductive.

Fruity: Silly, slightly crazy.

Get your ducks in a row: Get people or ideas organized.

Goes together like peas and carrots: Forms a natural pairing, or a combination that works well.

Goose: A silly person, witless; or poke someone from the rear.

Got a beef: Have a complaint.

Got his goat: To upset or frustrate someone.

Grass is always greener on the other side of the fence, The: What we don't have always seems more appealing than what we do have.

Gravy train: A secure supply of easy pleasure.

Greener pastures: Better prospects.

Half-baked: Not well thought out.

Ham: Show-off, melodramatic person.

Hard to swallow: Difficult to believe.

Hen pecked: Man dominated by a woman.

Hill of beans: An insignificant amount.

Hog heaven: Satisfaction from simple pleasures that others may not enjoy.

Hogwash: Not true or believable.

Hog wild: Out of control.

Honey (of a deal): A very favorable situation or offer.

Horse feathers: Not true or believable.

Hot dog: A person showing off; or an expression of happiness.

Hot potato: A sensitive issue that creates strong feelings on each side.

Hotter than Hell's half acre: Very warm place.

Hungry: Eager to acquire or achieve something.

In a nutshell: In a compact version.

In a pig's eye: A statement of frustration indicating disbelief or a refusal to agree.

Kick the bucket: Die.

Land of milk and honey: A plentiful place where life is good and easy.

Last roundup, The: The end, the final time something will be done.

Last straw, The: The little piece or action that makes the entire load too much to bear.

Lemon: A defective product.

Like bees to honey: With an overwhelming attraction.

Like lambs to the slaughter: Mindlessly following a path into trouble.

Living in the tall cotton: Well off, an easy and prosperous existence.

Living off the fat of the land: Surviving by consuming easily available goods.

Locking the barn after the horse is stolen: Deciding too late to take action.

Long in the tooth: Old, aged.

Main course: The central focus.

Making a silk purse from a sow's ear: Making the best of a bad situation.

Meal ticket: Source of supply or success.

Meat (of the story): The most interesting or important part.

Mighty oaks from little acorns grow: Small ideas can lead to big successes.

Milked dry: Drained of value.

Milk it for all it's worth: Get every bit of value from something.

Money doesn't grow on trees: Success does not come easily.

Nest egg: Financial reserve, or something of value saved for special situation.

No free lunch: Nothing comes without work.

Not from this neck of the woods: Not a local resident.

Nut: A person considered to be occasionally mentally unstable. (*See* fruitcake *and* vegetable)

Ol' homestead, The: Where a person lives.

Old McDonald had a farm: Part of a child's song that associates farmers with animals.

One bad apple spoils the barrel: A bad person can make associates do bad things.

Out in the north forty (acres): In a distant location.

Out to lunch: Missing one's senses, or being off-base in one's thinking.

Pay dirt: A highly profitable idea or venture.

Peachy: Very nice; or well (as in feeling well).

Pecking order: Hierarchy, ranking or relative status of people.

Piece of cake: Simple, easily accomplished.

Pig out: Eat large quantities.

Pig sty: A big mess, unsightly.

Pits, The: Depth of despair; or the unpleasant waste left after something nice has been consumed or has ended.

Playing chicken: Taking risks to see who will show fear first.

Plowing ahead: Proceeding despite obstacles.

Plucked like a chicken: Relieved of everything of value; thoroughly defeated.

Plumb full: Stuffed, unable to contain any more.

Pork barrel: Special source available only to selected few.

Pork out: Consume large quantities.

Proof is in the pudding, The: Trying something is the best way to determine its value.

Pull the wool over your eyes: Deceive.

Put out to pasture: Retired.

Ripe for the picking: Available or ready to be collected and consumed.

Roast: Ridicule.

Root around: Search for something.

Run with the pack: Conform, be a member of a group.

Running around like a chicken with it's head cut off: Having no direction or purpose, engaging in mindless activity.

Sacred cow: Untouchable object or program, something that is not to be harmed for reasons not always understood.

Seed money: Small investment expected to start something that will generate large returns.

Separate the wheat from the chaff: Distinguish between something or someone of value and that which is worthless.

Small potatoes: Small amount, relatively unimportant.

Sour grapes: Resentment, hard feelings.

Sow your wild oats: Actively pursue pleasure despite risks.

Spoon-fed: Given in small doses to assure success.

Stubborn as a mule: Obstinate, unwilling to compromise or move.

Sugarcoated: Artificially presented to disguise or soften the true purpose.

Sugar daddy: Wealthy benefactor with suspect motives.

That's the way the cookie crumbles: Things just happen in life that must be accepted.

Tighter than the skin of a new potato: Cheapskate; or a snug fit.

Too wet to plow: Too soon to begin work.

Trim the fat: Get rid of waste.

Trying to squeeze blood from a turnip: Attempting something impossible.

Vegetable: Person with no mental capacities. (*See* fruitcake *and* nut)

Wake up and smell the coffee: Acknowledge facts as given and unchangeable.

Walking on eggshells: Being very careful.

Weed out: Remove the undesirable components.

Wellspring (of happiness): Valuable source.

What's cooking?: Expression that inquires as to what events are in progress.

What's sauce for the goose is sauce for the gander: If it's okay for women it's okay for men.

What's the beef?: What is the person's problem.

When pigs fly: Expression indicating that something is most unlikely to occur.

Where's the beef?: What or where is the main point or object of value.

Whole hog: Entirely, without reservation.

Wild goose chase: Search for something that doesn't exist.

Wolf in sheep's clothing: Harmful person pretending innocence; or an idea that looks good but isn't.

Workhorse: Person who works hard for long hours.

Working for peanuts: Earning very little for one's efforts.

You animal: Strong or wild person.

You can lead a horse to water, but you can't make it drink: Some things cannot be controlled.

You can't have your cake and eat it too: Greedy people will not succeed.

You weren't born in a barn: Close the door.

Bibliography

AGRICULTURE: FIRST IN, FIRST OUT

Agence France-Presse. "Asia-Pacific Economies Grew an Average 7.7% in '94," April 18, 1995.

Anderson, G., J. Melville, and S. Waldhorn. "Creating Economically Competitive Regions: The New Comparative Advantage." Chapter 9 in S. Johnson and S. Martin, eds., *Industrial Policy for Agriculture in the Global Economy*, Ames: Iowa State University Press, 1993.

Associated Press. "Georgia Farmers Confront Labor Shortage," September 11, 1997.

Davis, C., and M. Langham. "Agricultural Industrialization and Sustainable Development: A Global Perspective." *Journal of Agricultural and Applied Economics* 27 (1995): 21-34.

Delmarva Farmer. "Bill to Control Illegal Immigration Hurts Agriculture," October 3, 1995.

Journal of Commerce. "Japan's Food Imports Increase," October 25, 1995.

Journal of Commerce. "Lumber Producers Fight Canadian Imports," November 3, 1995.

Knight-Ridder. "Germany Plans Aid for Alternatives to Shrinking Farm Sector," October 9, 1995.

Lee, H., J. Glauber, and D. Sumner. "Increased Industrial Uses of Agricultural Commodities: Policy, Trade and Ethanol." *Contemporary Economic Policy* 12, 3 (1994): 22-32.

New York Times. "Men Plead Guilty to Enslavement of Migrant Workers," May 8, 1997.

Reich, Robert. *The Work of Nations: Preparing Ourselves for 21st Century Capitalism.* New York: Alfred A. Knopf, Inc., 1991.

Reuters. "Austria's Dairy Farmers Reeling After EU Entry," January 19, 1995.

Reuters. "Farming Aggravates European Flooding," January 31, 1995.

Reuters. "Singapore Becomes Southeast Asia's First Developed Country," December 22, 1995.

Reuters. "EU Farm Workforce Slashed," April 18, 1996.

Reuters. "Chinese Workers Increasingly Seen Leaving the Land," January 7, 1997.

Thilmany, Dawn. "The Effect of Immigration Reform on the Farm Labor Market: Three Essays." Unpublished Ph.D. thesis, University of California, Davis, 1994.

Thilmany, D., and S. Blank. "FLCs: A Risk Management Option for the California Farm Labor Market." *Agribusiness: An International Journal* 12 (1996): 37-49.

U.S. Department of Agriculture. *Agricultural Income and Finance.* Rural Economy Division, Economic Research Service. AIS-63, December 1996.

U.S. Department of Agriculture. *Forces Shaping U.S. Agriculture: A Briefing Book.* Economic Research Service, July 1997.

Washington Post. "French Urged to Eat Bread." September 28, 1995.

Wharton, Clifton, Jr. "Malthus, Cousteau, and Schultz: Does Foreign Agricultural Development Have a Future?" *Choices* 10, 1 (1995): 19-21, 24.

ANY PORTFOLIO IN A STORM

Arizona Agricultural Statistics. University of Arizona, various issues.

California Fruit and Nut Statistics. California Agricultural Statistics Service, various issues.

Drury, R. and L. Tweeten. "Have Farmers Lost Their Uniqueness?" *Review of Agricultural Economics* 19, 1 (1997): 58-90.

Gale, F., and D. Harrington. "U.S. Farms: Diversity and Change—Six Myths of the Farming Sector." *Agricultural Outlook.* Economic Research Service, U.S. Department of Agriculture, 1992.

Hughes, D., and V. Litz. "Rural-Urban Economic Linkages for Agriculture and Food Processing in the Monroe, Louisiana, Functional Economic Area." *Journal of Agricultural & Applied Economics* 28, 2 (1996): 337-355.

Purdy, B., M. Langemeier, and A. Featherstone. "Financial Performance, Risk, and Specialization." *Journal of Agricultural & Applied Economics* 29, 1 (1997): 149-161.

Stam, J., and G. Wallace. "Indicators of Financial Stress in Agriculture." *Journal of Agricultural Lending* 7, 4 (1994): 34-39.

Tweeten, Luther. "The Twelve Best Reasons for Commodity Programs: Why None Stands Scrutiny." *Choices* 10, 2 (1995): 4-7, 43-44.

U.S. Department of Agriculture. *Agricultural Statistics, Annual Summary*, various issues.

Washington Post. "Don't Insult a Vegetable; It Could Sue You," April 17, 1996.

READING BETWEEN THE CURVY LINES

Blank, Steven. "Returns to Limited Crop Diversification." *Western Journal of Agricultural Economics* 15 (1990): 204-212.

Blank, Steven. "Income Risk Varies with What You Grow, Where You Grow It." *California Agriculture* 46, 5 (1992): 14-16.

Blank, Steven. "The New Risk Environment in California Agriculture." *Agribusiness: An International Journal* 11 (1995): 155-168.

Blank, S., J. Siebert, and T. Wyatt. "The Risk and Credit Environment Faced by Agricultural Borrowers." in S. Blank, ed., *Financing Agriculture in California's New Risk Environment*, 42-87. Agricultural Issues Center, University of California, 1994.

California Department of Food and Agriculture. *California Agriculture: Statistical Review, 1991* (and earlier issues), Sacramento.

Carter, H., and C. Nuckton, eds. *Agriculture in California: On the Brink of a New Millennium, 1990-2010.* Agricultural Issues Center, University of California, 1990.

Freund, R. "The Introduction of Risk Into a Programming Model." *Econometrica* 24 (1956): 253-263.

Johnson, Stan. "A Re-Examination of the Farm Diversification Problem." *Journal of Farm Economics* 49 (1967): 610-621.

Johnston, Warren. *California Field Crops: Location and Trends in Acreage, Yields, and Production, 1945-91.* Giannini Foundation Information Series no. 94-1, University of California, March 1994.

Khoju, M., C. Nelson, and P. Barry. "Debt Service Reserve Fund as a Response to Repayment Risk." *Review of Agricultural Economics* 15, 2 (1993): 217-232.

Miller, L., P. Ellinger, P. Barry, and K. Lajili. "Price and Nonprice Management of Agricultural Credit Risk." *Agricultural Finance Review* 53 (1993): 28-41.

Pederson, G., M. Duffy, M. Boehlje, and R. Craven. "Adjustable-Term Financing of Farm Loans." *Western Journal of Agricultural Economics* 16 (1991): 268-279.

Robison, L., and P. Barry. *The Competitive Firm's Response to Risk*, Chapter 12. New York: Macmillan, 1987.

Shi, Y., T. Phipps, and D. Colyer. "Agricultural Land Values Under Urbanizing Influences." *Land Economics* 73, 1 (1997): 90-100.

Sundell, Paul. "Determinants of Short-Term Agricultural Loan Rates at Commercial Banks." *Agricultural Income and Finance,* Economic Research Service, U.S. Department of Agriculture, December 1991, 42-45.

Tew, B., D. Reid, and G. Rafsnider. "Rational Mean-Variance Decisions for Subsistence Farmers." *Management Science* 38 (1992): 840-845.

Turvey, C., T. Baker, and A. Weersink. "Farm Operating Risk and Cash Rent Determination." *Journal of Agricultural and Resource Economics* 17 (1992): 186-194.

Turvey, C., and A. Weersink. "The Demand for Agricultural Loans and the Lender-Borrower Relationship." Paper presented at the NC 207 Agricultural Finance Conference, Chicago, October 1993.

U.S. Board of Governors of the Federal Reserve System. *Financing Agriculture in the 1990s: Structural Change and Public Policy.* Committee on Agriculture and Rural Development, 1991.

U.S. Department of Agriculture. *Agricultural Income and Finance: Situation and Outlook Report,* Economic Research Service, AIS-54, September 1994.

U.S. General Accounting Office. *Availability of Credit for Agriculture, Rural Development, and Infrastructure.* GAO/RCED-93-27, November 1992.

Weimar, M., and A. Hallam. "Risk, Diversification, and Vegetables as an Alternative Crop for Midwestern Agriculture." *North Central Journal of Agricultural Economics* 10 (1988): 75-89.

Western Grower & Shipper. "Credit Squeeze Continues," vol. 64, no. 3 (March 1993): 14-15.

LENDERS RIDE THE ROLLER COASTER

Barry, P., and J. Calvert. "Loan Pricing and Profitability Analysis by Agricultural Banks." *Agricultural Finance Review* 43 (1983): 21-29.

Blank, Steven. "Income Risk Varies with What You Grow, Where You Grow It." *California Agriculture* 46, 5 (1992): 14-16.

Bridge. "U.S. Pension Funds Investigating More in Farm Land," December 3, 1996.

Brunoehler, Ron. "Differential Loan Rates: Do They Pay?" *AgriFinance* (Sept. 1993): 46-48.

Ellinger, P., P. Barry. and M. Mazzocco. "Farm Real Estate Lending by Commercial Banks." *Agricultural Finance Review* 50 (1990): 1-15.

Hanweck, G., and T. Kilcollin. "Bank Profitability and Interest Rate Risk." *Journal of Economics and Business* 36 (1984): 77-84.

Klonsky, Karen. "It takes a lot of effort but . . . There's an 'Active Market' Today for Small Farm Loans." *California Agriculture* 47, 2 (1993): 23-26.

Klonsky, K., S. Blank, R. Thompson, T. Hazlett, and L. Shepard. "The Risk and Credit Environment Faced by Agricultural Borrowers." in S. Blank, ed., *Financing Agriculture in California's New Risk Environment*, 99-148. Agricultural Issues Center, University of California, March 1994.

Learn, E., and G. King. "The Direct and Indirect Effects of Commodity Price Support Programs on California Agriculture." in *Impacts of Farm Policy and Technological Change on U.S. and California Agriculture*, 253-270. Proceedings of a Symposium sponsored by the University of California Agricultural Issues Center, June 1986.

Peoples, K., D. Freshwater, G. Hanson, P. Prentice, and E. Thor. *Anatomy of an American Agricultural Credit Crisis: Farm Debt in the 1980s*. A Farm Credit Assistance Board publication. Lanham, Md.: Rowman and Littlefield Publishers, 1992.

Schmiesing, B., M. Edelman, C. Swinson, and D. Kolmer. "Differential Pricing of Agricultural Operating Loans by Commercial Banks." *Western Journal of Agricultural Economics* 10 (1985): 192-203.

Sharpe, Steven. "Asymmetric Information, Bank Lending, and Implicit Contracts: A Stylized Model of Customer Relationships." *The Journal of Finance* 45 (1990): 1069-1087.

Thompson, R., and S. Blank. "Criteria Used in Agricultural Loan Analysis in California." *Journal of Agricultural Lending* 7, 2 (1994): 12-14, 16-17.

U.S. Bureau of the Census. *Census of Agriculture*, various years.

U.S. Department of Agriculture. *Agricultural Finance Outlook*, February 1992.

U.S. Department of Agriculture. *Economic Indicators of the Farm Sector: State Financial Summary*, various issues.

U.S. Department of Agriculture, *Farm Real Estate Market Developments*. Economic Research Service (USDA, ERS), various years.

U.S. Federal Reserve Board of Governors. *Federal Reserve Bulletin*, various issues.

WILL AGRICULTURAL RISKS CHASE LENDERS BACK TO THE CITY?

Barry, P., and J. Calvert. "Loan Pricing and Profitability Analysis by Agricultural Banks." *Agricultural Finance Review* 43 (1983): 21-29.

Blank, Steven. "Will Agricultural Toxics Chase Lenders Back to the City?" *Agribusiness: An International Journal* 7 (1991): 577-583.

Briys, E., and H. Schlesinger. "Risk Aversion and the Propensities for Self-Insurance and Self-Protection." *Southern Economic Journal* 57 (1990): 458-467.

Brunoehler, Ron. "Differential Loan Rates: Do They Pay?" *AgriFinance* (September 1993): 46-48.

Ellinger, P., P. Barry, and M. Mazzocco. "Farm Real Estate Lending by Commercial Banks." *Agricultural Finance Review* 50 (1990): 1-15.

Hanweck, G., and T. Kilcollin. "Bank Profitability and Interest Rate Risk." *Journal of Economics and Business* 36 (1984): 77-84.

Klonsky, K., S. Blank, R. Thompson, T. Hazlett, and L. Shepard. "The Risk and Credit Environment Faced by Agricultural Borrowers." in S. Blank, ed., *Financing Agriculture in California's New Risk Environment*, 99-148. Agricultural Issues Center, University of California, March 1994.

Knight-Ridder. "Farm Group Opposes Wisconsin Bank Buyout," July 26, 1996.

Riemenschneider, C., and D. Freshwater. "Is a Revised Mandate for the US Farm Credit System Needed?" *Agribusiness: An International Journal* 11 (1995): 291-296.

Schmiesing, B., M. Edelman, C. Swinson, and D. Kolmer. "Differential Pricing of Agricultural Operating Loans by Commercial Banks." *Western Journal of Agricultural Economics* 10 (1985): 192-203.

Sharpe, Steven. "Asymmetric Information, Bank Lending, and Implicit Contracts: A Stylized Model of Customer Relationships." *The Journal of Finance* 45 (1990): 1069-1087.

U.S. Department of Agriculture, Economic Research Service, Rural Economy Division. *Credit in Rural America*, Agricultural Economic Report No. 749, 1997.

U.S. General Accounting Office. *Rural Credit: Availability of Credit for Agriculture, Rural Development, and Infrastructure*, 1992.

U.S. General Accounting Office. *Survey on Availability of Credit and Equity in Rural America*, 1996.

DUELING PORTFOLIOS

Blank, S., J. Siebert, and T. Wyatt. "The Risk and Credit Environment Faced by Agricultural Borrowers." in S. Blank, ed., *Financing Agriculture in California's New Risk Environment*, 42-87. Agricultural Issues Center, University of California, March 1994.

Daily Oklahoman. "Decline in Oklahoma Peanut Acreage," August 7, 1996.

Haley, Stephen. "Capital Accumulation and the Growth of Aggregate Agricultural Production." *Agricultural Economics* 6 (1991): 129-157.

Los Angeles Times. "California Farm Belt is Being Transformed," October 26, 1995.

Modesto Bee. "California Farmers Root Around With Permanent Crops," November 25, 1996.

Purdy, B., M. Langemeier, and A. Featherstone. "Financial Performance, Risk, and Specialization." *Journal of Agricultural & Applied Economics* 29, 1 (1997): 149-161.

Today's Farmer. "Editorial," October 1994.

LIVE POOR, DIE RICH

Blank, S., M. Shepherd, and L. Forero. *Estate Planning for Farmers and Ranchers.* University of California, DANR Publication 21515, 1993.

Harl, Neil. *Farm Estate and Business Planning*, 11th ed. Niles, Illinois: Century Communications, 1991.

Rhodes, Richard. *Farm: A Year in the Life of an American Farmer.* New York: Simon and Schuster, 1989.

Top Producer. "Loan Problems for Young Farmers," March 1995.

Tweeten, Luther. "The Twelve Best Reasons for Commodity Programs: Why None Stands Scrutiny." *Choices* 10, 2 (1995): 4-7, 43-44.

U.S. Department of Agriculture. *Agricultural Statistics.* Washington D.C., 1993.

WORKING WITHOUT A NET

Associated Press. "Payments for not Growing Crops," December 9, 1996.

Blank, S., and J. McDonald. *Crop Insurance as a Risk Management Tool in California: The Untapped Market.* Research Report for the Federal Crop Insurance Corporation, September 1993.

Blank, S., C. Carter and J. McDonald. "Is the Market Failing Agricultural Producers Who Wish to Manage Risks?" *Contemporary Economic Policy* 15, 3 (1997): 103-112.

Braschler, C., and G. Nelson, *Nonmetropolitan and Metropolitan Federal Transfer Payments.* Rural Policy Research Institute, University of Missouri, P97-2, April 1997.

Brooks, J., and C. Carter. *The Political Economy of U.S. Agriculture.* ABARE Research Report 94.8. Canberra, Australia, 1994.

Browne, W., J. Skees, L. Swanson, P. Thompson, and L. Unnevehr. *Sacred Cows and Hot Potatoes.* Boulder, Colorado: Westview Press, 1992.

Bullock, David. "Objectives and Constraints of Government Policy: The Countercyclicity of Transfers to Agriculture." *American Journal of Agricultural Economics* 74 (1992): 617-629.

Chicago Sun-Times. "Bitter Truth About Sugar Supports," May 22, 1995.

Des Moines Register. "Loans to Farmers Soar," November 24, 1994.

Des Moines Register. "Private Sources Pay for Ag Research," January 23, 1997.

Goetz, S., and D. Debertin. "Rural Population Decline in the 1980s: Impacts of Farm Structure and Federal Farm Programs." *American Journal of Agricultural Economics* 78 (1996): 517-529.

Heuer, Robert. "Sun Setting on Ag Research?" *AgriFinance* 37, 3 (March 1995): 23-25.

Hoffman, W., C. Campbell, and K. Cook. *Sowing Disaster: The Implications of Farm Disaster Programs for Taxpayers and the Environment.* Washington, D.C.: Environmental Working Group, 1994.

Innes, Robert. "Politics and the Public Interest in Farm Policy: Five Litmus Test Issues." *Choices* 10, 3 (1995): 17-21, 24.

Johnson, S. and S. Martin, eds. *Industrial Policy for Agriculture in the Global Economy.* Ames: Iowa State University Press, 1993.

Journal of Commerce. "Cotton as King," October 4, 1995.

Knight-Ridder. "USDA Not Consulted on Possible Farm Cuts in Rivlin Memo," October 25, 1994.

Lee, H., J. Harwood, and A. Somwaru. "How New Crop Disaster Policy Could Affect California." *California Agriculture* 49, 3 (1995): 7-13.

Los Angeles Times. "Coalition Seeks to Cut $6 Billion in California Projects," February 1, 1995.

Los Angeles Times. "Brazil Gets Set to Wire Rain Forest," October 19, 1995.

Modesto Bee. "Irrigation Subsidies Cost Taxpayers Billions," July 30, 1996.

Offutt, Susan. "Subsidizing Agriculture: The Road Ahead," *Choices* 11, 2 (1996): 30-

33.

Omaha World Herald. "Rural Counties Warned that Change Is Coming," November 10, 1994.

Philadelphia Inquirer. "Sugar Growers Fight Processors," October 18, 1995.

Reuters. "Jump in Farm Program Payments Possible," October 7, 1994.

Reuters. "Farmers May Refund Billions to U.S. for Overpayments," October 10, 1995.

Spitze, R. "A Continuing Evolution in U.S. Agricultural and Food Policy—The 1990 Act." *Agricultural Economics* 7 (1992): 125-139.

Tweeten, Luther. "The Twelve Best Reasons for Commodity Programs: Why None Stands Scrutiny." *Choices* 10, 2 (1995): 4-7, 43-44.

Unnevehr, Laurian. "Suburban Consumers and Exurban Farmers: The Changing Political Economy of Food Policy." *American Journal of Agricultural Economics* 75 (1993): 1140-1144.

Venner, R., and S. Blank. *Reducing Citrus Revenue Losses From Frost Damage: Wind Machines and Crop Insurance.* Giannini Foundation Information Series 95-1. May 1995.

Washington Post. "Resources Institute Backs 50% Crop Subsidy Cuts," April 29, 1995.

Washington Post. "Candy Politics," September 19, 1995.

Washington Post. "Peanut Program 'Quota Lords' Examined," October 6, 1995.

Washington Times. "Less Support for Farm Programs," November 22, 1994.

Washington Times. "What to Do With Farm Subsidies," March 29, 1995.

Washington Times. "Benefits of Sugar Program," September 30, 1995.

Washington Times. "Environmental Impacts of Farm Subsidies," October 12, 1995.

WHY NOT SWITCH RATHER THAN FIGHT?

Associated Press. "Kansas Woos California Dairies," November 13, 1994.

Associated Press. "Megafarms Concern Some Farmers," November 28, 1994.

Associated Press. "Farmers Want Simpler Crop Insurance," August 21, 1996.

Associated Press. "Michigan Losing Agricultural Land at Fast Pace," September 19, 1997.

Associated Press. "Report Documents Oregon Farmland Loss to Urban Development," September 23, 1997.

Associated Press. "State Lawmaker Proposes New Regulations for Largest Farms," September 23, 1997.

Batabyal, Amitrajeet. "The Timing of Land Development: An Invariance Result." *American Journal of Agricultural Economics* 78,4(1996): 204-212.

Blank, Steven. "Returns to Limited Crop Diversification." *Western Journal of Agricultural Economics* 15 (1990): 204-212.

Blank, S., C. Carter, and B. Schmiesing. *Futures and Options Markets: Trading in Financials and Commodities.* Chp. 8. Englewood Cliffs, New Jersey: Prentice Hall, 1991.

Business Wire. "Alarm Over California Urbanization," October 28, 1994.

Carriker, G., J. Williams, A. Barnaby, and R. Black. "Yield and Income Risk Reduction Under Alternative Crop Insurance and Disaster Assistance Designs." *Western Journal of Agricultural Economics* 16 (1991): 238-250.

Chicago Tribune. "Farm Succumbs to Urban Sprawl," November 14, 1994.

Chicago Tribune. "Farm Crunch Catches Small Towns," October 20, 1994.

Chicago Tribune. "Developers Dig Into Wisconsin," October 1, 1995.

Christian Science Monitor. "Farm Use of High Plains Water Poses Dilemma," November 28, 1994.

Delsohn, Gary. "Report: Ag Threatened by Growth," *Sacramento Bee,* October 26, 1995.

Des Moines Register. "Concern About Urban Sprawl," December 9, 1994.

Des Moines Register. "Objections to Swine Research Facility," January 8, 1995.

Des Moines Register. "Population Loss Continues in Farm Counties," April 24, 1995.

Des Moines Register. "What Farmers Want in a New Farm Bill," October 19, 1995.

Des Moines Register. "Millions Sought to Study Hog Lot Issues in Iowa," October 11, 1995.

Des Moines Register. "Livestock Odor a Serious Science," October 18, 1995.

Farm Journal. "When Urban Sprawl Chokes Agriculture," March 12, 1996.

Farmweek. "Sociologists Say Producers Get Short End at Market," October 5, 1994.

Farmweek. "Poultry Plans Ruffle Some Feathers," December 14, 1994.

Forero, L., L. Huntsinger and J. Clawson. "Land Use Change in Three San Francisco Bay Area Counties: Implications for Ranching at the Urban Fringe." *Journal of Soil and Water Conservation* 47, 6 (1992): 475-480.

Johnson, S. and S. Martin, eds. *Industrial Policy for Agriculture in the Global Economy.* Ames: Iowa State University Press, 1993.

Kline, J., and D. Wichelns. "Measuring Public Preferences for the Environmental Amenities Provided by Farmland." *European Review of Agricultural Economics* 23 (1996): 421-436.

Knight-Ridder. "Pork Group Decries Farm-Retail Spread," November 21, 1994.

Los Angeles Times. "Fresno on Brink of 'Land War,'" October 26, 1994.

Los Angeles Times. "California Farm Belt is Being Transformed," October 26, 1995.

Minneapolis Star Tribune. "Benefits to Preserving Farmland," November 17, 1994.

Morgan, Dan. *Rising in the West.* New York: Alfred A. Knopf, 1992.

New York Times. "Tomato Growers File Complaint," March 31, 1995.

Omaha World Herald. "Nebraska May Try to Improve Its Image," November 30, 1994.

OMNI. "Swine Odor Task Force," February 1995.

Successful Farming. "Looking at the Kansas Vote Against Corporate Farming," January 1995.

Thompson, R., and S. Blank. "Finance and Risk Characteristics of California Agricultural Cooperatives." *The Cooperative Accountant* 47, 2 (1994): 65-70.

United Press International. "Michigan Farms Hurt by Urban Growth," December 7, 1994.

USA Today. "EZ/EC Announcement," December 21, 1994.

Wall Street Journal. "Growth in Rural America," November 21, 1994.

Wall Street Journal. "It's Still No Cheaper to Bring Home the Bacon," November 30, 1994.

Washington Post. "Virginia Urban Growth," December 10, 1994.

Washington Times. "Radioactive Soil Could be Used to Raise Chickens," May 7, 1995.

Weimar, M., and A. Hallam. "Risk, Diversification, and Vegetables as an Alternative Crop for Midwestern Agriculture." *North Central Journal of Agricultural Economics* 10 (1988): 75-89.

Williams, J., J. Harper, and A. Barnaby. "Government Program Impacts on the Selection of Crop Insurance in Northeastern Kansas." *North Central Journal of Agricultural Economics* 12 (1990): 207-221.

Williams, J., G. Carriker, A. Barnaby Jr., and K. Harper. "Crop Insurance and Disaster Assistance Designs for Wheat and Grain Sorghum." *American Journal of*

Agricultural Economics 75 (1993): 435-447.

SUSTAINABLE AGRICULTURE: GOLF COURSES, NURSERIES AND TURF
FARMS

Associated Press. "Minnesota Farmers Work to Convert Alfalfa Into Electricity," April
15, 1996.
Associated Press. "Proposal to Keep Hogs Away From Golfing," February 8, 1997.
Associated Press. "Farmers Want to Diversify with Bike Trails," July 10, 1997.
Bloomberg. "USDA Clears Biotech Potatoes," March 24, 1995.
Browne, W., J. Skees, L. Swanson, P. Thompson, and L. Unnevehr. *Sacred Cows and
Hot Potatoes*. Boulder, Colorado: Westview Press, 1992.
Heimlich, R., and C. Barnard. *Agricultural Adaption to Urbanization: Farm Types in
United States Metropolitan Areas*. Paper presented at the Western Regional Science
Association Meeting, February 1991.
Heimlich, R., and D. Brooks. *Metropolitan Growth and Agriculture: Farming in the
City's Shadow*. USDA/ERS Agricultural Economic Report 619, 1989.
Hogs Today. "Diluting Waste Will Reduce the Odor," January 1995.
Knight-Ridder. "Business Is Blooming at Gardening Shops," January 15, 1997.
Los Angeles Times. "A History Wilts," October 9, 1995.
Los Angeles Times. "Ornamentals Overtake Foodstuff Production in Orange County,"
October 12, 1995.
Minneapolis Star Tribune. "Products From Soybeans," January 6, 1995.
Newsweek. "Calling All Cows," April 17, 1995.
New York Times. "Kitty Litter From Wheat," December 12, 1994.
New York Times. "Golf Course Cancels Goose Shoot," January 7, 1995.
New York Times. "Cool Cows Make Milk Hip," April 14, 1995.
Orlando Sentinel. "Central Florida's Foliage Industry Keeps Growing," May 20, 1996.
Patriot News. "Horse Industry Called Big Business for Pennsylvania," August 16,
1996.
Schuch, U., and G. Klein. "Wholesale Nursery Surveys Reveal Inventory, Customers
and Business Practices." *California Agriculture* 50, 5 (1996): 16-21.
Toman, Michael. "Economics and 'Sustainability': Balancing Trade-offs and
Imperatives." *Land Economics* 70, 4 (1994): 399-413.
Top Producer. "Cash From Trash," March 1995.
United Press International. "Grants Support Experimental Agriculture Products,"
December 30, 1994.
United Press International. "NASA Asks USDA for Help in Growing Crops in Space,"
January 26, 1996.
Unnevehr, Laurian. "Suburban Consumers and Exurban Farmers: The Changing
Political Economy of Food Policy." *American Journal of Agricultural Economics*
75 (1993): 1140-1144.
Wall Street Journal. "Biotech Plants Gain Approval," March 31, 1995.
Wall Street Journal. "Cow Milks Herself," May 8, 1995.
Wall Street Journal. "Guests May Pay Better than Cattle," August 1, 1997.
Washington Post. "The Skinny on a New Pig," October 18, 1995.
Whitten, Ron. "Best New Courses of the Year." *Golf Digest* 46, 1 (1995): 122-131.

WHAT TIME IS THE LAST DINNER BELL?

Associated Press. "China to Increase Agricultural Investment," December 27, 1994.

Bloomberg. "DuPont Forms Alliance to Study Ag Production in India," March 30, 1995.

Carter, C., and H. Carter, eds. *North American Free Trade Agreement: Implications for California Agriculture.* University of California Agricultural Issues Center, 1992.

Chicago Tribune. "Potatoes as Salvation of Third World Hunger," May 21, 1995.

Feedstuffs. "Milling Training Centers Open in Egypt and Morocco," December 26, 1994.

Journal of Commerce. "Turkey's Irrigation Project to Boost Farm Exports," November 10, 1994.

Journal of Commerce. "WTO Gives Stability, Says New Director," January 3, 1995.

Journal of Commerce. "India Seeks to Reduce Food-Grain Inventories," January 6, 1995.

Journal of Commerce. "North Carolina Port Expects Chilean Fruit to Surge," January 18, 1995.

Journal of Commerce. "Farm Equipment Exports Booming," September 29, 1995.

Journal of Commerce. "Grape Growers' Suit Dismissed," October 3, 1995.

Kansas City Star. "Counting on Careers in Farming," November 19, 1994.

Knight-Ridder. "Burger King to Up Australian Beef Imports," January 30, 1996.

Knight-Ridder. "Bolivia Unveils $2.8 Billion Plan to Revamp Agriculture," July 29, 1996.

Los Angeles Times. "Japan Looks Toward Asia," October 25, 1994.

New York Times. "Mubarak Inaugurates Project to Expand Crop Area," January 10, 1997.

Ning, Y. and M. Reed. "Locational Determinants of the US Direct Foreign Investment in Food and Kindred Products." *Agribusiness: An International Journal* 11, 1 (1995): 77-85.

Omaha World Herald. "Economist on GATT Benefits to Food Trade," November 19, 1994.

Reuters. "Japan's Vegetable Imports," December 25, 1994.

Reuters. "Agricultural Output Grew in Peru in 1994," January 6, 1995.

Reuters. "China Farm Export Sector Attracts $10 Billion in Foreign Capital," January 12, 1995.

Reuters. "Zimbabwe Exports Seen Up 27% in 1995," January 17, 1995.

Reuters. "Hungary Seeks Partners for Meat Ventures," January 17, 1995.

Reuters. "Algeria to Invest $3.8 Billion in Agriculture," June 2, 1996.

Reuters. "China Promotes its Own Fast Food," July 17, 1996.

Staten, Vince. *Can You Trust a Tomato in January?* New York: Simon and Schuster, 1993.

U.S. Department of Agriculture. *Agricultural Statistics,* Washington D.C., various issues.

U.S. Department of Agriculture. *Forces Shaping U.S. Agriculture: A Briefing Book.* Economic Research Service, July 1997.

Wall Street Journal. "Food Tastes Are Changing Around the World," October 11, 1995.

Washington Post. "Why Are People Getting Fatter?" December 30, 1994.

Washington Post. "Fighting Colonel Sanders in India," October 1, 1995.

Washington Times. "Canada Cultivates Canola Crop," January 4, 1995.

World Bank. *World Development Report.* New York: Oxford University Press, 1988.

STOP THE TRAIN, I WANT TO GET OFF!

Associated Press. "U.N. Recommends Using Vacant Lots to Feed Mega-Cities of the Future." February 13, 1996.

Barkema, Alan. "Reaching Consumers in the Twenty-First Century: The Short Way Around the Barn." *American Journal of Agricultural Economics* 75 (1993): 1126-1131.

Bloomberg. "China Acts to Limit Loss of Farmland in Development Zones," May 5, 1995.

Boehlje, Michael. "Industrialization of Agriculture: What are the Implications?" *Choices* 11, 1 (1996): 30-33.

Bridge. "Vietnam May Overtake India as 2nd Biggest Asia Rice Exporter," October 3, 1996.

Chicago Tribune. "Debate Over Farmland Preservation," November 1, 1994.

Chicago Tribune. "Off-Farm Ag Opportunities," November 27, 1994.

Chicago Tribune. "Millionaire Finances 11,000 Acres for Grazing," March 12, 1995.

Des Moines Register. "Hog Farms Stake New Turf," November 6, 1994.

Des Moines Register. "Large-Scale Hog Operations Could Hurt Ogallala Aquifer," March 29, 1995.

Des Moines Register. "Low Prices Put Hog Project on Hold," May 5, 1995.

Des Moines Register. "Traces of Herbicides Still in Water," September 28, 1995.

Des Moines Register. "Livestock Lots Spur Action by Counties," October 1, 1995.

Des Moines Register. "Court Limits Counties' Rule Over Hog Farms," October 26, 1995.

Des Moines Register. "Killer Fumes in the Countryside," November 29, 1995.

Drabenstott, Mark. "Industrialization: Steady Current or Tidal Wave?" *Choices* 9, 4 (1994): 4-8.

Drabenstott, Mark. "Agricultural Industrialization: Implications for Economic Development and Public Policy." *Journal of Agricultural and Applied Economics* 27 (1995): 13-20.

Gale, F., and D. Harrington. "U.S. Farms: Diversity and Change—Six Myths of the Farming Sector." *Agricultural Outlook.* Economic Research Service, U.S. Department of Agriculture, 1992.

Heimlich, R., and C. Barnard. *Agricultural Adaption to Urbanization: Farm Types in United States Metropolitan Areas.* Paper presented at the Western Regional Science Association Meeting, February 1991.

Heimlich, R., and D. Brooks. *Metropolitan Growth and Agriculture: Farming in the City's Shadow.* USDA/ERS Agricultural Economic Report 619, 1989.

Journal of Commerce. "Food to the U.S.," December 27, 1994.

Journal of Commerce. "Pesticide Ban Threatens Exports," October 3, 1995.

Journal of Commerce. "Herd Shot Round the World Will Herald New Trade Initiative," October 19, 1995.

Kansas City Star. "Counting on Careers in Farming," November 19, 1994.

Kansas City Star. "Zoning for Hog Farms?" November 29, 1994.

Kansas City Star. "Missouri Governor Calls for Tougher Supervision of Hog Farms," September 29, 1995.

Knoeber, Charles. "Explaining State Bans on Corporate Farming." *Economic Inquiry* 35, 1 (1997): 151-166.

Los Angeles Times. "U.S. Food Industry, A Star of World Trade," January 27, 1995.

Los Angeles Times. "Proposal to Sell Imperial Valley Water Angers California

Farmers," October 2, 1995.

Martin, L., and K. Zering. "Relationships Between Industrialized Agriculture and Environmental Consequences: The Case of Vertical Coordination in Broilers and Hogs." *Journal of Agricultural & Applied Economics* 29, 1 (1997): 45-56.

New York Times. "Land-Idling Programs Attacked," October 30, 1994.

New York Times. "Nation's Farm Count Lowest Since Before Civil War," November 10, 1994.

New York Times. "More Agricultural Research Gains Needed," February 5, 1995.

New York Times. "Battle Over Control of Federal Lands," April 8, 1995.

New York Times. "Boll Weevil Eradication Program Questioned," October 9, 1995.

New York Times. "Water Sales Meet Resistance," August 6, 1996.

Ning, Y., and M. Reed. "Locational Determinants of the U.S. Direct Foreign Investment in Food and Kindred Products." *Agribusiness: An International Journal* 11,1 (1995): 77-85.

Palmquist, R., F. Roka, and T. Vukina. "Hog Operations, Environmental Effects and Residential Property Values." *Land Economics* 73, 1 (1997): 114-124.

Pinstrup-Andersen, P., and R. Pandya-Lorch. "Enough Food for Future Generations?" *Choices* 9, 3 (1994): 13-16.

Reich, Robert. *The Work of Nations: Preparing Ourselves for 21st Century Capitalism.* New York: Alfred A. Knopf, 1991.

Rhodes, V. James. "The Industrialization of Hog Production." *Review of Agricultural Economics* 17 (1995): 107-118.

Ruttan, Vernon. "Sustainable Growth in Agricultural Production: Into the 21st Century," *Choices* 7, 3 (1992): 32, 34, 36-37.

Salt Lake Tribune. "Forest Service Noncompliance May Put West's Ranchers Out to Pasture," December 16, 1994.

U.S. Department of Agriculture. *Forces Shaping U.S. Agriculture: A Briefing Book.* Economic Research Service, July 1997.

Unnevehr, Laurian. "Suburban Consumers and Exurban Farmers: The Changing Political Economy of Food Policy." *American Journal of Agricultural Economics* 75 (1993): 1140-1144.

USA Today. "Washington Weighs Property Rights," November 2, 1995.

Wall Street Journal. "Voters to Settle Land Battle in Arizona," November 1, 1994.

Wall Street Journal. "Benefits of CRP," February 9, 1995.

Wall Street Journal. "Researchers Find Evidence of Global Spread of Old Pesticides," September 29, 1995.

Wall Street Journal. "China Puts Priority on Agriculture," September 29, 1995.

Wall Street Journal. "Chile Boosts Its Wine Making With Support From U.S. Vintners," April 5, 1996.

Washington Post. "A Mother Lode That Won't Play Out," October 26, 1995.

Washington Times. "Norway's Farmers Fear EU Membership," November 28, 1994.

Washington Times. "Southern California Looks at Desalination," February 6, 1995.

Washington Times. "Costs and Benefits of Logging in National Forests," October 3, 1995.

Washington Times. "Battlefields of the West," October 13, 1995.

Washington Times. "Betting on Doomsday." January 30, 1996.

Wharton, Clifton Jr. "Malthus, Cousteau, and Schultz: Does Foreign Agricultural Development Have a Future?" *Choices* 10, 1 (1995): 19-21, 24.

GUNS FOR HIRE

Armbruster, Walter. "The Future of Land Grant Universities and Agricultural Economists." *Review of Agricultural Economics* 15, 3 (1993): 591-602.

Business Week. "Cotton Consumption," January 16, 1995.

Christian Science Monitor. "Kinder, Gentler Chickens," October 4, 1994.

Crow, Michael. "The University as a Catalyst for Scientific and Industrial Development," in Johnson and Martin, eds., *Industrial Policy for Agriculture in the Global Economy*, 109-127, 1993.

Des Moines Register. "Hog Waste Research Aided," April 7, 1995.

Dobson, W. "Strategies for Declining Academic Enterprises," *Choices* 10, 3 (1995): 29-33.

Huffman, W., and R. Evenson. "Contributions of Public and Private Science and Technology to U.S. Agricultural Productivity." *American Journal of Agricultural Economics* 74 (1992): 751-756.

Iowa Farmer Today. "Ag-Link Program Gets Rolling in Iowa," February 11, 1995.

Jorgenson, D., and F. Gollop. "Productivity Growth in U.S. Agriculture: A Postwar Perspective." *American Journal of Agricultural Economics* 74 (1992): 745-750.

Lexington Herald-Leader. "Kentucky Tobacco Farmers Diversify into Vegetables," August 12, 1996.

Minnesota Star Tribune. "Dean Wants Citified School of Agriculture," October 17, 1995.

Olson, D., and D. Hadwiger. "University Centers, Technology Transfer, and Agricultural Development." in Johnson and Martin, eds., *Industrial Policy for Agriculture in the Global Economy*, 249-260, 1993.

OMNI. "Methane Detectors for Cattle," February 1995.

Scheuring, Ann. *Science and Service: A History of the Land-Grant University and Agriculture in California.* Division of Agriculture and Natural Resources publication 3360, University of California, 1995.

Wall Street Journal. "Difficulty Adding Diversity to Ag," September 19, 1995.

IS THE SKY FALLING?

Chicago Tribune. "'Fragmentation' Farming on the Rise in Midwest," May 15, 1995.

Des Moines Register. "What Do Farmers Want?" January 15, 1995.

Des Moines Register. "Cuts Expected Amid Low Farm Income," January 15, 1995.

Des Moines Register. "Impacts of Hog Operation Odor Assessed," January 20, 1995.

Des Moines Register. "Finding New Blood for Farms," February 19, 1995.

Des Moines Register. "Willie Nelson Sings to Save Rural America," March 15, 1995.

Des Moines Register. "Benefits of Urban Sprawl," March 16, 1995.

Farmweek. "Sociologists Say Producers Get Short End at Market," October 5, 1994.

Hightower, Jim. *Eat Your Heart Out*, New York: Vintage Books, 1975.

Kansas City Star. "'City' Farmers Get Billions," March 16, 1995.

Los Angeles Times. "Goat Ranchers Fear Extinction," March 27, 1995.

Minnesota Star Tribune. "Experts Say Shortages Will Force U.S. to Change Diet," February 18, 1995.

New York Times. "Potential for Growth in Food Demand," February 18, 1995.

New York Times. "New Jersey Farmland Tax Benefits May Widen," March 27, 1995.

New York Times. "Crop Contracts in Farming's Future," May 20, 1995.

Progressive Farmer. "Farmers of the Future," January 1995.

Texas Farmer-Stockman. "Saving America's Farmland," March 1995.

Top Producer. "Telecommuting Brings Corporate Jobs to Rural America," February 1995.

Wall Street Journal. "Cattle Ranching Is an Office Job," October 4, 1995.

Washington Times. "Farmers Fight for Way of Life," February 18, 1995.

Washington Times. "Poll Finds More Americans Are Overweight," February 27, 1995.

Wichita Eagle. "Farmland Values Threatened by Subsidy Cuts," March 17, 1995.

Index

About the Author

Steve Blank is a Cooperative Extension Economist in the Agricultural and Resource Economics Department at the University of California, Davis. A native Californian, he is the grandson of a farmer from Missouri and a butcher and grocer from Washington state. While growing up he worked as a farm laborer, picking fruit and vegetables, and occasionally as a cattle ranchhand. In college, he spent summers working numerous jobs in canneries. As a professional business consultant, he has advised—and learned from—varied agricultural and food companies in several states and in countries on every continent. These and other experiences gave him firsthand exposure to the "Economic Food Chain" on both a personal and global scale.

Dr. Blank holds a Bachelor's degree in business administration from California State University, Stanislaus; a Master's of Business Administration degree from the University of Massachusetts; and a Masters of Science and Ph.D. in Agricultural Economics, both from the University of Hawaii. He held faculty positions at California Polytechnic State University—San Luis Obispo, South Dakota State University, and the University of Arizona prior to his current position at the University of California. He has held varied positions in industry. His international experience includes a multiyear stint as a Section Head in the Australian government's Bureau of Agricultural Economics in Canberra, plus short-term research and consulting assignments all over the globe. Finally, he continues to be an active business consultant to maintain the learning process that comes with working in agribusiness.

ISBN 1-56720-165-2

HARDCOVER BAR CODE